Mustapha Abiodun Akinkunmi

Central Bank Balance Sheet and Real Business Cycles

Mustapha Abiodun Akinkunmi

Central Bank Balance Sheet and Real Business Cycles

—

DE
G
PRESS

ISBN 978-1-5474-1667-7
e-ISBN (PDF) 978-1-5474-0057-7
e-ISBN (EPUB) 978-1-5474-0059-1

Library of Congress Control Number: 2018952174

Bibliographic information published by the Deutsche Nationalbibliothek
The Deutsche Nationalbibliothek lists this publication in the Deutsche Nationalbibliografie;
detailed bibliographic data are available on the Internet at http://dnb.dnb.de.

© 2018 Mustapha Abiodun Akinkunmi
Published by Walter de Gruyter Inc., Boston/Berlin
Printing and binding: CPI books GmbH, Leck
Typesetting: MacPS, LLC, Carmel

www.degruyter.com

To My Father
Mr. Mustapha Kehinde Gbaja-Biamila

DOI 10.1515/9781547400577-201

About De|G PRESS

Five Stars as a Rule

De|G PRESS, the startup born out of one of the world's most venerable publishers, De Gruyter, promises to bring you an unbiased, valuable, and meticulously edited work on important topics in the fields of business, information technology, computing, engineering, and mathematics. By selecting the finest authors to present, without bias, information necessary for their chosen topic *for professionals*, in the depth you would hope for, we wish to satisfy your needs and earn our five-star ranking.

In keeping with these principles, the books you read from De|G PRESS will be practical, efficient and, if we have done our job right, yield many returns on their price.

We invite businesses to order our books in bulk in print or electronic form as a best solution to meeting the learning needs of your organization, or parts of your organization, in a most cost-effective manner.

There is no better way to learn about a subject in depth than from a book that is efficient, clear, well organized, and information rich. A great book can provide life-changing knowledge. We hope that with De|G PRESS books you will find that to be the case.

DOI 10.1515/9781547400577-202

Acknowledgments

I owe a great debt to my colleagues at Brickfield Road Associates Limited, Mr. Saheed Bello and Mr. Lanre Sanni. I am exceptionally grateful to these gentlemen.

Valuable suggestions were made by my publisher, Mr. Jeffrey M. Pepper of De|G PRESS, an imprint of De Gruyter.

—Mustapha Abiodun Akinkunmi
Chair, Accounting and Finance
School of Business and Entrepreneurship
American University of Nigeria
Yola, Nigeria

DOI 10.1515/9781547400577-203

About the Author

Dr. Mustapha Abiodun Akinkunmi is a Financial Economist and Technology Strategist. He has over 25 years of experience in estimation, planning, and forecasting using statistical and econometric methods, with particular expertise in risk, expected utility, discounting, binomial-tree valuation methods, financial econometrics models, Monte Carlo simulations, macroeconomics, and exchange rate modeling. Dr. Akinkunmi has performed extensive software development for quantitative analysis of capital markets, revenue and payment gateway, predictive analytics, data science, and credit risk management. He has a record of success in identifying and implementing change management programs and institutional development initiatives in both public and private sector organizations. He has been in high profile positions as a Consultant, Financial Advisor, Project Manager, and Business Strategist to AT&T, Salomon Brothers, Goldman Sachs, Phibro Energy, First Boston (Credit Suisse First Boston), World Bank, and Central Bank of Nigeria. He is an internationally recognized co-author (*Introduction to Strategic Financial Management*, May 2013), authored *Data Mining and Market Intelligence: Implications for Decision Making*, May 2018 and leader in demand analysis, specializing in working with very large databases. Furthermore, he has conducted teaching and applied research in areas that include analyses of expenditure patterns, inflation and exchange rate modeling for Manhattan College, Riverdale, NY; Fordham University, New York, NY; University of Lagos, Lagos, Nigeria; State University of New York-FIT, New York, NY; Montclair State University, Montclair, NJ; and American University, Yola, Nigeria. In 1990, he founded Technology Solutions Incorporated (TSI) in New York, which focused on data science and software application development for clients including major financial services institutions. After ten years of successful operations and rapid growth under Dr. Akinkunmi's leadership, TSI was acquired by a publicly

DOI 10.1515/9781547400577-204

traded technology company based in the U.S. in a value-creating transaction. Dr. Akinkunmi was the former Honorable Commissioner for Finance, Lagos State, Nigeria. He is now an associate professor of finance and chair of the accounting and finance department at the American University of Nigeria, Yola, Nigeria.

Contents

DOI 10.1515/9781547400577-205

Preface

This book directly responds to the ongoing debate surrounding the impact of unconventional monetary policies, especially in relation to the size and composition of central banks' balance sheets. In addition, it provides a thorough analysis of the link between central bank balance sheets and the macroeconomic environment using secondary data. Therefore, the book is a guide for policy makers, practitioners, and academics whose areas of interest are financial economics, monetary economics, international economics, financial institutions, and applied econometrics.

This book also provides in-depth diagnostics of central bank balance sheets through a disaggregated analysis of its components, and their implications on the financial stability and effective functions of the economy. This is written to fill the existing knowledge and analytical gaps in issues related to the size of central bank assets and their composition, as well as their influence on macroeconomic performance. Moreover, it presents a broad framework for understanding and analyzing information on real business cycles in relation to potential output and output gaps, and how the objectives of policy makers can be met through the use of appropriate techniques, considering dynamic economic environments.

DOI 10.15159781547400577-206

Chapter 1
Global Genesis of the Central Bank

1.1 Origin of the Central Bank

The pioneering central banks were established to boost the financial capacity of governments. For instance, the Sveriges Riksbank was created in 1668 as an instrument of managing Swedish financial resources. The Bank of England was set up in 1694 by William III during a war against France. The European Central Bank (ECB) came on board in January 1999 as a result of the creation of the Euro-zone. The U.S. financial crisis of 1907 led the U.S. Congress to pass the Federal Reserve Act of 1913, which mandated the creation of the Federal Reserve. The Federal Reserve was established with the understanding that the Fed would explore its balance sheet to support a currency that could respond elastically to meet the needs of a growing economy, and lessen the impact of future economic downturns. In creating the Federal Reserve System, the U.S. Congress hoped to minimize the occurrence of panics that would lead to bank runs, and maintain the stability of the U.S. financial system.

The great challenge facing the U.S. financial system was too many government constraints. It was believed then that private banking was not stable. Therefore, the result of the National Monetary Commission led to the origin of the Federal Reserve. However, the Federal Reserve failed to prevent the Great Depression of the 1930s, and there were periods of significant inflation since World War II.

Central banks, even with their technocratic expertise, could not predict the 2007–2008 global financial crisis or the euro zone's debt crisis. In light of this, the future of central banks remains uncertain as their autonomy is not guaranteed, and because governments depend on them in a crisis and ignore their suggestions when economies recover (*The Economist*, 2017).

1.2 Roles of the Central Bank

Central banks around the world serve as the ultimate means of settlement in an economy. For instance, balances held in commercial banks can be exchanged on-demand for banknotes; this support of direct convertibility in terms of central bank liabilities ensures some level of trust in the value of such money. Some countries—for example, the UK—allow private banks to issue banknotes, with the endorsement of the monetary authority. Prior to the establishment of the Federal

DOI 10.1515/9781547400577-001

Reserve System, the United States implemented various measures to regulate banks and manage the money supply at a national level. Owing to the recurring financial panics during the nineteenth and early twentieth centuries, the National Monetary Commission was set up in 1908 to investigate the problem and provide a recommended solution. The outcome of this study made the U.S. Congress pass the Federal Reserve Act in December 1913. Before 1914, the U.S. financial system was confronted with the problem of too many government restrictions.

As observed throughout history and as recently as the 2007–2008 financial crisis, central banks have explored their balance sheets and exercised their power to intervene in the financial markets, particularly when facing systemic threats arising from the failure of financial institutions.

The ECB has been tasked with the responsibility of conducting monetary policy for the euro area since its creation in January 1999. The creation of the euro area led the transfer of responsibility of monetary policy from the national central banks to the ECB.

Central banks have wielded monopoly power to issue notes and have served as a lender of last resort since their conception. In times of severe illiquidity, the central bank acts as a credible lender of last resort, and has the capacity to create the monetary liabilities needed to provide liquid assets to imperiled institutions. In addition, most central banks often have supervisory and regulatory powers to ensure financial institutions' solvency, prevent bank runs, as well as reckless or fraudulent behavior by commercial banks.

Commercial bank reserves can be equivalent to a commercial bank's current accounts held at the central bank. Settlement of monetary transactions between two commercial banks is accomplished by moving reserves across the central bank's balance sheet with one commercial bank's reserve account being debited, and the other being credited. This payment flow is always balanced by interbank transactions in order to prevent excessive withdrawals at the central bank.

Thus, the central bank creates confidence in commercial bank deposits as a means of settlement. This confidence enhances the efficiency of financial systems by freely encouraging commercial banks. Thus, it serves as intermediaries between agents in the economy and creates money by offering credit.

The central bank balance sheet presents the financial position of monetary authority in any economy. It has both an asset side and a liability side. The asset side mainly contains foreign and domestic assets, while the liability side consists of nonmonetary liabilities (such as banknotes) and monetary liabilities.

This book will specifically focus on composition and evolution of central balance sheets, and their implications on real business cycles and the macroeconomic environment.

Questions

1. What is the history of the central bank?
2. What led to the establishment of the Federal Reserve?
3. What are the roles of the central bank?
4. What is the concept of the "central bank balance sheet"?

Chapter 2
Relevance of the Central Bank Balance Sheet

2.1 Understanding Relevance of Central Bank Balance Sheet in Functions of Economy

The analysis of the central bank balance sheet is important in designing and understanding the policies needed to support an economic recovery in post-financial crisis years. This book asserts that a deeper comprehension of changes to the central bank balance sheet can lead to more effective policymaking. We support this assertion by highlighting the challenges and controversies faced by central banks in the past and present when implementing policies, and analyze the links between these policies, the central bank balance sheet, and the consequences to economies as a whole.

Every country has a central bank with specific features in terms of name, organizational structure, monetary policy targets, ownership, and level of autonomy. Some countries like Nigeria, name their central bank by adding the country name to the phrase "Central Bank of" while other such as the United Kingdom and Ghana attach the phrase "Bank of" to their country name (Bank of England, Bank of Ghana). Countries such as the United States and South Africa adopt the use of "Federal Reserve."

Most central banks have institutionalized inflation targeting. Recently, about seventy economies were regarded as inflation targeting countries. The creation of money has been considered a common feature of central banks in the world and their establishment was legally backed up.

Before the book delves deeper into its main theme, it is essential to provide readers with the fundamental information required to comprehend the content of this book. Therefore, the next subsection will be dedicated to that purpose, but this may be skipped by those readers who have a basic understanding of the balance sheet.

2.1.1 Similarities and Differences between a Company's Balance Sheet and a Central Bank Balance Sheet

A balance sheet of any organization provides information on financial status at a specific point in time. This implies that balance sheets can be created weekly,

DOI 10.1515/9781547400577-002

monthly, quarterly or annually. The balance sheet also provides an insight into an entity's fiscal health, enabling stakeholders to assess previous performance and predict future trends.

However, different types of entities such as corporations and banks explore different types of information on their respective balance sheets. This creates many differences between a central bank's balance sheet (see Figure 2.1) and a corporation's balance sheet. These differences are as follows:

1. A central bank's balance sheet is prepared in line with the established guideline whereas a company's balance sheet is prepared in relation to the regulation of the International Accounting Standards Board (IASB).

2. The main objective of the central bank balance sheet is to ensure a stable financial system, while a company's key objective is to present the accurate financial position of an organization to the stakeholders.

3. The scope of a central bank's balance sheet covers the financial system of the whole economy whereas the counterpart's scope is applicable for all sorts of companies.

4. A central bank's assets and liabilities are very different from any regular company.

5. The economic situation influences the composition of the central bank's balance sheet; however, this is insignificant in a company's balance sheet.

Bank of Canada
Statement of Financial Position
As at December 31, 2017
(Millions of dollars)   UNAUDITED

ASSETS			LIABILITIES AND EQUITY		
Cash and foreign deposits		14.6	Bank notes in circulation		85,855.9
Loans and receivables			**Deposits**		
Securities purchased under resale agreements	9,478.5		Government of Canada	21,454.2	
Advances	-		Members of Payments Canada	500.3	
Other receivables	4.5		Other deposits	2,274.3	
		9,483.0			24,228.8
Investments			Securities sold under repurchase agreements		.
Treasury bills of Canada	18,370.4				
Government of Canada bonds	82,087.0		Other liabilities		520.0
Other investments	403.6				110,604.7
		100,861.0			
Property and equipment		569.0	**Equity**		
Intangible assets		40.1	Share capital	5.0	
Other assets		132.6	Statutory and special reserves	125.0	
			Available-for-sale reserve	365.6	
					495.6
		111,100.3			**111,100.3**

Figure 2.1: Bank of Canada balance sheet

At the onset, governments set up central banks with the aim of creating reliable payment systems. Over time, the central bank's responsibility increased to managing entire financial systems and economies. Their key method has been to influence the cost of money through a change in interest rates. This was initially applied in an effort to boost or slow the economy, and then as a means of ensuring stability.

Any transaction engaged in by the central bank—for example, issuing currency, conducting foreign exchange operations, investing its own funds, intervening to provide emergency liquidity assistance, and carrying out monetary policy operations—influences its balance sheet. Despite the relevance of the balance sheet, many central banks have largely ignored balance sheet movements, such as assets and liabilities and instead have focused on implementing price targets—establishing targets for a price index like the consumer price index. In addition, economists generally do not favor analyzing balance sheets for patterns that could inform policy decisions. However, analysis of the composition and evolution of the central bank balance sheet provides a valuable basis for understanding the needs of an economy, and is an important tool in developing strategies that would most effectively achieve policy goals.

The fundamental aim of this book is to provide a sound framework for comprehending a central bank's balance sheet. The importance of the central bank's balance sheet also extends to its main liabilities in the functions of the economy. The strength (or weakness) of a central bank's balance sheet provides the trust (or lack thereof) that supports or undermines the legitimacy of most forms of money circulating in an economy.

Monetary policy can be defined as actions of central banks, which affect the size and rate of money supply growth in an economy. Its instruments for implementing these actions include interest rates, forward guidance, large scale asset purchases (QE), and additional liquidity operations such as repurchase agreements. Setting an interest rate would directly influence cost of borrowing, thus affecting economic conditions—lower borrowing cost would stimulate economic growth and vice versa.

Price level targeting is a monetary policy framework designed to ensure price stability. It establishes targets for a price index like the consumer price index. As inflation targeting is forward looking, the price-level targeting is applied to correct any short-term deviations from the target rate of inflation. For instance, in the latter half of the twentieth century, Peru experienced a long inflationary challenge. This led to the International Monetary Fund (IMF) imposition of austerity policies on the country. Its economy suffered stagflation at that time, and gave Alan Garcia the opportunity to become president in 1985. Alan's economic reforms weakened the economy and drove Peru out of global credit markets. This condition hindered access to credit, and worsened the economic situation, and transformed high inflation into hyperinflation in Peru (http://www.businessinsider.com/worst-hyperinflation-episodes-in-history-2013-9?IR=T#china-october-1947-may-1949-6). Deflation in the Eurozone occurred when European prices declined and imports of European goods became cheaper. This made imports into Europe more expensive and pushed inflation up in Europe.

2.2 Trajectory Relevance of the Central Bank Balance Sheet

The lack of attention paid to central bank balance sheets can be attributed to the actions of central banks in moving away from quantitative targets such as money targets and moving toward price targets like inflation, using exchange rates as a means of guiding monetary policy. In the late 1970s and early 1980s, central banks used narrow measures of money supply as an operational target, thus leading to a greater focus on the central bank's balance sheet. The status of the reserves balance, as reported on the central bank's balance sheet, was of great interest to both practitioners and observers. Figure 2.2 indicates a long-run interest rate for G7 economies. As shown in the figure, G7 real interest rates move closely to the convergence point in recent years. Since the early 1960s, the trend patterns were characterized by three episodes. The first episode was a decline in the interest rate up to the mid-1970s; followed by the second episode of a rise until the late 1980s, and then the third episode recorded a fall since the late 1980s.

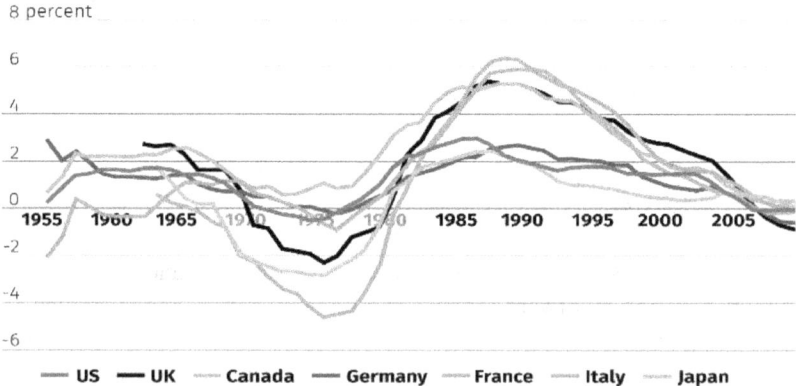

Note: 11-year centered moving average
Source: IMF, Haver and authors' calculations

Source: Excerpted from Yi & Zhang (2016).

Figure 2.2: Real interest rates in G7 nations

However, many central banks abandoned quantitative targets such as a money target because of their relatively poor performance in guiding sound policy. The failures of this policy framework were associated with two factors. First, the central bank has limited influence on the size of its liabilities in the short run. Demand for both banknotes and reserves is exogenous in the very short term, and any attempt to influence in the form of short-term liabilities would result in considerable market instability. Second, there is no clear justification for the central bank to control the quantity of its liabilities.

The money multiplier is closely related to the ratios of commercial bank money to central bank money under fractional-reserve banking. The money multiplier is used to measure the maximum amount of commercial bank money that can be created, given a certain amount of central bank money. Money supply can take the form of narrow and broad money. Narrow money is a type of money supply that includes all physical money such as coins and currency, demand deposits, and other liquid assets held by the central bank. Broad money is defined as the sum of assets that can be used to make payments or held as short-term investments such as currency, funds in bank accounts, and anything of value resembling money.

Key explanations mainly focused on the concept of the money multiplier, which both oversimplifies the importance of commercial banks in money creation and wrongly specifies the causality between narrow and broad monetary aggregates. Without the money multiplier, targeting the quantity of money has no sufficient theoretical justification for a central bank. The money multiplier captures the amount of money banks generate given a certain amount of central bank money. Countries such as Canada, the UK, Australia and Sweden set no legal reserve requirements, compared to those countries such as USA where the reserve requirement is expressed as a ratio of deposits held.

The abandonment of quantitative targets in the late 1980s and early 1990s led many central banks to use either an explicit inflation target as their monetary policy framework or a closely related framework.

These frameworks explore a short-term interbank rate as the operational target of monetary policy, implying that central banks focus on the local price of money and the ways in which the local price of money affects the ultimate objective: inflation. Small open economies, as well as large commodity exporting countries, choose an exchange rate target as their monetary policy target with the purpose of providing a better nominal anchor. Under such a framework, the operations of money markets are implemented to enhance the exchange rate or the external price of money. Proponents of both frameworks believe that the quantity of money does not influence the short-term price level, but does allow commercial banks to access central bank liabilities that are important in attaining the targeted price (the target for the consumer price index).

The renewed interest in the central bank balance sheets has arisen because of the 2007–2008 financial crisis. Responses to the crisis, which were often unconventional in nature, fueled significant increases in the size of central bank balance sheets.

Worldwide, there were substantial disparities in the actions taken by economic authorities during the initial stages of the financial crisis. Many economies halted their participation in interbank markets in order to smooth the dissemination of reserve balances among commercial banks. This caused many commercial banks to hoard reserves instead of lending in interbank markets, partly as a means of safeguarding them against potential negative shocks, and partly to heighten credit risk fears in the potential start-up banks. A slowdown in fund dissemination experienced by interbank markets hindered the ability of commercial banks to settle transactions in commercial bank deposits. In response to the crisis, central banks explored various measures to increase the supply of reserves in order to ensure the smooth settlement of transactions. This response is viewed as liability-driven. By attaining their effective lower bounds of desired prices, central banks readjusted to broaden policies designed to boost economic growth. Desired prices are set to include lower and upper bounds. As the lower bound is attained, the central banks can decide how to reach the upper bound in order to further boost economic performance. These approaches are common to those central banks that adopt band targets rather than a point target. A band target has a range while a point target does not. Consequently, many central banks implemented asset-buying policies to lower longer-term interest rates (both lowering risk-free rates and the spread between risk-free rates and other rates), and affect the portfolio composition of agents in the economy.

The creation of reserves was used to finance the purchase of assets. This led to continual rises in the size of central bank balance sheets, and thus resulted in asset-driven growth.

Exchange rate targeting economies were confronted with the effects of the global financial crisis through additional channels. The fluctuations in global capital flows dramatically affected the exchange rates of many currencies. At the apex of the crisis, emerging economies experienced varying degrees of capital flight as investors sought safe havens for their currency. This resulted in the depreciation of many developing economy currencies, thus forcing monetary authorities (central banks) to intervene and protect the value of their currency. As financial markets witnessed improving conditions, the amount of liquidity increased. Improving liquidity conditions were partly supported by the success of unconventional policies (including the use of asset purchasing measures based on the central bank balance sheet) adopted by many advanced economies. Eventually, this led to the resumption of capital flows into emerging economies and triggered central banks to respond to appreciation pressure. This timeline of events renewed interest in the size and composition of the central bank's balance sheet.

The Great Depression of the 1930s was the aftermath of the failure of major central banks to address fully the consequences of debt deflation. Central banks failed to utilize their balance sheets to sufficiently reduce long-term rates (as discussed above) and counter a cascading sequence of bankruptcies. The policy-making failures during the Great Depression served as a cautionary lesson for monetary authorities in responding to the 2007/2008 financial crisis.

It is historically proven that central banks allowed balance sheets to expand excessively, with the aim of financing profligate government spending. This led to high inflation; however, central banks were reluctant to tighten monetary policy when conditions improved.

The Asian financial crisis of 1997–1998 convinced monetary authorities that building up foreign exchange reserves would safeguard against future crises, or perhaps mitigate the effects of a financial downturn. This led to a huge rise in forex reserves held by central banks in emerging Asian economies—from $2 trillion at the beginning of 2006 to more than $5 trillion today—proportionally equivalent to 45 percent of emerging Asian economy gross domestic product (GDP). Rising foreign exchange reserves also reflected the exchange rate targeting regimes and export-oriented growth measures implemented by many countries. The effectiveness of this measure translates into the greater economic performance experienced in many emerging Asian countries. As illustrated in Figure 2.3, the Fed commenced purchasing longer-term Treasury securities as well as the debt and the mortgage-backed securities (MBS) in December 2008. About US$75 billion of longer-term Treasuries was intended to be purchased by the Fed on a monthly basis in November 2010. This amount increased to nearly US$85 million per month in September 2012 under QE3. During this period, the Fed decided to continue the purchase of securities to the point where there was sufficient improvement in the labor market.

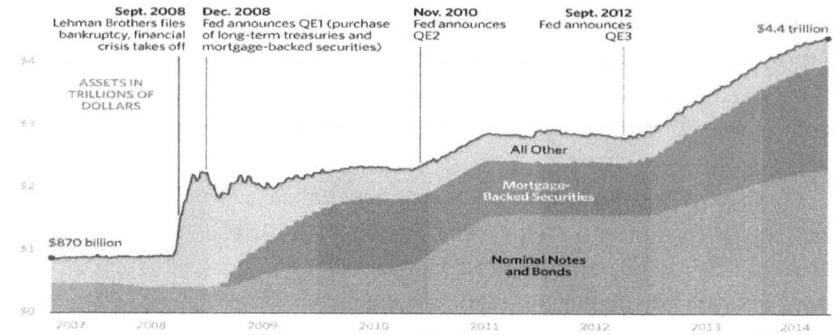

Source: Board of Governors of the Federal Reserve System, "Credit and Liquidity Programs and the Balance Sheet: Total Assets of the Federal Reserve," http://www.federalreserve.gov/monetarypolicy/bst_recenttrends.htm (accessed August 5, 2014).

BG 2938 ☎ heritage.org

Figure 2.3: Federal Reserve assets

Figure 2.4 presents the cumulative change in central bank balance sheets since August 2008. All central banks excluding the Reserve Bank of Australia witnessed a positive cumulative change in the related period. However, the Reserve Bank of Australia continued to record a negative cumulative change in its balance sheets since August 2009.

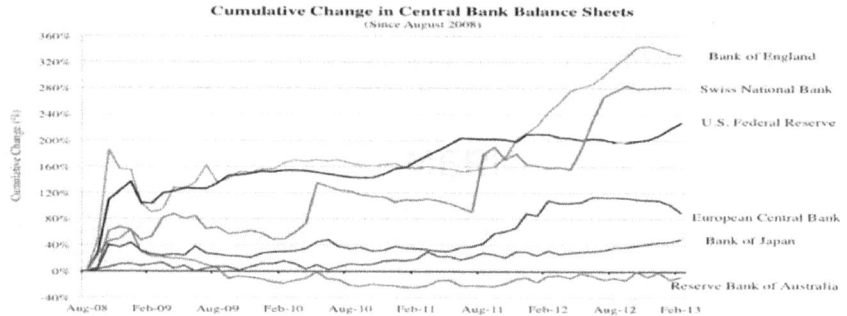

Figure 2.4: Comparative change in central bank balance sheets

2.3 Externality of the Central Bank Balance Sheet Size

The global financial crisis of 2007–2008 triggered the zeal of central banks to buy "unconventional" assets on a large scale such as purchases of long-term government bonds, particularly in advanced economies. Central banks started by purchasing short-term assets and engaging in short-term lending, but gradually moved toward purchasing long-term paper. The total size of central bank balance sheets in advanced economies was about US$20 trillion in 2017, the equivalent of more than 20 percent of global GDP. Lower, zero-bound interest rates meant little room to maneuver through traditional means, so monetary policy was directed toward large-scale asset buying programs (such as TARP in the United States) as a fundamental tool to prevent any renewed financial meltdown that may have been caused by a severe credit crunch. These policies generated an additional monetary stimulus through reducing the long-term interest rate on government bonds, even with short-term interest rates near zero.

A negative aspect of sustained expansions in their balance sheets is that central banks become increasingly exposed to market fluctuations. For instance, a fall in the value of foreign assets or a rise in long-term interest rates could decrease the value of their assets, while the value of their liabilities remains unchanged. This would put the capital of the central bank at risk and may even undermine the central bank's credibility, perhaps leading to greater market instabilities and panic.

Thus, central bank policies that increase the size of a central bank's balance sheet have the ability to generate broader policy risks such as inflation, financial instability, distortions in financial markets, and conflicts with government debt managers.

Exploring balance sheet-related risk is a useful guide in designing suitable exit strategies from monetary policy positions such as asset-purchasing programs, and addresses the following sets of questions:
- Does the expansion of the central bank balance sheet lead to inflation risk?
- What is the correlation between the expansion of the central bank balance sheet and inflation in the past and recent years?
- Are advanced, emerging, and low-income developing economies differently impacted by an expansion in the central bank's balance sheet?

The following chapters in this book will explore the answers to the questions above, and aid in developing our understanding of central banking and the impact of balance sheet changes on the economy as a whole.

Questions

1. What are the similarities and differences between central bank balance sheets and company balance sheets?
2. What is the money multiplier?
3. What is monetary policy?

4. What is the relevance of central bank balance sheets?
5. What influences the use of central bank balance sheets in decision making?
6. What are negative and positive externalities of central bank balance sheets?

Chapter 3
Components of Central Bank Balance Sheets

As discussed in Chapter 1, understanding the composition and size of a central bank's balance sheet is at the core of comprehending the strength of an economy, the range of monetary policy decisions that can be explored, and the possible outcomes of these decisions. However, there are no unified standards that dictate how often a central bank balance sheet should be disclosed to the public, how the sheet should be formatted, or which items are to be included on the balance sheet.

Table 3.1: Publication of central banks' balance sheets in advanced economies, emerging and developing countries

Country	Frequency	Income-Group	Region
Argentina	Weekly	Middle income	Latin American and Caribbean
Australia	Weekly	High income	East Asia and Pacific
Brazil	Monthly	Lower middle income	Latin American and Caribbean
Canada	Weekly	High income	North America
China	Monthly	Upper middle income	East Asia and Pacific
European Union	Weekly	High income	Europe
France	Monthly	High income	Europe and Central Asia
Germany	Monthly	High income	Europe and Central Asia
India	Weekly	Lower middle income	South Asia
Indonesia	Annual	Lower middle income	East Asia and Pacific
Italy	Monthly	High income	Europe and Central Asia
Japan	Ten days	High income	East Asia and Pacific
Mexico	Weekly	Lower middle income	Latin American and Caribbean
Nigeria	Monthly	Lower middle income	Sub-Saharan Africa
Russia	Monthly	Upper middle income	Europe and Central Asia
Saudi Arabia	Monthly	Upper middle income	Middle East and North Africa
South Africa	Monthly	Upper middle income	Sub-Saharan Africa
South Korea	Monthly	Upper middle income	East Asia and Pacific
Turkey	Weekly	Upper middle income	Europe and Central Asia
United Kingdom	Weekly	High income	Europe and Central Asia
United States	Weekly	High income	North America

Source: Central Bank Website and World Bank.

Many central banks publish their balance sheets inside their annual report, and usually at a substantial lag from their current real position. To supplement annual reporting, central banks also publish their balance at more frequent intervals as

DOI 10.1515/9781547400577-003

a separate item on their websites. For instance, the Bank of England, European Central Bank (ECB), and the Federal Reserve publish their balance sheets on a weekly basis with minimal lag, while others such as Central Bank of Nigeria and the Hong Kong Monetary Authority publish their balance sheets on a monthly basis. Table 3.1 indicates the publication frequency of central bank balance sheets across a number of advanced and emerging economies.

It is easy to see the variations that can occur in balance sheets. Let's take Malaysia's central bank balance sheets for the month of February 2018 in Table 3.2 and compare it to that of Nigeria in Table 3.3. Malaysia's central bank does not disaggregate its foreign asset holdings as it is reflected in its counterpart balance sheet (Nigeria). In addition, about 80 percent of Malaysia's central banks assets were held in foreign assets compared to 50 percent in Nigeria. However, deposits by financial institutions accounted for the largest share in their liabilities.

Table 3.2: Malaysia's central bank balance sheets for the month of February 2018

Assets	RM
Gold and Foreign Exchange and Other Reserves including SDR	419,549,797,551
Malaysian Government Papers	4,463,229,458
Deposits with Financial Institutions	5,598,818,970
Loans and Advances	7,493,903,885
Land and Buildings	4,179,614,080
Other Assets	9,516,489,885
	450,801,853,829

Capital and Liabilities	RM
Paid-Up Capital	100,000,000
Reserves	137,234,486,113
Currency in Circulation	108,303,399,938
Deposits by:	
Financial Institutions	167,881,909,188
Federal Government	11,105,958,177
Others	1,112,181,442
Bank Negara Papers	12,992,576,427
Allocation of Special Drawing Rights	7,759,395,868
Other Liabilities	4,311,946,676
	450,801,853,829

Source: Central Bank of Malaysia

Table 3.3: Nigeria's central bank balance sheets for the month of November 2017(000' Naira)

Date	11/30/2017
Gold	19,009
Convertible Currency	12,010,447,867
IMF Gold Tranche	22,623
Special Drawing Rights	631,681,317
Total External Reserve	**12,642,170,816**
Federal Govt Sect.	**1,667,227,008**
Other Securities	**4,330,538,381**
Rediscount & Advance	**1,906,224,520**
Other Assets	**4,229,102,626**
Fixed Assets	**459,108,596**
Total Assets	**25,234,371,947**
Capital Subscribed	5,000,000
General reserve	220,068,958
Other Reserves	40,764,187
Total Capitalisation	265,833,145
Currency in Circulation	1,896,585,425
Government Deposits	904,622,429
Bankers Deposit	3,568,164,797
Other Deposits	16,128,321,448
Subtotal Liabilities	20,601,108,674
Other Liabilities	2,470,844,703
Total Equity and Liabilities	**25,234,371,947**

Source: Central Bank of Nigeria.

3.1 Factors Influence the Reporting Frequency of Central Bank Balance Sheets

The level of detail at which balance sheet items are reported differs across countries. These differences are due to accounting practices and local idiosyncrasies. For instance, central banks that implement a floating exchange rate might report their foreign exchange reserves more precisely, perhaps using subsidiary items (creating additional reports to provide more details) for each currency. This contrasts with regimes that fix their exchange rate, thus holding a smaller amount of such assets. Some balance sheet accounts may be uniquely specific to a certain country. For example, the transfer of cash management to the UK Debt Management in 2000 remains as an item on the Bank of England's balance sheet to this day.

Despite these differences, a central bank's balance sheet has a general format as indicated in Table 3.4.

Table 3.4: Generalized form of central bank balance sheets

Liabilities	Assets
Banknotes	Net foreign assets
Commercial bank reserves	Net government balances
Capital and reserves	Net central bank operations Other items

Items on the liability side of the balance sheet capture central bank money while items on the asset side are reported in a net format. Each component fulfills a critical responsibility in the functioning of both the central bank and the whole economy. Variations in the balances of these accounts consequently influence the quantity of reserves available to the banking system. Thus, a clear understanding of the wider economy depends on understanding the nature and changes in the components of the central bank's balance sheet.

3.2 Components of Central Bank Assets and their Composition Analysis

This subsection explains various forms of assets that can be held by a central bank and how the composition of these assets can change in response to different situation.

3.2.1 Foreign Assets

Foreign assets are expressed in non-local currency. The principal form of foreign assets kept by central banks is foreign exchange reserves. The reasons for holding foreign exchange reserves by central banks include intervention to support the domestic currency, to fulfill external obligations on foreign currency debt (public and/or private), and to cover trade balances.

A central bank can intervene to address the issue of appreciation of domestic currency strength by raising its holding of foreign exchange reserves. To accommodate this, the central bank can intervene by selling domestic assets (likely reserves) in exchange for foreign currency denominated assets, with the consequent balance sheet change illustrated in Figure 3.1. This leads to increasing the supply of domestic currency assets and increasing the demand for foreign currency assets, which (ceteris paribus) alleviates appreciation pressure.

The quantity of foreign exchange reserves accumulated by the central bank dictates its ability to intervene to offset depreciation in the domestic currency (see Figure 3.2). In the case of a depreciating domestic currency, the central bank may intervene by selling foreign assets in exchange for domestic currency denominated assets. This jointly results in a rise in the supply of foreign assets, and a drop in the supply of domestic assets, offsetting depreciation pressure. This has a corollary effect of shortening the central bank's balance sheet.

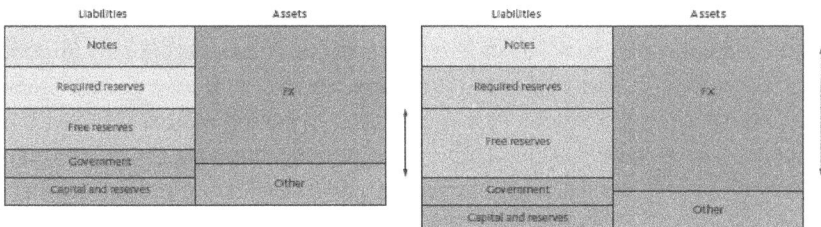

Figure 3.1: Currency appreciation situation

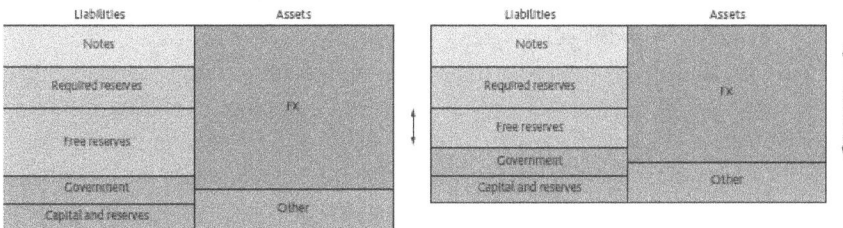

Source Excerpted from BIS.

Figure 3.2: Currency depreciation situation

The amount of foreign exchange reserves that central banks hold is likely to be proportional to the frequency and magnitude of foreign exchange interventions that a central bank is inclined to make. This is largely based on the territory's exchange-rate regime. For central banks that follow a free-float regime, reserves may be relatively small; market supply and demand dictate the value of a currency and interventions are usually rare. Other countries, particularly those facing substantial and prolonged appreciation pressures, may hold relatively much larger quantities of foreign reserves. In particularly strict exchange rate targeting regimes, monetary authorities may establish a currency board. The tasks of a central bank currency board focus on ensuring direct convertibility between domestic and a target foreign currency. In this situation, a currency board ensures adequate foreign exchange reserves to satisfy the demand for exchange. Over recent years, there has been a significant rise in the volume of foreign exchange reserves held by central banks, especially in emerging economies.

Foreign exchange reserves are usually kept in the form of liquid and safe assets, such as developed economy cash and government bonds. Naturally, central banks are risk averse and intervention often requires a quick response, which makes it necessary to hold foreign assets that are in wide demand and can thus be quickly liquidated or traded. In addition, central banks decide to hold assets in a foreign currency that is directly critical for trade and investment in their countries. For the aforementioned reasons, the U.S. dollar most frequently forms the majority of central bank foreign reserve currencies, particularly for commodity exporting countries. Furthermore, the central bank may perform some of its balance sheet operations in foreign currency liabilities. This is linked to a number of central bank policies and other factors. In many countries where there is substantial foreign exchange activity, but underdeveloped financial markets, the central bank creates foreign currency facilities to support its commercial banks (which may want to lend in a foreign currency). Since it is not possible for a central bank to create foreign currency, such facilities have to be matched either by expanding existing holdings of foreign currency assets or through agreeing to an exchange line with the central bank of the currency provided.

Foreign liabilities capture the funding of foreign exchange reserves. The central bank needs to decide whether to build foreign exchange reserves through the issuance of domestic currency assets or other means. Any decision on this will have a direct influence on the current exchange rate (as it will lead to a rise in the supply of domestic currency assets and a rise in the demand for foreign currency assets). In order to keep currency neutral, the central bank might exchange for foreign assets through issuing foreign currency liabilities. Then, it can also exchange the received funds for more suitable assets in additional currencies if required.

3.3 Components of Central Bank Liabilities and their Composition Analysis

In this section, we look at different components of central bank liabilities in a consensus way. We also discuss how different economic activities can influence each of these components.

3.3.1 Banknotes

This item includes banknotes issued by the central bank that are circulating through the economy, either being held in vaults by commercial banks, in automatic teller machines (ATMs), or by individuals. These banknotes are circulated through commercial banks in some countries (note that money in circulation excludes notes printed but still held by the central bank or those returned to the central bank). This allows commercial banks to withdraw banknotes in exchange for reserve balances held at the central bank. The wider population has access to banknotes by directly withdrawing notes from commercial banks or indirectly from other agents. Most price targeting economies will supply banknotes on demand to commercial banks. The volatility of banknote demand in the short term has been attributed to seasonal variables, at weekly, monthly, and yearly periods.

3.3.1.1 Drivers of Short-Term Volatility of the Demand for Banknotes

On a weekly basis, the demand for banknotes increases as the weekend approaches and decreases at the beginning of the week as businesses deposit cash at commercial banks. A rise and a fall in banknote balances occurs days before and after the weekend as commercial banks prepare for the usual outflow and inflow of notes around a weekend.

Monthly fluctuations in banknote demand depend on the share of the country's population that has access to banking facilities. Within-month volatility will be low if a large proportion of the population obtains their salary in the form of commercial bank deposits. Conversely, within-month volatility will be high if a large share of the population lacks access to banking facilities, necessitating the payment of salaries in cash. This implies that the demand for banknotes will be more pronounced around common payment dates, and will then decline as people expend their wages and invariably return to commercial banks.

Banknote demand also rises around public holidays, significantly during Christmas or Eid al-Fitr. In addition, countries with popular tourist destinations might witness a rise in demand for banknotes around the peak tourist season.

3.3.1.2 Drivers of Long-Term Volatility of the Demand for Banknotes

The long-run relationship between demand for banknotes and nominal gross domestic product (GDP) has been established. As both the value and volume of payments in an economy rise, banknote demand also increases over time. Other long-term drivers of banknote demand include the opportunity cost of holding cash and payment technology. The amount of this opportunity cost differs based on the central bank's interest rate. Under low interest rate conditions, the cost of holding banknotes (as an alternative to depositing the cash in a bank account) will be lower due to reduced interest yields. However, carrying bank notes or keeping cash at home can be risky; the person holding large amounts of physical cash may be robbed. Receiving compensation for cash losses arising from theft is often extremely problematic. Furthermore, attempts to safeguard banknotes pose an additional cost, for example, the cost of buying a safe.

Money held in electronic form is significantly more difficult to steal. Even in the situation of bank robberies or electronic fraud, the loss of physical banknotes is not attached to specific accounts, and banks insure against these losses so individual account holders would not suffer personal cash losses if their bank branches were robbed. In addition, in many nations, the government insures bank deposits up to a certain limit, in the case of bank failures. For instance, the Federal Deposit Insurance scheme of the United States insures balances up to US$250,000. However, agents may prefer to hold cash and bear the risks if there is low trust in commercial banks, fearing losses of liquidity in the banking system may result in the inability to withdraw funds. These aggregated factors, complemented by growth in the informal economy, are responsible for a rise in demand for cash in many countries through a global financial meltdown, despite declining nominal GDP growth.

Payment technology also determines demand for banknotes. Advances in payment technology in the form of debit cards, contactless payments, and mobile phone technology have changed the means of settling transactions that traditionally settled in cash. However, demand for banknotes continues to rise despite predictions that cash would become increasingly marginalized as a means of settlement due to technological advances. The effect of payment technologies on cash balances is more pronounced in developing countries. In Kenya, M-Pesa, a mobile application for payment services, has recorded tremendous progress by including a significant proportion of the rural population into its payment technology, and has allowed individuals to hold smaller amounts of physical cash.

The demand for banknotes denominated in the domestic currency is also driven by the confidence level in the central bank. If people have low confidence in the central bank's ability to protect currency value from inflation or devaluation, they will explore other channels to settle transactions that do not involve using the domestic currency. This often leads to dollarization (named such because the U.S. dollar is often the most common currency employed, but could potentially be any foreign currency employed), when another country's currency circulates either in an unofficial manner or semiofficial way alongside the domestic currency as a means of settling transactions. Change in the volume of dollarization over time is a significant moderator for the demand of domestic banknotes.

3.3.2 Commercial Bank Reserves

Reserves are regarded as overnight balances that banks hold in an account at the central bank (Clews, Salmon, and Weeken, 2010). In addition, these balances form a claim against the central bank. Reserves and banknotes are the most liquid and risk-free assets in the economy. They are used in settling payments and enabling banking transactions among clients of different commercial banks directly or indirectly by conducting transfers between reserve accounts at the central bank. Reserves are viewed as a current account balance held by commercial banks at the central bank, conceptually similar to current account balances held by individuals at commercial banks. There are many misconceptions surrounding the function of reserve balances, despite the crucial economic role that reserve balances play.

3.3.2.1 Misconceptions Regarding Commercial Bank Reserves
All commercial banks can decide to pick between reserves and other assets. This implies that the aggregate amount of reserves held at the central bank at any period is determined by commercial banks. Though this determination is only possible for individual commercial banks, system-wide levels of reserves depend on accounting identities on the central bank's balance sheet. This clarification is better understood if we consider what occurs when an individual commercial bank decides to reduce its reserve balance.

3.3.3 Capital

The structure of the central bank's balance sheet is similar to private corporation balance sheets in several ways. According to Cukierman (2010), central banks share some similar features, in terms of legal aspects and accounting principles. Central banks place capital on their balance sheets as practiced in the private sector institutions. The capital buffer or net worth based on the gap between the value of total assets and total liabilities is identified as the channel through which the central bank absorbs losses (which is based on the value of the capital).

However, regulatory capital requirements are not applicable to central banks. This contrasts with commercial banks and other financial institutions, which are required to hold capital buffers in direct relation to the size and riskiness of their lending activities, as stipulated by international and domestic regulations. There are no such regulations applied to central banks. Furthermore, private institutions can only raise required amounts of capital through accumulating retained earnings or transacting with financial markets to increase additional funds (for example through share offerings). Although central banks are not constrained by official capital requirements, there is some debate as to an optimal level of capital that should be held by central banks. The capital portion of the balance sheet should not be ignored as consistently operating under negative equity conditions can have serious implications for the integrity of the central bank.

3.3.3.1 Debate on Optimal Capital Level for Central Banks

Several works have attempted to determine the optimal level of capital for a central bank. The conclusion of Cukierman (2010) and Derbyshire (2010) is that there is no simple correct answer. Stella (2010) observed that central banks' policy choices are limited by the size of their capital. In addition, she stated that central banks loosen policies in order to prevent huge losses for reputational or political reasons. The optimal capital level for a particular central bank is influenced by factors related to the situation it faces, as well as institutional and political structures.

Certain policy goals might create scenarios where the central bank has to lose money or take greater risks to attain socially optimal results. For instance, a central bank might implement a quantitative easing program by purchasing government debt with likely low yields (high prices) as investors want safety over risky assets. This may happen in an era of economic recession in the country, with inflation either undershooting or being forecast to undershoot its target. Economic recovery and closing inflation targets are indicators for the success of such a program. On the other hand, when the economy recovers, the yields on government bonds have a tendency to rise (prices fall) as investors decide to buy riskier assets and policy rates are increased. When the central bank intends to sell its bond holdings, it will likely trade at a loss. It will be socially optimal for the central bank to implement this program as it has attained its goal of enhancing growth and/or achieving its inflation target, despite the financial loss. The former deputy governor of the Bank of England, Charlie Bean, states that quantitative easing and the asset purchase facility (APF) are aimed at attaining macroeconomic objectives such as hitting the inflation target without stimulating undue volatility in output. The failure of the APF in solving these overall macroeconomic costs or benefits creates the need to evaluate the impact of quantitative easing on demand and inflation.

Questions

1. What are the components of central bank assets and liabilities?
2. What is non-monetary liability in the central bank balance sheet?
3. How does banknote circulation influence inflation in the economy?
4. What are the short-term and long-term drivers of volatility of the demand for banknotes?
5. What are the misconceptions related to commercial bank reserves?

Chapter 4
Analytical Framework of Central Bank Balance Sheets

4.1 Structure of Central Bank Balance Sheets

Analyzing the evolution of the central bank's balance sheet has important practical applications when evaluating the performance of the central bank in meeting policy goals. The structure of central bank balance sheets differs from those of private sector firms. A simplified structure of central bank balance sheet is portrayed in Figure 4.1.

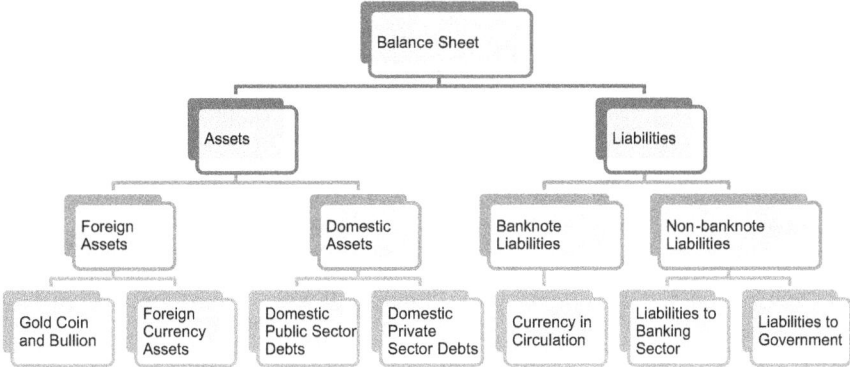

Source: Adapted from Christiaan Pattipeilohy (2016).
Figure 4.1: A simplified structure of central bank balance sheets

As illustrated in Figure 4.1, the foreign assets category covers assets denominated in foreign currency and assets issued by foreign counterparties, as well as central bank holdings of precious commodities like gold. Domestic assets cover domestic public sector debt (G) that take the form of collateralized lending or repurchase agreements, and domestic private sector debt (P), which is defined as loans to or debt securities issued by banks and other financial intermediaries. For the classification of central bank liabilities, the balance sheet delineates between base money, that is, banknotes in circulation (N) and reserve balances from commercial banks, and non-monetary liabilities. From a practical perspective, the definition of what is covered in base money in addition to banknotes significantly differs across central banks. For instance, most central banks issue debt

DOI 10.1515/9781547400577-004

certificates to sterilize the impacts of asset purchases on the formal definition of base money, but the Bank of Indonesia regards its debt instruments as secondary reserves and includes them in the formal definition of base money.

Similarly, the problem also arises in dealing with how to classify term deposits issued by central banks. Borio and Disyatat (2010) suggest that what is entailed in base money in practice is largely a matter of semantics, with different outcomes across times and regions.

This book adopts a Bank for International System (BIS) approach to address the practical issues in relation to the theoretical differentiation between monetary and non-monetary liabilities. The nonbanknote central bank liabilities are given separate classifications as liabilities to banks (LB) that cover term deposit and debt certificates, as distinct from liabilities to the government (LG). The distinction between monetary and non-monetary liabilities plays a role in the development of monetary policy frameworks.

4.2 Balance Sheet Indicators

To explain the nature of central bank balance sheets in relation to its components, this subsection presents different indicators used to understand this pattern. These indicators are generally utilized to discuss the central banking system.

4.2.1 Computation of Indicators

Based on BIS (2016), it is possible to compute four balance sheet indicators, of which two pertain to the asset side, and the remaining two to the liability side. These indicators jointly reflect the central bank balance sheet structure.

For the asset side, the relative distribution between foreign assets and domestic assets is derived as follows:

Domestic asset (DA) = domestic government debt (DGD) + domestic private sector debt (DPD)

Domestic assets in terms of foreign assets = DA/FA where FA denotes foreign assets

$$= \frac{(DGD + DPD)}{FA}$$

The decision as to whether a central bank's domestic asset portfolio assigns more weight to domestic government debt or domestic private sector debt depends on the actual data computation. A similar decision is applied to the composition of central bank liabilities.

On the liability side, the relative distribution between banknotes in circulation and total non-banknote liabilities is specified as:

$$\frac{(LG + LB)}{N}$$

Where LG is liabilities to government, LP represents liabilities to banks, and N denotes banknotes in circulation.

In addition, a decision is taken whether a central bank's deposit liabilities are geared more toward the banking sector or the domestic government by calculating LG in terms of LB.

Quick question: Compute these indicators using central bank balance sheets of your country or your region.

4.2.2 Significance of these Indicators

The indicators explained above provide concise information on balance sheet composition with the aid of a limited number of parameters. In addition, it will provide a guide in designing taxonomies of central banks based on balance sheet structure (see Table 3.2). Quantitative assessment on the dynamic nature of balance sheet composition is done using these indicators, as well as the relative differences among central banks.

4.2.3 Underlying Assumptions of Four Indicators

The derivations of these indicators require a set of basic assumptions. Therefore, the fundamental assumptions related to the indicators are as follows:
1. There is no correlation among the four indicators.
2. A central bank does not face any constraints in deciding the size of any of the four indicators, regardless of the effect on the other three.

Example 4.1
Consider a case in which the central bank intends to raise its public debt holding by purchasing government bonds from the banking sector. This situation would affect all four indicators, holding all other things constant. DGD enters in both asset-side indicators, while the Ls record in both liability-side indicators.

The central bank can increase the DGD/DPD by concomitantly increasing DGD and reducing L, keeping all other indicators constant. However, it is practically impossible to have an unconstrained central bank. Therefore, it faces a challenge in deciding the size of every balance sheet item; the central bank views many developments as exogenous shocks and responds to them by endogenously adjusting its balance sheet.

4.3 Determinants of Central Bank Balance Sheet Composition

Structural and policy-related factors influence the composition of a central bank balance sheet (BIS, 2009). The structural factors include behavioral, operational, and institutional factors. These factors are regarded as autonomous liquidity factors, as suggested in Ho (2008) or ECB (2011). Examples of behavioral factors affecting central bank balance sheets may be associated with the supply of banknotes. A central bank has no control over the demand for banknotes but ensures that the implications of changes in demand are fully understood.

The payment systems of the central bank are an important determinant of its balance sheet and are considered as an example of an operational factor. Settling large value interbank payments on a day-to-day basis depends on bank deposits at the central bank (CPSS, 2003). This implies that interbank payments can be responsible for a large intraday volatility within the central bank balance sheet. In addition, the design of payment and settlement systems also influences the composition of central bank balance sheets. More intraday liquidity is needed if a central bank operates a real-time gross settlement system compared to a system of end-of-day netting (BIS, 2009).

Central bank operating frameworks influence the functioning of money markets and hence the level of liabilities. Central banks may also adjust their instruments to the money market configuration with the aim of achieving their effective policies.

In many economies, the central bank maintains the government's main account. In this situation, incoming and outgoing payments from the government will also determine the composition of central bank liabilities.

Institutional factors, such as the prevailing exchange rate regime, influence central bank balance sheet composition. The well-known impossible trinity in international macroeconomics explains that in a fixed exchange rate regime with free capital mobility, autonomous monetary policy is no longer feasible (Obstfeld and Taylor, 1998). Owing to this, domestic monetary policy is subject to the monetary policy of the anchor currency within the exchange rate regime, both in terms of conventional (interest-rate setting) and unconventional (balance sheet) policies. With reference to balance sheet policies, the central bank may need to intervene in the foreign exchange market at specific predetermined levels of the exchange rate, making the balance sheet endogenous to capital flows. This is the reason behind the huge accumulation of foreign currencies by many EMEs (Obstfeld et al., 2010). To illustrate, the Swiss National Bank set a unilateral cap for the Swiss franc against the euro from September 2011 to January 2015, and decided to defend the cap by purchasing foreign exchange in unlimited amounts.

Aside from the aforementioned factors, monetary policy decisions, as well as financial stability intervention measures, will also influence the central bank balance sheet (BIS, 2009). For instance, monetary policy operations pertaining to the buying of either domestic or foreign currency assets or entering into repo agreements with banks may influence the asset side of a central bank balance sheet. Setting reserve requirements or issuing longer-term liabilities (including term deposits or central bank bills) are actions that can be explored by the central bank to manage commercial banking reserves; these policies invariably affect the liability side of the balance sheet.

Financial stability interventions can include extending short-term emergency facilities for distressed private sector financial institutions. Although this type of intervention is conducted with the aim of stabilizing conditions in the short term, these decisions might affect the central bank balance sheet composition more persistently, as showcased during the recent global financial crisis. It took until 2014 for the U.S. Treasury to sell all of its shares in U.S. companies, six years after the original bailout package was agreed to as part of the TARP program.

The end result of central bank decisions that affect (or utilize) its balance sheet may differ across different monetary authorities and is likely to be time-variant. These results may be moderated by factors such as monetary policy regime, the central bank's mandate, the structure and maturity of the financial system, and financial market conditions.

4.4 Classification of Central Bank Balance Sheet Components

Using the set of indicators described above as a guideline, the composition of central bank assets and liabilities is classified as per the underlying principles detailed in Table 4.1. Based on asset composition, a central bank may be categorized as a foreign exchange holder, treasury holder, or private sector lender. On the liability side, a central bank can be identified as a note issuer, government banker, or bankers' banker. These definitions are for illustrative purposes only and will be decided by the actual data of balance sheet composition. The classification principles assume discrete thresholds to differentiate between types (see Figure 4.2).

Table 4.1: Framework for extracting data in standardized IFS reporting of central banks

Assets		Liabilities	
Items	**Description**	**Items**	**Description**
Foreign Assets(FA)	Claims on non-residents	**Banknotes in circulation(N)**	Currency in circulation
Domestic Government debt(DPD)	Claims on central government Claims on state and local government Claims on public non-financial corporations	**Liabilities to government (LG)**	Liabilities to central government
Domestic Private sector debt(DPD)	Claims on other depository corporations Claims on other financial corporations Claims on private sector Claims on other sectors	**Liabilities to banks(LB)**	Liabilities to other depository corporations Liabilities to other sectors Liabilities to other depository corporations not included in monetary base Deposits and securities other than shares excluded from monetary base

Source: Excerpted from BIS (2017).

Asset Category

- —Foreign asset holder: *More than 50 percent of central bank assets are foreign assets.*
- —Treasury holder: *More than 50 percent of central bank assets are domestic assets, and domestic public assets account for more than 50 percent of domestic assets.*
- —Private sector holder: *More than 50 percent of central bank assets are domestic assets, and domestic private assets account for more than 50 percent of domestic assets.*

Liability Category

- —Note issuer: *Total deposits at the central bank are less than 10 percent of currency in circulation.*
- —Government's banker: *Total deposits at the central bank are more than 10 percent of currency in circulation. Of total deposits, more than 50 percent are linked to the domestic government.*
- — Bankers' banker: *Total deposits at the central bank are more than 10 percent of currency in circulation. Of total deposits, more than 50 percent are linked to the domestic banking sector.*

Source: Modified from Christiaan Pattipeilohy (2016).

Figure 4.2: Categorizations of central bank sheets

4.5 Theoretical Landscape: Quantity Theory of Money versus Quality Theory of Money

During the twentieth century, conventional monetary economics has dealt with the value of a monetary unit using the quantity theory.

4.5.1 Quantity Theory of Money

Modern monetary economics focuses on the use of the quantity theory of exchange in establishing the purchasing power of money. The Fisherian equation of exchange is used to back this theory mathematically in a simple expression:

$$MV = PY$$

Where M represents the quantity of money, V is its velocity, that is, rate of circulation; Y denotes real output and P is the price index of this output.

V and Y are assumed to be constant in the long run, implying that the quantity of money directly influences money's value (representing the inverse of the general price index). In this theory, qualitative measures are irrelevant.

Its disadvantage is the failure to address the real problem in relation to the value of and demand for the monetary unit. The importance attached to transaction is determined by the value of the monetary unit, while the demand for the monetary unit is a function of expected future prices used when making purchases (regression theorem of money[1]). Owing to the fact that future prices are driven by the interplay between the demand for money and its future supply, the analysis of the balance sheet can provide an insight into investors' expectations of what the central bank's target might be for the quantity of money.

4.5.2 Quality Theory of Money

The quality theory of money identifies the significance of qualitative factors in the aspect of money demand. The famous proponents of the quality theory are Irving Fisher (1911) and Milton Friedman (1956).

---

[1] Regression theorem of money is the theorem that links the subjective theory of money value to the objective-exchange value or purchasing power of money.

According to the theory, quality of money refers to the ability of a currency to fulfill money's three functions: as a medium of exchange, store of value, and unit of account. Quality is a subjective concept based on the fact that users assign different degrees of importance to the extent to which a good is able to fulfill these three functions. In the absence of changes in the money supply, the subjective valuation of money can vary. A shift in the demand for money can be responsible for the change in the purchasing power of money, but with the expectation of a constant money supply, the subjective valuation of money can even change. For instance, the currency support (i.e., central bank reserve) can change, and hence influence the subjective valuation of the currency by altering expectations regarding the future rate of inflation or changing perceptions regarding the ability of the central bank to act as a lender of last resort to the private banking system.

4.5.2.1 Drivers of the Quality of Money as a Unit of Account and Medium of Exchange

Changes in the perceived quality of money arise from how well it is performing its three core roles. The unit of account role remains stable and reasonably predictable in a situation of low and stable inflation. However, this can change suddenly when an economy experiences hyperinflationary conditions, pushing users to commence recording the value of goods in an alternative manner that does not use the domestic currency. For example, during the mid-1920s, Germans calculated the value of goods using foreign currencies due to massive hyperinflation that resulted from flooding the economy with newly-printed domestic currency, exacerbated by a loss of productive capacity. In recent times, Zimbabwean hyperinflation reached a monthly inflation rate of 80 billion percent by November 2008, forcing suppliers to price goods in a more stable standard, that is, U.S. dollars or gold, at the expense of their devalued local currency. Furthermore, the domestic currency received from a sale at the start of the business day would be almost worthless by the close of business, which leads to the discussion of money's value as a medium of exchange.

In terms of the medium of exchange function, the following necessary conditions are put forward by classical economists: lower transportation and storage costs, easier divisibility, greater recognizability, stronger durability, and superior homogeneity of the money units. Although historically many currencies were linked with a gold standard, modern economists argue that fiat money meets these conditions. Of course, as noted above with the Zimbabwe and Germany examples, money loses its value as a medium of exchange when it is thinly traded due to devaluation.

4.5.2.2 Drivers of the Quality of Money as a Store of Value

Individuals keep their wealth in a way that is efficient, allowing them to defer future purchases of goods and services or obtain cash in order to facilitate current consumption. The better a good conserves its value, the better it will execute a role as currency, holding all other things constant. Even with wide demand, perishable goods like fish or potatoes perform poorly as store of value, as trading these items can only be completed in a limited timeframe before they lose all their value. With the recent advent of cryptocurrency, this might pose significant impacts on the potential store of value of these commodities.

There are five ways through which the quality of money can change in its effectiveness as a store of value. First, changes in the quantity of money substantially influence money's quality. Quantities of issued fiat money (in the form of paper currencies) can be dramatically increased, if the central bank decides to run its printing presses. If the supply of goods remains the same, the prices of these goods would eventually increase to reflect the increased amount of cash circulating in the economy available for consumption (more money chasing the same amount of goods). The store of value function is affected by the present quantity of money and the quantity anticipated in the future. Expectations about the evolution of the quantity of money are not the only determinant of money's store of value function.

Second, changes in the redemption ratio[2] may determine the quality of money even when holding expectations about the future quantity of money constant. For example, a dollar bill can currently be converted to 1/20 of an ounce of gold and at a future date this redemption ratio may be altered to 1/35 of an ounce of gold, or 1/20 of an ounce of silver, or redemption may be suspended altogether. Under this situation, the quantity of money in circulation is the same, but money's function as a store of value is adversely affected, as it can be used to obtain a smaller amount of valuable goods. Redemption changes may affect the valuation of the currency unit relative to other goods even if expectations about future quantity of money remain unchanged. The valuation of the currency unit in relation to other goods may not be as high as it might be with the change in the backing of the currency. Also, in an extreme case, a war can affect the value of a currency; if users expect that a government will fall and no longer be able to back the fiat currency, the currency will experience massive depreciation.

---

2 A redemption is the return of a principal in a fixed-income security or the sale of units in a mutual fund. The redemption amount at maturity is calculated by multiplying the face value by the index factor. The calculation of the redemption ratio is out of the scope of this book.

Third, the general condition of the banking system also determines the quality of currency as a store of value. For instance, an illiquid banking system triggers the risk of a bail-out that finally raises the quantity of money. Signs of an imperiled banking system can be noted on the central bank's balance sheet through sharp rises in overnight lending or loan rates. This leads to a decrease in the quality of money, and creates expectation-based inflationary pressures.

Fourth, the configuration of the monetary authority is an important driver of the quality of money. A central bank that is not independent from the government is more likely to be inclined toward monetizing government debts. Attempts to influence the decision of an independent central bank may harm the quality of money, even in the absence of commensurate changes in the quantity of money in circulation, as individuals may become worried that monetary policy will be directed toward fulfilling certain political goals rather than improving the whole economy in an efficient manner.

Amendments to a central bank's constitution in regard to its philosophy or doctrine may result in changes in the quality of money. For instance, if a central bank alters its stated target growth rate of the money supply from 5 to 10 percent, this announcement immediately changes the quality of money through increased inflationary expectations. Similarly, if a central bank terminates a rule-based monetary policy and switches to targeting asset prices, this action will instantly affect the quality of money as a store of value. Other policies supported by the central bank—such as full employment or financing educational expenditures—will also affect the quality of money. If the original constitutional objective is focused on price stability, and it is amended to entail other aims like achieving full employment, increasing asset prices, or maintaining a currency union (a pact among members of that union-countries to share a common currency and a single monetary policy and foreign exchange policy), this will influence the quality of money: the aim of price stability might be less of a priority relative to another goal. This leads to uncertainties among the business community as to what the dominant aim of the central bank will be.

The credentials, experience and ability of central bank employees is also an important driver of the quality of money. Chairmen of central banks set monetary policy based on building consensus, a role which directly influences the credibility of a proposed monetary policy. Particularly in an economy where the central bank lacks independence, a weak chairperson will be viewed as incapable of enacting efficient policies. The normative economic preferences of a chairperson can also affect the quality of money. Replacing a chairperson with a record of favoring conservative monetary policy with a new chairperson who is known to prefer expansionary monetary policy may decrease the quality of money on the day the replacement is announced, regardless of any changes in the money supply.

4.5.2.3 The Quality of the Central Bank's Balance Sheet as a Driver of the Quality of Money as a Store of Value

Changes to the reserves and assets of the central bank are another determinant of changes in the quality of money. In relation to the soft factors mentioned above, the assets of the central bank are objective variables that can be assessed directly in analyzing its balance sheet. For instance, the monetary base is directly observable as the central bank's non-equity liabilities.

Therefore, indirect analysis of the quality of money can be investigated through the assets (domestic assets) that support the monetary base. The average-supporting asset of the monetary base is critical for the quality of money and is observable on the balance sheet. In a fractional-reserve banking system, the average backing of the currency in circulation can fall or rise based on changes in the monetary base. The average quality of the backing assets (domestic assets) rises when newly purchased assets are of a higher quality than the average of the existing assets. The average quality of the backing assets falls as newly purchased assets are of a lower quality than the average existing assets, a process known as "qualitative easing." Quantitative changes to the monetary base affect the quality of money as its backing reserves may be diluted. On the other hand, the quality of assets of the central bank can deteriorate even with a constant money supply as the central bank replaces its high quality assets by buying lower quality assets.

Central bank assets are crucial because they act as collateral for its liabilities and "back" the currency. In almost every fiat money regime, no legal obligation is imposed to redeem the currency against the central bank's assets. The central bank assets reflect the capacity of the central bank to safeguard the price of the currency domestically and globally in foreign-exchange markets. For instance, the central bank can utilize its reserves to back its currency through foreign-exchange interventions. It can also use its reserves as a de facto redemption tool; reserve assets are used to purchase currency and holders redeem their currency units against the reserves.

Furthermore, the central bank may utilize its assets to support the banking system by purchasing troubled assets from the banking system to restore confidence in the banking system's solvency. This will only reassure investors if the central bank owns sufficient amounts of high quality assets that can be exchanged for the banking system's troubled assets.

The quality of the central bank's assets is significant for its ability to credibly assist a struggling banking system. In rare cases, its assets can be utilized for monetary reform (such reforms were noted in ex-Soviet bloc countries after 1992–1993, and in the dissolution of Czechoslovakia in 1991). Higher asset quality indicates that a new currency will be stronger and less volatile (and individuals will be confident in its ability to fulfill the three aforementioned roles of money) (see Box 4.1).

The importance of the central bank's assets becomes readily apparent when a currency collapses in value. The decomposition of the monetary system lessens the value of currency. Temporarily, its assets may retain value, and can be allocated to creditors and currency holders, or used in exchange for imports. Currency holders in a normal situation prefer a central bank that holds liquid assets (i.e., foreign exchange or gold) as its main reserves to a central bank that holds illiquid assets (i.e., subprime mortgages) in the case of a monetary breakdown.

Insolvency will happen only in rare situations; the domestic government or foreign creditors like the International Monetary Fund (IMF) can be approached to recapitalize the central bank. The government recapitalizes the central bank through debt-finance funded monetary expansion. A fall in quality of the central bank's assets triggers the danger of a recapitalization by monetary expansion. Hence, the quality of money decreases as a store of value as inflationary pressures ensue.

Box 4.1: Icelandic crisis

"The recent Icelandic crisis illustrates this point. The króna fell sharply even though the money supply did not increase correspondingly. It became apparent that the banking system´s liabilities were backed by low quality assets. Lacking a sufficient amount of quality assets, the central bank could not compensate the losses incurred by the banking system. The central bank was unable to be recapitalized by the Treasury as the creditworthiness of the Icelandic government was already negatively shaken. The market realized that the Icelandic króna was backed mainly by credits to an insolvent banking system and that the central bank and the banking system could not be saved by the domestic government. The króna collapsed and the inflation rate increased without a correspondent change in the quantity of money." (*Source*: Yale Insights)

Expectations about the quality of currency's backing are another important factor. Suppose that a central bank sells gold reserves to purchase mortgages of dubious quality; this leads to a change in the quality of money in the absence of concurrent change in its quantity. In this case, currency users will expect that central bank liabilities (mainly currency and member bank reserves) will be supported by assets of lesser average quality.

In summary, the relationship between central bank assets and the quality of money is crucial. While the quantity of money is naturally an important determinant of the usefulness of cash as a store of value, medium of exchange, and unit of accounting, we must not ignore the importance of qualitative factors, which can affect the ability of money to perform its three core roles, despite any changes to the money supply.

Questions

1. What determines the composition of the central bank balance sheet?
2. What is the concept of quantity theory of money?
3. What are disadvantages of the quantity theory of money?
4. What are the drivers of the quality of money as a medium of exchange and as a unit of account?
5. How does the central bank balance sheet affect the quality of money?

Chapter 5
Evolution of Central Bank Balance Sheets and Their Heterogeneous Dimensions

An increased size of central bank balance sheets arose from the financial crisis of 2007–2009. This chapter discusses what makes central bank balance sheets different across regions and countries, and how they have evolved over time. Furthermore, factors that will bring more evolution to central bank balance sheets in the future are examined.

5.1 What Makes Central Bank Balance Sheets Special?

Central bank balance sheets consist of assets and liabilities, like any other balance sheet. But, the composition of central bank balance sheets is somewhat different. Figure 5.1 shows typical assets and liabilities common to central banks. The mix of these assets and liabilities varies quite a bit from country to country. In addition, there are differences in assets and liabilities that some countries utilize in their balance sheet that others do not and the naming of the assets also varies from country to country, making comparisons slightly more difficult. However, by comparing the balance sheets, a lot can be learned about the situation of these countries, their policies, and their motives. History plays an important role in the condition of the balance sheet of any country and so it is important to compare different points of history, which is the intention of this chapter and the next. In doing so, you can gain a good understanding of how events, policy, and time shape the balance sheets and therefore the range of economies of the countries we have selected. Data availability as well as the means of reporting the data in terms of language influence the number of countries utilized in this chapter and the subsequent one. The Organization for Economic Cooperation and Development (OECD) countries were selected based on access to data and how easy it is to transform the data for comparative analysis. In light of this, eight central banks' balance sheets are utilized for this purpose. Five of these belong to advanced economies while the remaining three are linked to emerging countries. Currencies of these selected central banks are mostly traded in the international currency market except for Mexico and Chile, which might influence their balance sheets.

DOI 10.1515/9781547400577-005

Central bank balance sheets entail the following unusual features:
- Owing to the central bank's role as an issuer of banknotes, notes in circulation are a significant component of a central bank's liabilities.
- Their operation can work with negative equity. For instance, central banks of countries like Chile, the Czech Republic, Israel, and Mexico were able to attain their policy aims effectively even with technical insolvency in recent years.
- An appropriate yardstick of central bank performance is not only profit but includes much wider objectives such as financial and monetary stability.

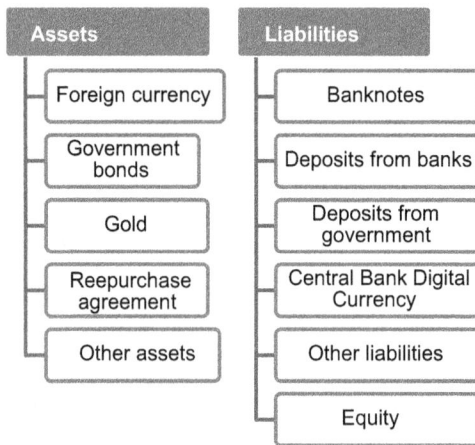

Figure 5.1: Hypothetical central bank balance sheet

Apart from the above-mentioned features, there are peculiarities associated with the accounts of any one central bank. For example, the Bank of England separates its issue department from the rest of the bank, that is, the "banking department." This separation is mainly based on an accounting deceit, which, according to the Bank Charter Act of 1844, was to ensure that the bank's note issue was supported by gold. However, the bank no longer abides by the rule of gold standard. In terms of the profit formula, 50 percent of the banking department's profits are allocated to the government while the remaining percent are used to cover operational expenses. The entire profit of all issue departments goes to the Treasury on the basis that seigniorage income belongs to the sovereign.

5.2 Historic Uses of Central Bank Balance Sheets

All central banks in the world responded to the global financial crisis of 2007–2009 through expansion of their balance sheets as depicted in Figure 5.2. New liabilities were formed to purchase assets from other economic agents in a channel called quantitative easing (QE). The increasing size in central bank balance sheets was implemented to prevent the recession from becoming even more severe.

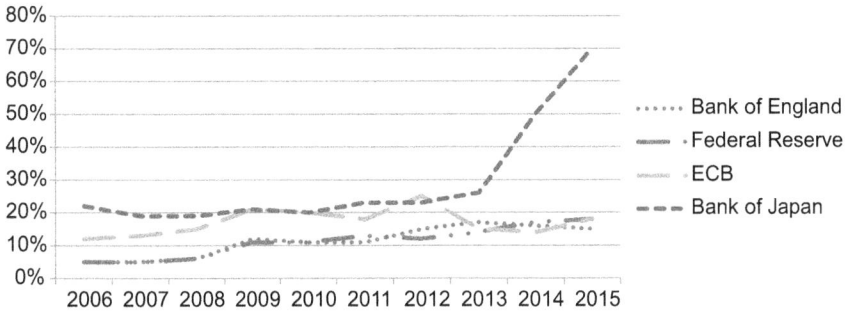

Figure 5.2: Central bank balance sheet's response to global financial crisis 2007–2009

QE is commonly considered as unconventional monetary policy from a longer-term perspective. The Bank of England has used its balance sheets to implement policy for a very long time. Therefore, it is necessary to show how the bank has previously utilized its balance sheets in response to crises of 1847, 1857, and 1866.

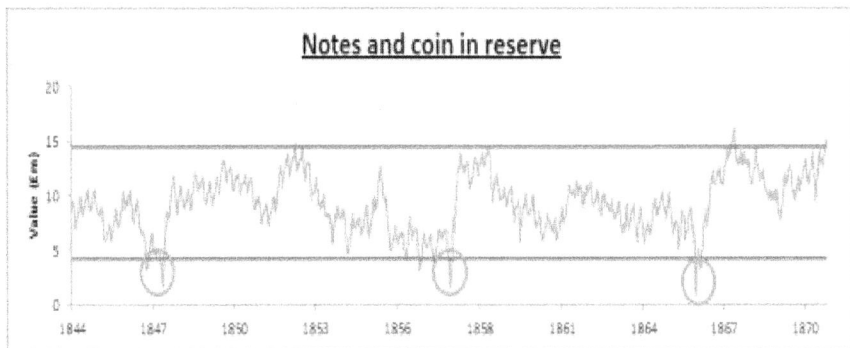

Figure 5.3: Notes and coin in reserve

In Figure 5.3, the horizontal lines capture two standard deviations from the mean holdings while normal values lie between the two lines. In the period of crises (circled), safe assets like banknotes witnessed a rise in their demand, thus the banking department sought to meet this demand out of its note reserve (see Figure 5.3).

In order to satisfy the demand for the notes, assets were purchased from the private sector (known as discounting of bills) or loans were secured on those assets (known as advances). Figure 5.4 depicts discounts and advances spiking in the period of crises of balancing the decline in notes and coins in reserve.

Figure 5.4: Discounts and advances

On the other hand, the failure of the Bank of England's note reserve in satisfying public demand for money during the crisis, resulted in a problem. In reference to the 1844 Bank Charter Act, the issue department was only permitted to print extra notes providing they were supported by gold.

In the time of crisis, successive governments permitted the bank to temporarily avoid this rule in order to meet the additional demand for notes. This indemnity was usually sufficient in itself to bring back stability in the markets and end the crises. The breaking of the rule only occurred in 1857, indicating the potential use of central bank balance sheets as powerful policy instruments.

5.3 Composition of Central Bank Balance Sheet Liabilities

Central banks' usefulness has expanded beyond the basic operations and collateral generally thought of as the mandate of the central bank. In studying their balance sheets in recent years, we have witnessed a significant number of uncommon uses. The activity beyond the fundamental ones is regarded as "unconventional" or "non-standard" or "non-traditional."

Therefore, along with the reasons already discussed, there is a need to understand a normal central bank balance sheet, how central bank asset and liability compositions differ across countries, and how the crisis affected this composition—all require extensive explanation. This will be the main focus of both chapters 5 and 6 of this book. In order to achieve this, the main features of central bank balance sheets before the crisis, and how this composition has changed in response to the crisis, are analyzed. The remainder of Chapter 5 will look at the liability side of the ledger and Chapter 6 will look at the assets.

5.3.1 Central Bank Liabilities in Normal Times

The major liabilities of central banks are mainly currency (banknotes) and reserves (deposits from banks and government kept at the central bank). Reserves are used to make payments among banks and to the central bank. Furthermore, some central banks issue deposits to the government, which are regarded as the government's checking account at the central bank. The general central bank liabilities are depicted in Table 5.1.

Table 5.1: Typical central bank liabilities

Assets	Liabilities
	Currency
	Bank's reserves
	Government deposits
	Capital

Source: Eisner et al. (2018.)

In the analysis that follows, you will see large tables that include balance sheets of the United States, Europe, Switzerland, Australia, Norway, Mexico, South Africa, and Chile beginning with Table 5.2 for 2005 and 2006 (pre-recession), then moving on to Table 5.3, which covers recession years 2008 and 2009, and ending with looking at most recent data for 2016 and 2017 in Table 5.4. You should look carefully at these tables and see how each country differs and the impact that the recession had on the balance sheets. We will comment on the highlights in the text that follows. In Chapter 6, we will go through the same exercise for assets in the balance sheet. You will note that data may not be included for some countries in years where inclusion would not have significantly added to the discussion.

We hope that in the process of reviewing these balance sheets you will learn a great deal about country-by-country variations, the impact of history and policy by looking at the balance sheets of this diverse group of countries.

5.3.2 Snapshot of Selected Economies' Performance before the 2007–2008 Crisis

As indicated in Figure 5.5, the economic performance of the concerned regions and countries improved from 2005 to 2006, with the exception of Australia, Norway and the USA. A substantial rise in economic growth was noticeable for Mexico and the Euro zone. For instance, the economic growth rate in Mexico increased to about 5 percent in 2006 from 3 percent in 2005. Similarly, the Euro area witnessed a rise in its growth rate from about 1.8 percent in 2005 to nearly 3.5 percent in 2006. However, the United States experienced a significant drop in its economic growth rate from about 3.5 percent to 2.5 percent in 2006. Other countries like Norway and Australia witnessed a slight fall of about 0.5 percentage point in their growth rate.

During these periods, the Fed's liabilities were mainly made of currency in circulation, which constituted of 90 percent, whereas liability-side composition of other central banks like the European Central Bank (ECB), the Reserve Bank of Australia (RBA), and the Swiss National Bank (SNB) was diversified in the sense that banknotes in circulation did not exceed 50 percent of their total liabilities in these periods. However, their banknotes still accounted for the largest share.

For the case of emerging economies, their liability composition pattern replicated the structure observed in the advanced countries. South Africa's economy was improved in 2006 despite a shift in the leading role from banknotes to deposit accounts. In addition, the composition of the Mexico's central bank liabilities remained the same between 2005 and 2006.

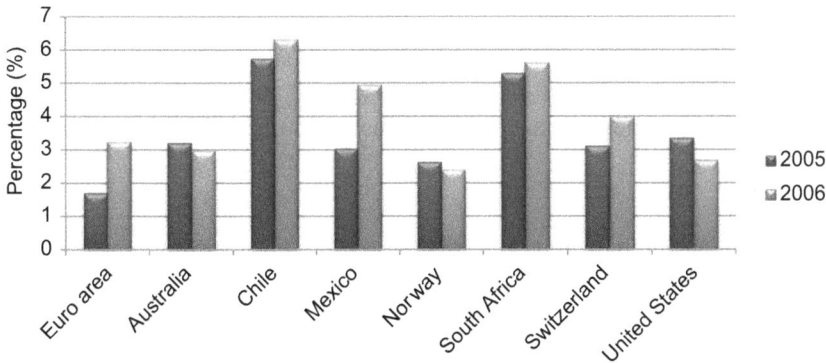

Source: World Bank World Development Indicator (2017).
Figure 5.5: Gross domestic product (GDP) growth rate

5.3.3 Country-by-Country Snapshots of Economic Structure Since 2005

We will start with an analysis of the economic structures of each selected central bank so that we have a general sense of the economies and variables pertinent to the central banks.

United States
The Federal Reserve ended adding to its balance sheet through bond buying programs and commenced the process of normalizing interest rates in 2015. Any rise in interest rates needs to be in line with inflation to reach the Fed's inflation target in order to not trade-off the economic recovery.

The ending of unconventional monetary policy implies more tasks for its fiscal policy in stimulating domestic demand through well-targeted public investment. In addition, structural policies would support the normalization of monetary policy through boosting potential output growth and a neutral interest rate. These policies would provide resilience for monetary policy in addressing negative shocks, as well as mitigating the risk related to the lower bound of the target.

The fragmented nature of the financial regulatory system still exists in the United States and this might make necessary macroprudential policy measures complicated. In addition, the Federal Reserve is constrained in acting as a lender of last resort outside the banking sector.

The country was able to reduce the general government deficit in terms of gross domestic product (GDP) from 10.5 percent in 2009 to 4.4 percent in 2015, reflecting both the improving economy and a period of sustained and substantial consolidation since 2011. Similarly, the federal deficit declined from a peak of

9.5 percent of GDP to only 2.5 percent in 2015. The suspension of the federal debt ceiling until March 2017, and the approval of the Bipartisan Budget Act of 2015 that fully funded the government during 2016, would improve financial stability and support a path toward long-term fiscal sustainability.

Switzerland

During the recession time, the SNB adopted an ultra-low interest rate policy, and in 2011 put a cap on the domestic currency, franc against the euro. The quick economic recovery after the 2009 recession was substantially led by exports. Many immigrants are attracted to the country because of its dynamic and open economy. This also contributed to a significant part of the country's robust economic growth. However, the policy of mass immigration initiated in February 2014 put quotas on immigration by 2017. This initiative poses a big challenge to a key source of Switzerland's growth model, and reflects weak confidence.

The economy witnessed an internal shock when the SNB removed the franc ceiling in January 2015. This led to a sharp appreciation of the franc especially against the euro. Indirectly, it has affected its exports and growth as nearly as 70 percent of Swiss exports go to Europe, and the appreciation has been reducing consumer prices in the country.

The Swiss economy was adversely affected by the sharp 15 percent appreciation of the franc against the euro in early 2015, following the removal of the currency ceiling. The appreciation put an end to the trade-led drive in 2014. However, robust domestic demand led to 0.2 percent growth in mid-2015. There was a shift from consumption-related components to manufacturing, and Swiss households utilized the opportunity of strong domestic currency through involving cross-border shopping of about 30 percent (Bloomberg, 2015).

The declining global oil prices as well as currency appreciation contributed to a fall in consumer prices of 1 percent year-on-year in mid-2015. In order to be competitive with imports, Swiss companies were forced to reduce their prices.

Expansionary monetary policy with near-zero policy rates have been implemented since 2009; and the placing of ceilings on its domestic currency against the euro were observed between mid-2011 and the early 2015. Recently, the presence of negative interest rates was noted. However, with persistent negative inflation, real policy rates were relatively tight compared to nominal rates.

In late 2014, the SNB intervened in foreign exchange markets in order to protect the currency ceiling through accumulation of more reserves and expansion of its balance sheets. In December 2014, foreign currency reserves increased to about 7 percent of GDP because of interventions.

Owing to the presence of divergence in monetary policy between the United States and the euro area, this posed a challenge to the sustainability of the exchange rate ceiling. This resulted in the abandonment of the franc ceiling in January 2015. At the same time, the SNB reduced its policy rate further by imposing 0.75 percent on all deposits above a specific exemption threshold. The threshold was twenty times the minimum reserve requirement for domestic banks and was adjusted in relation to the amount of cash held. A threshold of Chf 10 million was placed on other account holders.

This expansionary policy is suitable for long-term very low or negative inflation, but it poses a challenge to pension funds in meeting their legal target returns on portfolios. In addition, this might lead to low-quality investment in other assets. This would lead to a situation where individuals and institutions hold cash instead of bank deposits (a "rush to cash").

As the Swiss removed the exchange rate ceiling in January 2015, its domestic currency appreciated intensively against the euro but then reached about 1.05, which recorded a 12.5 percent appreciation. The value of the franc against the euro has fallen since September 2015 because of a decline in the volatility of the exchange rate market. This lowered safe haven effects, and the interest rate differential effect became more pronounced.

Norway

With the strong recovery in Europe, if continued, Norway's exports would be further enhanced. Furthermore, Norway is not immune from the risks emerging in China and geopolitical risks. The movements in the global financial market influence the value of the sovereign wealth fund. A little change in the fund's value poses short-term effects on the economy by influencing fiscal policy because its fiscal rule is connected to the value of the fund.

The country is in a very strong position to mitigate risks and shocks because of flexible monetary policy with a floating exchange rate that mixes with the wealth fund and fiscal framework. These measures reduce exposure to oil-price-related (and other) risks.

Its flexible inflation-targeting regime provides a good track record in achieving low and stable inflation. Its policy rate has been reduced recently, as of September 2015, the policy rate was 0.75 percent. Inflation had temporarily increased due to currency depreciation but is declining due to remaining economic slack.

Australia

The country's current account deficit is huge but poses insignificant economic risks because a large share of foreign-held debt is either denominated in Australian dollars or is hedged against exchange rate volatility. In addition, the Australian government only issues in Australian dollars.

However, changes in U.S. monetary policy, uncertainties about Brexit, rising protectionism and revisions to China's exchange rate may increase the global exchange-rate volatility that could influence the country's trade.

The main measure for boosting aggregate demand in recent years has been monetary policy. Fiscal policy is used to address the issue of deficits following the huge fiscal expansion during the global financial crisis and thus a rise in public debt. The inflation rate in Australia has been low and its interest rate is higher than in the United States or the euro area. This makes the monetary stimulus consistent with the RBA's medium-term inflation target band of 2 to 3 percent.

The present supportive stance of monetary policy remains effective especially in the absence of inflationary pressures. Nevertheless, accommodative policy might pose a risk of increasingly distorting financial markets, and particularly house prices, which have risen to very high levels. The normalization of rates is required but the timing and pace will be subject to developments in growth, employment, inflation, and the housing market.

The global financial crisis did not result in systemic bank failures in Australia but encouraged tighter regulation and alteration in banking practices. This led to adjustment of banks' funding composition from short-term debt toward deposits.

Chile

The large depreciation of the exchange rate puts a lot of pressure on prices despite well-anchored inflation expectations. Inflation increased to 4.7 percent in 2014, beyond the central bank's target range of 2 to 4 percent. High inflation has remained for a number of quarters in recent years. The exchange rate depreciation significantly influences net exports mainly through its impact on imports. However, the stimulus to export could not yield the expected result because of the following: the appreciation of the dollar influenced all currencies including the peso in Latin America, relatively high currency depreciation was notable in Brazil and Colombia; weakening external demand in China and Latin America exceeded the expansionary effect of the peso depreciation; and the continuous decline in the exchange rate elasticity of industrial exports arising from the further integration of trade linkages.

The Chile's central bank increased its interest rates from 3 to 3.25 percent in mid-October 2015 due to the headline inflation above the policy target. However, further increases in interest rates might not be effective because the recent inflation has been substantially attached to exchange rate depreciation. Slow domestic and external activity as well as a recent fall in commodity prices indicate the likely chance of a reduction in price pressures. Nevertheless, if expectations are continuously above the target, this might require some further monetary tightening.

The country had a current account surplus because of a fiscal rule, which allowed fiscal surplus to be saved in the sovereign wealth fund during much of the commodity boom. Its fiscal surplus increased from 2 percent in 2004 to over 7 percent of GDP in 2007, encouraging the country to keep more than 10 percent of GDP in its sovereign wealth fund. Then the surplus turned to deficits due to the counter-cyclical response to the 2009 global financial crisis, reconstruction spending related to the 2010 earthquake and tsunami, and the rise in production costs in mining. However, the government was able to respond counter-cyclically to the 2014 slowdown in activity, as well as sustain aggregate demand because of the near absence of net debt.

Mexico

Its economic performance is good in the midst of these shocks. The good performance is driven by domestic demand as well as structural reforms that support a low inflation environment and strong expansion of credit, resulting in gains in real wages and employment. The great depreciation of the peso further boosts the competitiveness of Mexican non-oil exports and does not lead to high inflation. In addition, it generates a positive effect on the fiscal balances, indicating the dollar denominated oil receipts and the low exposure to foreign currency debt. Concomitantly, the sufficient resources that have been saved in the oil stabilization fund put the country on the appropriate track with its fiscal consolidation trajectory without additional measures.

The huge depreciation of the peso during 2016 will continue to boost international trade, with insignificant pass-through to domestic prices, pushing inflation to converge toward Mexico's central bank target band (3% + or –1%).

Oil-related activities constituted about 13 percent of GDP in Mexico until the mid-2000s. However, falling oil extraction from the national oil company (PEMEX) for the past decade has significantly affected the oil-GDP contribution, which declined to nearly 8 percent in 2016. The main source of Mexican government revenue is oil-related receipts and exports. The oil sector also serves as the key source of foreign exchange receipts. The country's revenue dramatically reduced in recent years because of the collapse of oil prices. The tax reforms boosted the government revenue from taxation.

The Bank of Mexico has been able to control inflation within its target band despite the large depreciation of the peso. The policy rate was increased to 5.75 percent in December 2016. The purpose of this rise was to manage inflationary pressure arising from the significant depreciation of the peso. These actions were done based on the related monetary decision of the U.S. Federal Reserve and the output gap. The country halted foreign exchange intervention in February 2016, which was aimed at providing liquidity to the peso market and preserving its orderly functioning. Mexico reestablished and raised its access under the IMF flexible credit line (FCL) in May 2016. These measures allowed the central bank to control inflation expectations.

A wide range of macroprudent measures were enacted following the Tequila crisis in the mid-1990s. In addition, the country implements some appropriate regulation in relation to foreign exchange (FX) exposure such as limits to FX net open position of banks. Nevertheless, the country needs to closely monitor currency mismatches and balance sheet risk, given the recent significant depreciation of the peso.

South Africa

Its current account deficit has shrunk due to a slowdown in growth that reduced imports, but low saving rates made it huge. The country's terms of trade (price of exports/price of imports) figures were favorable because of currency (rand) appreciation in 2016 and the pick-up of global commodity prices. Portfolio investment flows are used to finance the current account, which leads to high exposure to a reversal in capital flows. In 2016, South Africa witnessed huge equity outflows partially covered by bond inflows, indicating investors' portfolio arbitrage and political uncertainty.

Foreign-owned debt at 41 percent of GDP in 2016 is higher than the percentage of the other emerging countries. Most of the external debt of the government is denominated in rand while external debt related to state-owned enterprises (SOEs), banks, and corporates are in foreign currency. SOEs are demanded to hedge their foreign currency risk, but the cost of doing that might rise because of the downgrade of the SOE's credit ratings.

The country's inflation rose from 4.6 percent in 2015 to 6.4 percent in 2016 due to currency depreciation and the drought-related rise in domestic food prices. From the domestic view, the confidence level in the economy is shaken given changes in the political environment. Private investment could further be constrained by a rise in political tension. From the global perspective, the local currency is highly sensitive to U.S. interest rates, thus increasing its exposure. Furthermore, with the United Kingdom, being its largest European trading partner, mean that the country's imports and financial flows may be affected by uncertainty about the Brexit.

The monetary policy operation takes place in a difficult environment of high inflation and low growth. Inflation exceeded the Reserve Bank's target band (3–6 percent) throughout 2016. This was as a result of delayed exchange rate pass-through following the substantial depreciation of the rand throughout 2015. A long-lasting drought further created pressure on agricultural prices in 2016 but there was a huge fall in prices, which pushed the headline inflation down into the target band. Stable core inflation was witnessed throughout 2016 but at the upper limit of the target band.

The reserve bank maintained the purchase rate at 7 percent from March 2016 until reducing it by 25 base points in 2017. With a long-term fall in inflation, monetary policy would have room for adopting accommodative measures. On the other hand, if the rand value falls as U.S. monetary policy continues to tighten, this would impose pressure on inflation.

The country's stock market exhibits more volatility than many other emerging countries due to the fact that its currency is mainly driven by external factors such as U.S. monetary policy, and national policy uncertainty.

ECB

The ECB was established on June 1, 1998. A year after the creation of ECB, the common currency euro was launched in January 1999. The ECB was tasked with the responsibility of maintaining price stability in the region. The extent of attaining the mandate influences its credibility and the public confidence in it. The procedures on the law related to the European System of Central Banks (ESCB) and the ECB supplied the financial resources in terms of capital, foreign reserve assets, and monetary incomes, that was required for the functioning of the ECB.

The ECB executes its tasks through conducting monetary policy, with the main aim of not generating profit. The successful implementation of its tasks is strongly attached to solid financial means. New activities emerged as new EU member states adopted the euro. This led to the transfer of the foreign reserves from the Eurosystem national central banks (NCBs) that created a remunerated EUR-denominated claim of the NCBs on the ECB. In addition, the ECB was exposed to the interest rate gap between the interest earned on investments (mainly in U.S. dollars) and the interest paid on the foreign reserves to the NCBs (in EUR) because of this transfer approach. Seigniorage (interest income from the allocation of euro banknotes within the Eurosystem) mainly boosted the ECB interest income since 2002.

The ECB is involved in different activities connected to these special operations, which influenced its balance sheet. The two important factors that influence the changes in the composition and values of the foreign reserves and own-fund portfolios, are financial market development and portfolio management. The ECB provided liquidity operations by acting as an intermediate in the provision of foreign currency to Eurosystem counterparties, and the supply of euro to other central banks. This operation led to a rise in the level of the balance sheet that occurred at the end of 2008.

The key driver of the ECB operation is the ECB banknotes issuance, which has significantly risen over time and gradually increased the balance sheet. The ECB's foreign reserve holdings are made up of gold and net assets in foreign currency, which account for their considerable size on the balance sheet. These foreign reserve holdings allow the ECB to execute foreign exchange operations, which are among its fundamental mandates. Intervention on the foreign exchange market as well as decisions relating to the ECB foreign reserve management influence the amount of these holdings. The value is attached to asset price movements while the euro equivalent of the external reserve holdings relies on exchange rate developments for the underlying assets.

The ECB manages its own funds in terms of its paid-up capital and reserves. These funds are invested in euro-denominated assets whose value depends on asset price movements. The foreign reserves accounted for 66 percent of the ECB total assets in 1999 but its share reduced to 35 percent by 2006 as other items especially banknotes, which were added to the total in 2002, witnessed strong growth thereafter. The significant share of the ECB foreign reserve is kept in foreign currency mainly in U.S. dollars and Japanese yen while the remainder of its holding are in gold.

At the commencement of 1999, the ECB foreign reserves were made up of nearly US$35 billion, JPY 445 billion and 24 million ounces of gold. The amount changed as its capital, which determines the contribution of each ESCB member altered or an EU member state adopted the euro. This led to small structural breaks. However, the key reason the central bank keeps foreign exchange reserves is to serve as potential interventions on the currency markets, in order to protect their own currency. In the autumn of 2000, the ECB executed this purpose in the foreign exchange market because of the continuous depreciation of the euro since the onset of 1999. The effort was exerted by the ECB in September 2000, together with the monetary authorities of the United States and Japan, but the ECB executed its own measure in November 2000. These actions were responsible for the fall in the dollar and yen reserve volumes at the end of 2000. Shortly thereafter, the yen reserves were restored at the expense of U.S. dollars.

The revenue generated from the sales of the ECB gold was mainly invested in Japanese yen. This contributed to a sharp rise in the Japanese yen reserves in the ECB foreign reserve holdings. Foreign currency portfolios were composed of 90 percent in U.S. dollars and 10 percent in Japanese yen in 1999. The composition pattern remained the same until 2003, with the exception of 2000 when the ECB intervention led to the sale of the Japanese yen but later readjusted against the U.S. dollar.

The decision of the Governing Council created a rebalancing of the foreign currency reserves, which was executed from the first half of 2004. The gradual adjustment of foreign currency shares resulted in 80 percent in the U.S. dollar and 20 percent in the Japanese yen by early 2008, and then to respectively 78 percent and 22 percent at the end of 2009 because of the depreciation of the dollar against the Japanese yen.

In addition to ongoing investment gains and losses in the volume and composition of foreign reserves, liquidity and security are the key drivers for the investment of the ECB reserves. The foreign reserve management is based on ensuring liquid resources for any foreign intervention at any point in time. In 2000, the interest income gained was utilized to stabilize the currency split but this policy ended afterward mainly due to the intervention later in 2000, thus leading to huge U.S. dollar outflows.

The first weakening of the euro against the dollar occurred up to 2001. The euro began to appreciate following the foreign exchange intervention in late 2000. Strong appreciation of the euro was observed between 2002 and 2004 mainly connected to a deterioration of the growth outlook for the United States, the widening U.S. current account deficit, and geopolitical tensions. The euro depreciated in 2005 but gained its strong currency value at the onset of 2008. The continued appreciation of the euro was linked to a dynamic market evaluation of the relative cyclical outlook for the economic areas in favor of the euro area, as well as developments in interest rate differentials. On the other hand, the weakness of the U.S. currency is driven by the persistently huge current account deficits. In the period of the financial crisis of 2008, the euro value substantially dropped against the United States up to the first quarter of 2009, but rose by the end of 2009.

The price of gold continued to witness an upward trend since 2004, because its price gained from the rise in inflation and commodity prices as well as from the U.S. dollar depreciation. This served as a safe haven during the global financial distress that commenced in mid-2007. The persistent rise in the price of gold accounted for an increase in the euro equivalent of the gold holding by 78 percent at end 2009 despite the gold sale strategy adopted by the ECB. The shares of different assets in the composition of foreign reserve holdings changed in favor of gold and the yen.

From mid-2007 onward, the challenge of much higher liquidity needs from the banking sector manifested in the Eurosystem and other central banks because of disruption of the euro and other money markets. The Eurosystem responded to the challenge by providing the necessary liquidity to direct the short-term interest rate to its target, performing the role of a lender of last resort, and extending its operations in order to maintain financial stability.

The ECB plays the role of coordinating monetary policy of the ECB while NCBs are saddled with the execution. In addition, the ECB performs other roles in order to provide foreign currency to Eurosystem counterparties. These additional operations commenced at the end of 2007, and made a significant impact on the size of the ECB balance sheet.

The ECB initiated U.S. dollar-liquidity providing operations in connection with the U.S. dollar term auction facility (TAF) during the period of December 2007–January 2010. This measure was used to provide a temporary reciprocal currency arrangement. The magnitude of the arrangement was sometimes adjusted in order to accommodate rises in needs. The initial arrangement ended in February 2008, but relaunched after a month due to rising tensions in the run-up to the rescue of U.S. investment bank Bear Stearns. The tensions increased further because of the uncertainty created by the collapse of Lehman Brothers.

Foreign exchange swap tenders were established by the Eurosystem with its counterparties against euro cash at a fixed price agreed in swap points. Foreign exchange swaps with the United States were ended in January 2009 because of limited demand.

The ECB experienced difficulty in accessing Swiss currency funding. This led to the establishment of a swap arrangement with the SNB in order to provide Chf to counterparties against EUR. After January 2009, one-week EUR/Chf foreign exchange swaps continued to supply Swiss francs with the aim of improving liquidity in the short-term Swiss franc money market. The SNB kept an account with the ECB for the placement of EUR funds obtained by the SNB from the same type of operations with other central banks and from its counterparties.

5.3.4 A Look at the Balance Sheets: 2005 and 2006

Let's start with the United States. Currency accounted for the largest share of U.S Federal Reserve balance sheet liability before the crisis. In December 2006, currency constituted 90.2 percent of the Fed's liabilities, while reserves and government deposits accounted for the remaining percent. Currency is a significant liability on most central bank balance sheets in normal periods, but the U.S. dollar's use as a standard (of sorts) around the world, accounts for this significantly high percentage (see Table 5.2).

In the same vein, about 50 percent of the ECB liabilities were linked to banknotes in circulation in 2005 and 2006. The banknotes in circulation accounted for the largest share for the European union, followed by the intra-Eurosystem liabilities, while the liabilities to noneuro area residents had the lowest share (see the second section of Table 5.2).

More than 40 percent of the SNB (Swiss) liabilities were banknotes in 2005 and 2006. In addition, as total liabilities of the SNB increased by CHF 2825.3 million between 2005 and 2006, its banknotes in circulation rose to CHF 43,182.2 million in 2006 with an increase of CHF 1,815.7 million. However, the largest share of a rise in the two periods was attributed to the distribution reserve component (see the third section of Table 5.2).

Australian notes on issue (banknotes available and put in circulation) accounted for the largest share of RBA liabilities in 2005, but in 2006, deposits took the leading role, followed by the banknote component. Other components constituted less than 15 percent of the RBA aggregate liabilities (see the fourth part of Table 5.2). The reason behind this is that the RBA are in charge of issuing and distributing banknotes to commercial banks. Commercial banks directly buy banknotes from the RBA. In addition, the RBA holds a certain amount of banknotes in order to meet seasonal and other fluctuations in demand. The country's current account deficit is huge, but poses insignificant economic risks because a large share of foreign-held debt is either denominated in Australian dollars or is hedged against exchange rate volatility. Furthermore, the Australian government only issues in Australian dollars.

Deposits including the government pension fund, recorded the largest share of the Norges Bank balance sheet liabilities with about 80 percent in 2005 and 2006. Treasury deposits accounted for the largest of the Norges Bank domestic liabilities in 2005 and 2006, while borrowing took the leading role in the total foreign liabilities (see Table 5.2). The Norges Bank was the only advanced central bank that witnessed a fall in its deposits in 2006. This decline is as a result of changing its financial system which was initially dominated by domestic banks. At the end of 2005, there was a considerable increase in the activities of foreign-owned banks in Norway to the extent that they had a market share of over 30 percent of the total assets. In addition, their lending growth was relatively high for several years. However, it poses a big challenge to the Norges bank in terms of supervision and crisis management. The inclusion of the borrowing item on the Norges Bank liabilities can be traced to the growth rate of foreign bank activities in the country.

Table 5.2: Central bank liabilities (2006 and 2005)

Country	Name of Bank	Liabilities	2006	2005	Currency	Source
USA	Federal Reserve	FR Banknotes	783,000.0		Dollar (million)	Federal Reserve website
		Reserves repos w/ foreign entities	30,000.0		Dollar (million)	
		Bank deposits	19,000.0		Dollar (million)	
		Government deposits	5,000.0		Dollar (million)	
		Capital and reserves	31,000.0		Dollar (million)	
		Total	868,000.0		Dollar (million)	
Europe	European Central Bank	Banknotes in circulation	50,259.5	45,216.8	Euro (million)	European Central Bank website
		Liabilities to other euro area residents denominated in euro	1,065.0	1,050.0	Euro (million)	
		Liabilities to non-euro area residents denominated in euro	105.1	649.3	Euro (million)	
		Liabilities to non-euro area residents denominated in foreign currency. Deposits, balances and other liabilities.	331.0	855.9	Euro (million)	
		Intra-Eurosystem liabilities. Liabilities equivalent to the transfer of foreign reserves	39,782.3	39,782.3	Euro (million)	
		Other liabilities				
		Accruals and income collected in advance	1,262.8	919.3	Euro (million)	
		Sundry	899.2	632.0	Euro (million)	
			2,162.0	1,551.4	Euro (million)	
		Provisions	2,393.9	1,027.5	Euro (million)	
		Revaluation accounts	5,578.4	8,108.6	Euro (million)	
		Capital and reserves capital	4,089.3	4,089.3	Euro (million)	
		Profit for the year	0.0	0.0	Euro (million)	
		Total liabilities	105,766.5	102,331.1	Euro (million)	

Table 5.2 (continued)

Country	Name of Bank	Liabilities	2006	2005	Currency	Source
Switzerland	Swiss National Bank (SNB)					Swiss National Bank website
		Banknotes in circulation	43,182.2	41,366.5	Chf (million)	
		Sight deposits of domestic banks	6,716.0	5,852.7	Chf (million)	
		Liabilities toward the Confederation	1,056.2	3,126.3	Chf (million)	
		Sight deposits of foreign banks and institutions	421.7	483.9	Chf (million)	
		Other sight liabilities	-	189.9	Chf (million)	
		Liabilities from Swiss franc repo transactions	-	-	Chf (million)	
		Foreign currency liabilities	1.8	230.8	Chf (million)	
					Chf (million)	
		Other liabilities	81.9	90.7	Chf (million)	
		Provisions for operating risks	11.1	11.7	Chf (million)	
		Provisions for currency reserves	38,635.7	37,841.0		
		Share capital	25.0	25.0	Chf (million)	
		Distribution reserve	16,473.4	6,948.4	Chf (million)	
		Annual result	5,045.3	12,821.2	Chf (million)	
		Total liabilities	111,813.5	108,988.2	Chf (million)	
Australia	Reserve Bank of Australia (RBA)	LIABILITIES				Reserve Bank of Australia website
		Deposits	43,204.0	29,228.0	AUD$(million	
		Distribution payable to Australian Government	1,477.0	1,683.0	AUD$(million	
		Other	11,493.0	9,133.0	AUD$(million	
		Australian notes on issue	38,065.0	35,624.0	AUD$(million	
		Total Liabilities	94,239.0	75,668.0	AUD$(million	

Table 5.2 (continued)

Country	Name of Bank	Liabilities	2006	2005	Currency	Source
Norway	Norges Bank	FOREIGN LIABILITIES				Norges Bank website
		Deposits	87.0	377.0	NOK (million)	
		Borrowing	99,348.0	61,002.0	NOK (million)	
		Other liabilities	402.0	334.0	NOK (million)	
		Equivalent value of allocated Special Drawings Rights, IMF	1,575.0	1,620.0	NOK (million)	
		Total foreign liabilities	101,412.0	63,333.0	NOK (million)	
		DOMESTICS LIABIL-ITIES				
		Notes and coins in circulation	54,838.0	51,910.0	NOK (million)	
		Treasury deposits	159,679.0	109,627.0	NOK (million)	
		Deposits from banks etc.	24,030.0	42,699.0	NOK (million)	
		Borrowing	2.0	0.0	NOK (million)	
		Other liabilities	252.0	10,488.0	NOK (million)	
		Total domestic liabilities	238,801.0	214,724.0	NOK (million)	
		Total liabilities excl. Government Pension Fund-Global	340,213.0	278,057.0	NOK (million)	
		Deposits in krone account Government Pension Fund-Global	1,782,139.0	1,397,896.0	NOK (million)	
		Total liabilities	2,122,352.0	1,675,953.0	NOK (million)	
Mexico	Central Bank of Mexico	LIABILITIES				Central Bank of Mexico website
		International mone-tary fund	0.0	0.0	Dollar (million)	
		Monetary base	449,821.0	380,034.0	Dollar (million)	
		Bills and coins and circulation	449,821.0	380,034.0	Dollar (million)	
		Bank current account deposits	0.0	0.0	Dollar (million)	

Table 5.2 (continued)

Country	Name of Bank	Liabilities	2006	2005	Currency	Source
		Monetary regulation bonds	111,828.0	260,109.0	Dollar (million)	
		Federal government current account deposits	192,671.0	113,838.0	Dollar (million)	
		Other federal government deposit	44,197.0	11,447.0	Dollar (million)	
		Monetary regulation deposits	339,110.0		Dollar (million)	
		Banks	278,981.0		Dollar (million)	
		Government securities	60,129.0		Dollar (million)	
		Other bank deposits and debtors from repo operations	100.0	279,856.0	Dollar (million)	
		Trust funds' deposits	0.0	0.0	Dollar (million)	
		Special drawing rights	4,717.0	4,408.0	Dollar (million)	
		Other liabilities	45,856.0	43,683.0	Dollar (million)	
		Total liabilities	1,188,300.0	1,093,375.0	Dollar (million)	
South Africa	South Africa Reserve Bank	Liabilities				South Africa Reserve Bank website
		Deposit accounts	81,164.1	41,664.8	Rand (million)	
		Amounts due to subsidiaries	0.0	0.0	Rand (million)	
		South African Reserve Bank debentures	6,367.9	13,035.6	Rand (million)	
		Foreign loans	21,739.7	21,806.2	Rand (million)	
		Current taxation liabilities	4.1	8.3	Rand (million)	
		Notes and coin in circulation	52,822.9	49,439.7	Rand (million)	
		Employment benefit liabilities and other provisions	678.4	604.9	Rand (million)	
		Gold and Foreign Exchange	0.0	0.0	Rand (million)	
		Contingency Reserve Account	1,824.4	0.0	Rand (million)	
		Deferred taxation liabilities	111.5	102.5	Rand (million)	
		Forward exchange contract liabilities	307.8	628.4	Rand (million)	

Table 5.2   (continued)

Country	Name of Bank	Liabilities	2006	2005	Currency	Source
		Other financial liabilities	167.2	170.3	Rand (million)	
		Total liabilities	165,188.0	127,460.8	Rand (million)	
Chile	Bank of Chile	Foreign liabilities	202,329.1		Dollar (million)	Bank of Chile website
		Reciprocal loan agreements	7,819.8		Dollar (million)	
		Loans	93.4		Dollar (million)	
		Accounts with international organizations	88,423.2		Dollar (million)	
		Special drawing rights (SDR) allocations	105,992.7		Dollar (million)	
		Domestic liabilities	16,569,622.3		Dollar (million)	
		Monetary base	3,657,626.4		Dollar (million)	
		Banknotes and coins in circulation	3,031,980.5		Dollar (million)	
		Deposits from financial institutions (domestic currency)	194,971.9		Dollar (million)	
		Deposits for technical reserves	430,674.0		Dollar (million)	
		Deposits and obligations	3,744,931.6		Dollar (million)	
		Deposits and obligations with the Treasury	1,146,848.9		Dollar (million)	
		Other deposits and obligations	2,598,082.7		Dollar (million)	
		Instruments issued by Central Bank of Chile	9,167,064.3		Dollar (million)	
		Central Bank bonds in UF (BCU)	2,099,836.1		Dollar (million)	
		Central Bank bonds in Chilean pesos (BCP)	1,918,403.0		Dollar (million)	
		Indexed promissory notes payable in coupons (PRC)	2,055,701.3		Dollar (million)	
		Central Bank discountable promissory notes (PDBC)	1,853,187.0		Dollar (million)	
		Indexed coupons (CERO) in UF	776,513.3		Dollar (million)	

Table 5.2 (continued)

Country	Name of Bank	Liabilities	2006	2005	Currency	Source
		Central Bank bonds expressed in US dollars (BCD)	462,802.3		Dollar (million)	
		Other	621.3		Dollar (million)	
		Other liabilities	383,109.9		Dollar (million)	
		Provisions	7,643.4		Dollar (million)	
		Other securities	201.6		Dollar (million)	
		Temporary liabilities	71,221.0		Dollar (million)	
		Creditors on foreign currency purchased with resale agreements	304,043.9		Dollar (million)	
		Capital and reserves	(2,302,325.1)		Dollar (million)	
		Capital	(2,311,321.5)		Dollar (million)	
		Surplus (deficit) for the year	8,996.4		Dollar (million)	
		Total liabilities	14,852,736.2		Dollar (million)	

In other central banks, reserves accounted for a much larger share of their liabilities before the crisis. The reason for the large amount of reserves in normal times is to encourage a smooth running of interbank payments. If reserve supply is small, the focus of banks would be on running out of reserves at the end of the day. Thus, this might lead to a delay in payments to other banks, which can create "gridlock" and affect the confidence in the banking system.

For example, the Norges Bank balance sheet had liabilities in which about 50 percent was attributed to treasury deposits at the end of 2006. Only 16 percent of them were represented by currency. Currency and reserves are considered as immediate maturity liabilities because of instant transfer to other parties for payment. It is worth noting the extreme difference between the currency numbers in the United States and that of Norway.

In addition, some central banks issue term maturity liabilities, in the form of either term deposits (available to counterparties that have a central bank account) or term repos (which are collateral and available to counterparties beyond depositing institutions who do not have a central bank account).

Some central banks can issue bills to non-account holders in the secondary market while others limit primary issue to account holders. Term liabilities are issued to decrease the quantity of reserves in the system and also to control the central bank's target interest rate. For example, the ECB, the Fed, and the RBA have been adjusting term deposit facilities and repo instruments to have longer maturities than overnight.

5.3.4.1 Central Banks' Balance Sheet Liabilities of Emerging Economies

Thus far we have examined the balance sheets of influential established economies albeit with different histories. We now look at countries that are considered in some ways as emerging, having diverse histories. We will start with Mexico. In Mexico, currency in circulation constituted about 40 percent of the Bank of Mexico's balance sheet liabilities as of the end of 2006. Monetary regulation deposits, for historical reasons, recorded a very significant share in the composition as indicated in Table 5.2. The historical reasons emanated from the two significant financial crises occurring in Mexico in 1982 and 1994. Prior to the early 1980s, the Mexican economy adopted strong protectionist economic policies that included high trade barriers in several key industries like the automotive industry. After the 1982 debt crisis, the country's trade policy shifted toward unilateral trade liberalization to attract foreign investment. This made Mexico more competitive in non-oil exports. However, the country suffered another financial crisis in 1994–95 that was caused by a number of complex financial, economic, and political factors. Its monetary stimulus to the crisis was to replace the fixed exchange rate policy with a floating exchange rate regime. This led to strong depreciation of the peso by nearly 50 percent with six months, thus putting the country into a deep recession. Its currency steadily weakened through the end of the 1990s, which resulted in greater exports, and boosted its exporting industries. Nevertheless, there was a sharp increase in import prices along with low terms of trade. The United States and International Monetary Fund provided a supporting mechanism to the Mexican government through an emergency financial support package made up of US$50 billion loans, in which the U.S. Treasury provided the largest share. In addition, Mexico adopted tight monetary and fiscal policies to stem inflation and mop up some of the costs of the banking crisis. In order to prevent the occurrence of the financial crises, monetary regulation deposits took the huge share of its liabilities.

The largest share of the South Africa Reserve Bank (SARB) liabilities was attached to notes and coin in circulation in 2005 but shifted to deposit accounts in 2006. In addition, the contingency reserve account increased from 0 in 2005 to 1,824,430 rand in 2006 (see Table 5.2). The shift toward deposit accounts in 2006 can be traced to the modification of SARB's repo-based refinancing system adopted in March 1998. The system was adjusted in September 2001 and later in May 2005 in order to provide liquidity to the private sector. This allowed private sector banks to meet their daily liquidity requirements.

Table 5.2 shows that the significant portion of the Bank of Chile's liabilities was attached to its banknotes and coins in circulation in 2006. This could be linked to the implementation of monetary easing in Chile with the purpose of ensuring consistency with the inflationary outlook rather than to reestablish the operation of credit as done in other countries. Reductions in the Bank of Chile's interest rate have been consistent with the prevailing economic circumstances. This also reflects its negative capital and reserves on bank liabilities.

5.3.5 Snapshot of Selected Economies' Performance during the 2007–2008 Crisis

With the inception of the global financial crisis in 2007, all concerned countries and regions excluding Australia, witnessed a huge fall in their economic growth rate. The sharpest decline was observed in the United States, Euro area, and Norway between 2007 and 2008 (see Figure 5.6). The economic performance was even worse in 2009 when all countries with the exception of Australia experienced a negative growth rate, as indicated in Figure 5.6. The worst economic performance was observed in Mexico and the Euro area with a negative growth rate of more than 4 percent in 2009.

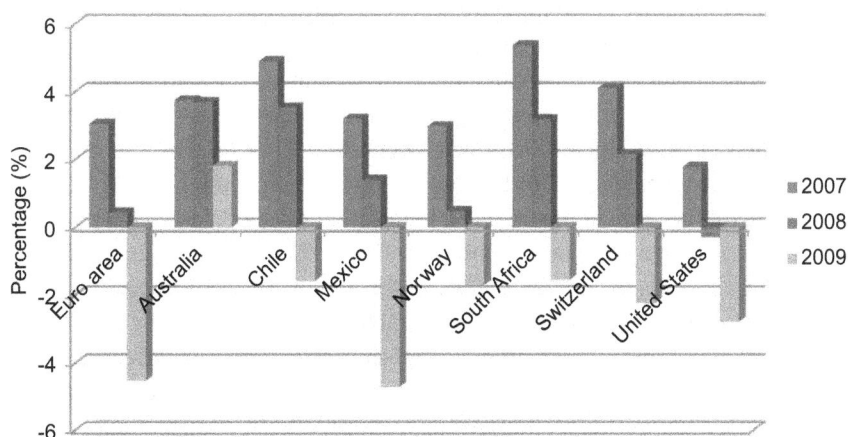

Source: World Bank World Development Indicator (2017).
Figure 5.6: GDP Growth rate during the 2007–2008 crisis

5.3.5.1 Central Bank Liabilities during the 2007–2008 Crisis

In the period of the global financial crisis, about 90 percent of the Fed liabilities were banknotes, while other components accounted for the remaining share. This implies that there was no change in the composition of the Fed liabilities before and during the crisis. In addition, the Fed initiated its bond buying program in 2008, in order to inject capital into the market with the aim of boosting the economy. This set the pace for the use of unconventional monetary policies especially QE in stimulating economic activities.

The banknotes accounted for almost 40 percent of the ECB liabilities in 2007 and 2008, indicating a decline in the banknotes share compared to 2005 and 2006. The total liabilities of the ECB recorded an increase from about £102billion in 2005 to £2,075 billion in 2008. The components of the ECB liabilities witnessed an increase with exception of deposits and fixed term deposits (see Table 5.3). The ECB's balance sheet expanded gradually because of the strong demand for euro banknotes. According to the EU Treaty, the ECB is given the exclusive right to authorize the issuance of euro banknotes. In reality, the NCBs circulate the euro banknotes while a share of 8 percent of the total banknotes in circulation is assigned to the ECB. Since 2002, euro banknotes were in circulation, and the ECB's share is indicated on its balance sheet, thus implying a claim by the ECB on the NCBs, as the ECB itself does not put banknotes in circulation. The decline in the ECB banknotes was a result of low demand for banknotes in the region. The demand for banknotes influence the ECB notes, which are based on fixed percentage shares of the region's banknotes.

As at the end of 2008, the banknotes in circulation accounted for the largest proportion of the SNB with about 20 percent as in Table 5.3. Cash in Switzerland has restored its value since 2008 due to a persistently low level of interest rates, which increased the demand for banknotes. Furthermore, cash holdings became more attractive because of the financial market and sovereign debt crises.

The banknotes and deposits components had a share of more than 80 percent in the RBA liabilities in 2007 and 2008. At the end of 2008, Australian notes on issue constituted the largest share of the total liabilities, seconded by the deposit component (see Table 5.3). As other advanced central banks experienced a rise in their deposit accounts, RBA recorded a drop in its deposits because the global financial crisis did not result in systemic bank failures in Australia but encouraged tighter regulation and alteration in banking practices. This led to the adjustment of the banks' funding composition.

Unlike other central banks in selected developed economies, the Norges Bank reduced its banknotes in circulation between 2007 and 2008. This may be attributed to the pattern of conducting monetary policy in Norway. The Norges Bank implements its monetary policy by weighing the inflation outlook against developments in output and employment. Therefore, it is less worried about inflation than if real economic prospects are also weak. The flexible inflation targeting adopted by the Norges Bank makes monetary policy significant in stabilizing the economy. This encouraged rapid adjustment in the policy rate in response to the crisis in 2008.

Table 5.3: Central banks' liabilities (2008 and 2007)

Country	Name of Bank	Liabilities	2008	2007	Currency	Source
Europe	European Central Bank	Banknotes in circulation	762,921	676,678	Euro (million)	European Central Bank website
		Liabilities to euro area credit institutions related to monetary policy operations denominated in euro	492,310	379,183	Euro (million)	
		Current accounts (covering the minimum reserve system)	291,710	267,337	Euro (million)	
		Deposit facility	200,487	8,831	Euro (million)	
		Fixed-term deposits	0	101,580	Euro (million)	
		Fine-tuning reverse operations	0	0	Euro (million)	
		Deposits related to margin calls	113	1,435	Euro (million)	
		Other liabilities to euro area credit institutions denominated in euro	328	126	Euro (million)	
		Debt certificates issued	0	0	Euro (million)	
		Liabilities to other euro area residents denominated in euro	91,077	46,183	Euro (million)	
		General government	83,282	38,115	Euro (million)	
		Other liabilities	7,794	8,069	Euro (million)	
		Liabilities to non-euro area residents denominated in euro	293,592	45,094	Euro (million)	

Table 5.3 (continued)

Country	Name of Bank	Liabilities	2008	2007	Currency	Source
		Liabilities to euro area residents denominated in foreign currency	5,723	2,490	Euro (million)	
		Liabilities to non-euro area residents denominated in foreign currency	10,258	15,553	Euro (million)	
		Deposits, balances and other liabilities	10,258	15,553	Euro (million)	
		Liabilities arising from the credit facility under ERM II	0	0	Euro (million)	
		Counterpart of special drawing rights allocated by the IMF	5,465	5,279	Euro (million)	
		Other liabilities	166,500	123,076	Euro (million)	
		Revaluation accounts	175,735	147,123	Euro (million)	
		Capital and reserves	71,200	67,101	Euro (million)	
		Total liabilities	2,075,107	1,507,887	Euro (million)	
Switzer-land	Swiss National Bank (SNB)	Banknotes in circulation	49,160.8		Chf (million)	Swiss National Bank website
		Sight deposits of domestic banks	37,186.2		Chf (million)	
		Liabilities toward the Confederation	8,803.7		Chf (million)	
		Sight deposits of foreign banks and institutions	3,799.8		Chf (million)	
		Other sight liabilities	1,383.7		Chf (million)	
		Liabilities from Swiss franc repo transactions	-		Chf (million)	
		SNB debt certificates	24,424.9		Chf (million)	
		Other term liabilities	29,414.5		Chf (million)	

Table 5.3 (continued)

Country	Name of Bank	Liabilities	2008	2007	Currency	Source
		Foreign currency liabilities	420.1		Chf (million)	
		Contractual agreements	948.1		Chf (million)	
		Other liabilities	1,934.4		Chf (million)	
		Provisions for operating risks and other provisions	6.2		Chf (million)	
		Provisions for currency reserves	40,275.3		Chf (million)	
		Capital	25.0		Chf (million)	
		Distribution reserve	22,871.7		Chf (million)	
		Annual result	(4,729.1)		Chf (million)	
		Foreign currency transaction differences	(16.8)		Chf (million)	
		Total liabilities	215,908.5		Chf (million)	
Australia	Reserve Bank of Australia (RBA)	Deposits	39,006.0	65,830.0	AUD$(million)	Reserve Bank of Australia website
		Distribution payable to Australian Government	1,403.0	1,085.0	AUD$(million)	
		Other	9,786.0	16,072.0	AUD$(million)	
		Australian notes on issue	42,064.0	40,289.0	AUD$(million)	
		Total Liabilities	92,259.0	123,276.0	AUD$(million)	
Norway	Norges Bank	FOREIGN LIABILITIES				Norges Bank website
		Deposits in NOK	55,873.0	85.0	NOK (million)	
		Borrowing in foreign currency	85,673.0	85,201.0	NOK (million)	
		Cash collateral received	27,222.0	36,797.0	NOK (million)	
		Other liabilities in foreign currency	4,491.0	3,296.0	NOK (million)	

Table 5.3 (continued)

Country	Name of Bank	Liabilities	2008	2007	Currency	Source
		Equivalent value of allocated Special Drawing Rights	1,811.0	1,442.0	NOK (million)	
		Total foreign liabilities	175,070.0	126,821.0	NOK (million)	
		DOMESTIC LIABIL-ITIES				
		Notes and coins in circulation	55,159.0	55,685.0	NOK (million)	
		Treasury deposits	147,359.0	148,494.0	NOK (million)	
		Deposits from banks etc	100,951.0	53,517.0	NOK (million)	
		Borrowing in foreign currency	52.0	0.0	NOK (million)	
		Other liabilities in NOK	16,765.0	5,114.0	NOK (million)	
		Total domestic liabilities	320,286.0	262,810.0	NOK (million)	
		Total liabilities excl. Government Pension Fund-Global	495,356.0	389,631.0	NOK (million)	
		Deposits in krone account Government Pension Fund-Global	2,273,289.0	2,016,955.0	NOK (million)	
		Total liabilities	2,768,645.0	2,406,586.0	NOK (million)	
Mexico	Central Bank of Mexico	International monetary fund	0		Dollar(million)	Central Bank of Mexico website
		Monetary base	577,543		Dollar(million)	
		Banknotes and coins and circulation	577,542		Dollar(million)	
		Bank current account deposits	1		Dollar(million)	
		Monetary regulations bonds	1,240		Dollar(million)	
		Federal government current account deposits	112,502		Dollar(million)	

Table 5.3 (continued)

Country	Name of Bank	Liabilities	2008	2007	Currency	Source
		Other federal government deposits	159,628		Dollar(million)	
		Monetary regulation deposits	528,397		Dollar(million)	
		Banks	280,000		Dollar(million)	
		Government securities	248,397		Dollar(million)	
		Other bank deposits and debtors from repo operations	4,100		Dollar(million)	
		Trust funds' deposits	0		Dollar(million)	
		Special drawing rights	6,179		Dollar(million)	
		Other liabilities	52,926		Dollar(million)	
		Total liabilities	1,442,515		Dollar(million)	
		Capital	6,817		Dollar(million)	
		Previous year operational surplus	0		Dollar(million)	
		Fiscal years' operational surplus	95,000		Dollar(million)	
		Income statement	247,522		Dollar(million)	
		Amortization past fiscal year losses	(77,197)		Dollar(million)	
		Amortization IPAB loans	(63,570)		Dollar(million)	
		Reserves	(11,755)		Dollar(million)	
		Total equity	101,817		Dollar(million)	
		Total liabilities and equity	1,544,332		Dollar(million)	
South Africa	South Africa Reserve Bank	Liabilities				South Africa Reserve Bank website
		Deposit accounts	131,278.3	100,471.2	Rand (million)	
		Amounts due to subsidiaries	0.0	0.0	Rand (million)	
		SARB debentures	16,928.7	5,478.5	Rand (million)	
		Foreign loans	11,311.5	19,585.9	Rand (million)	

Table 5.3 (continued)

Country	Name of Bank	Liabilities	2008	2007	Currency	Source
		Current taxation liabilities	214.5	3.1	Rand (million)	
		Notes and coin in circulation	63,372.0	58,469.0	Rand (million)	
		Provisions	100.2	84.0	Rand (million)	
		Gold and Foreign Exchange	0.0	0.0	Rand (million)	
		Contingency Reserve Account	72,189.5	28,482.3	Rand (million)	
		Deferred taxation liabilities	121.4	110.7	Rand (million)	
		Forward exchange	9.9	69.0	Rand (million)	
		contract liabilities	407.9	356.4	Rand (million)	
		Post-retirement medical benefits	805.0	682.3	Rand (million)	
		Total liabilities	296,738.8	213,792.4	Rand (million)	
Chile	Bank of Chile	Foreign liabilities	212,439.4	179,264.8	Dollar (million)	Bank of Chile website
		Reciprocal loan agreements	7,273.1	6,313.2	Dollar (million)	
		Accounts with international orga-nizations	88,953.3	76,961.9	Dollar (million)	
		Special drawing rights (SDR) allo-cations	116,213.0	95,989.7	Dollar (million)	
		Domestic liabilities	16,376,075.4	12,865,125.0	Dollar (million)	
		Monetary base	4,132,501.7	3,672,153.3	Dollar (million)	
		Banknotes and coins in circulation	3,600,978.4	3,315,835.6	Dollar (million)	
		Deposits from financial institu-tions (domestic currency)	531,523.3	326,317.7	Dollar (million)	
		Deposits for techni-cal reserves	-	30,000.0	Dollar (million)	
		Deposits and obligations	1,860,080.0	1,499,301.4	Dollar (million)	
		Deposits and obligations with the Treasury	132,399.7	206,352.3	Dollar (million)	

Table 5.3 (continued)

Country	Name of Bank	Liabilities	2008	2007	Currency	Source
		Other deposits and obligations	1,727,680.3	1,292,949.1	Dollar (million)	
		Instruments issued by Central Bank of Chile	10,383,493.7	7,693,670.3	Dollar (million)	
		Central Bank bonds in UF (BCU)	5,411,652.7	2,556,394.6	Dollar (million)	
		Central Bank bonds in Chilean pesos (BCP)	2,212,432.6	1,935,120.0	Dollar (million)	
		Indexed promissory notes payable in coupons (PRC)	1,133,766.1	1,488,343.9	Dollar (million)	
		Central Bank discountable promissory notes (PDBC)	1,098,702.3	852,300.0	Dollar (million)	
		Indexed coupons (CERO) in UF	522,061.5	663,313.5	Dollar (million)	
		Central Bank bonds expressed in US dollars (BCD)	2,803.1	198,177.2	Dollar (million)	
		Central Bank indexed-promissory notes (PRBC)	2,054.7		Dollar (million)	
		Other	20.7	21.1	Dollar (million)	
		Other liabilities	635,421.6	72,900.8	Dollar (million)	
		Provisions	12,966.9	7,887.3	Dollar (million)	
		Other securities	284.9	995.0	Dollar (million)	
		Temporary liabilities		64,015.5	Dollar (million)	
		Repurchase agreements	622,169.8			
		Creditors on foreign currency purchased with resale agreements		-	Dollar (million)	
		Capital and reserves		(2,176,826.5)	Dollar (million)	
		Net equity	803,434.1			
		Capital	(1,875,748.0)	(1,894,368.8)	Dollar (million)	
		Surplus (deficit) for the year	2,679,182.1	(282,457.7)	Dollar (million)	
		Total liabilities	18,027,370.5	10,940,464.1	Dollar (million)	

In the era of the 2007–2008 Global financial crisis, the composition of the Norges Bank balance sheet liabilities remained similar to the pre-crisis composition. This implies no significant changes in the liability-side composition from 2005 to 2008 (see Table 5.3).

5.3.5.2 Central Banks' Balance Sheet Liabilities of Emerging Economies

With reference to Table 5.3, currency in circulation still had the largest share of the Bank of Mexico aggregate liabilities, followed by government securities deposits. The pattern of South Africa's SARB liability composition remained unchanged in 2007 and 2008, as deposit accounts still made up the largest percent. As at the end of 2007, banknotes and coins in circulation maintained its leading role in the composition of the Bank of Chile's balance sheet liabilities. However in 2008, central bank bonds accounted for the largest share (see Table 5.3). The Chilean economy was able to wipe out its negative capital to zero value in 2008. There was a remarkable deterioration on Chile's external demand and financial conditions between August 2007 and August 2008. A rise in global inflation from high global food and energy prices caused the country's inflation to rise to 9 percent by mid-2008. The tight monetary policy from the Bank of Chile in response to the crisis led to substantial appreciating pressure on the peso during 2008. This contributed to turning the negative value of capital into positive value at the end of 2008.

5.3.6 Snapshot of Selected Economies' Performance Today

As illustrated in Figure 5.7, all economies witnessed a positive economic growth rate by the end of 2015. In Figure 5.7 the locations are listed in the order they are presented in the chart (front to back). The United States economy (in the back of Figure 5.7) experienced the highest growth rate of about 3 percent, followed by Mexico with about 2.5 percent, while South Africa and Switzerland recorded the lowest rate with less than 1.5 percent. By the end of 2016, all the countries witnessed a decline in their economic growth rate with the exception of Australia whose economy grew from 2 percent in 2015 to about 2.5 percent in 2016. A substantial fall was recorded for the economy of South Africa from 1.5 percent in 2015 to less than 0.5 percent in 2016. During these periods, the liability-side of the central banks' balance sheets were structurally changed except for the case of Australia whose banknotes still accounted for the largest share. For instance, in the ECB liability components, half of its total liabilities were shared by banknotes and liabilities to euro area credit institutions, while SNB's liabilities were mainly made up of domestic banks' deposits.

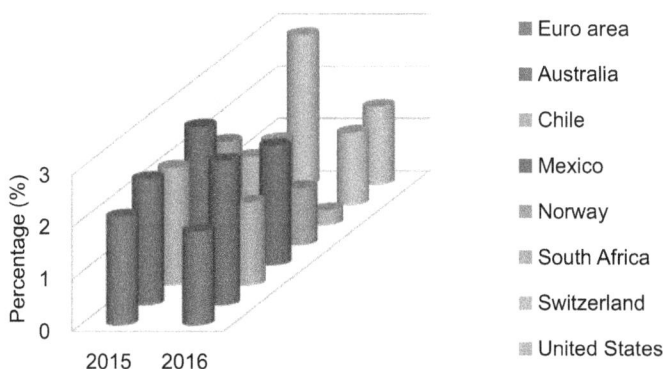

Source: World Bank World Development Indicator (2017).

Figure 5.7: GDP growth rate in 2015 and 2016

United States

The U.S. economy has been able to restore its economic growth rate seven years after the global crisis. This made its economic growth outweigh its pre-crisis peak by 10 percent. The country recorded robust private-sector employment gains that significantly reduced its unemployment level, and the restoration of fiscal sustainability. The improvement in its economic performance is attributed to robust monetary policy support and an early fiscal expansion. The creation of many private-sector jobs reduced unemployment to its pre-crisis level, thus providing consumers with higher incomes and enhancing their confidence. However, the country has not addressed its long-term puzzles especially the continuous slowdown of productivity growth since the mid-2000s. The slow speed of its economic recovery is a result of the severity and depth of the financial crisis, world trade stagnation driven by the slowdown of China and lower demand from oil-exporting countries. The effective exchange rate has significantly appreciated since mid-2014 in real effective terms. Its fiscal policy has had no significant effects after several years of budget consolidation. Monetary policy is highly accommodative even after the Federal Reserve halted the expansion of its balance sheets and commenced with a gradual increase in its interest rates from very low levels.

Switzerland

The Swiss economy recorded robust economic growth after the 2009 recession. This growth was mainly driven by low interest rates, high immigration, and an exchange rate ceiling until early 2015, which enhanced robust export growth. The Swiss economy has been witnessing low or negative inflation over the past four years, as a result of its strong currency. Its short-term economic performance was hurt by the sharp appreciation following the end of the currency ceiling.

Norway

The discovery of commercially viable offshore oil and gas fields in the late 1960s contributed to the economic transformation in Norway. This led to the achievement of its high per capita GDP. The improvement in its living standard was attributed to good macroeconomic management of the oil wealth through the sovereign wealth fund and the associated fiscal rule. Its economic activity has been enhanced by inflows of labor from other European Economic Areas (EEA).

A sharp fall in the global oil prices in mid-2014 provided a timely reminder of the relevance of a flexible, competitive, and productive mainland economy as well as floating exchange rate in addressing external shocks and developing balanced growth, once the income from petroleum commences to fade. The aggregate output growth in Norway continued to fall in 2015 as the sharp drop in oil prices in 2014 hampered oil-related activity. Oil sector investment began falling prior to the decline in oil price as a result of cost-reduction campaigns by the oil industry.

Australia

Over the recent decades, Australia witnessed robust economic growth driven by strong macroeconomic policy, structural reforms, and the long commodity boom. Low interest rates boosted its aggregate demand, triggered risk-taking by investors, and drove house prices as well as mortgage lending to historical highs. The country recorded an impressive twenty-five consecutive years of output growth. The rebalancing of the economic activity from commodity investment to other activities is well-implemented through monetary and fiscal policies, currency depreciation, and flexible labor and product markets. Despite this, its economy shares the global risk of a low-growth trap; the country's productivity is in line with its longer-term average.

At present, the country faces the risk of low growth and lackluster private-sector investment arising from pessimistic expectations and weakening global trade.

Chile

Chile's economy recorded a long period of strong growth as well as improved living standards, which significantly reducing its poverty level. Its growth was safeguarded from the large commodity price volatility including the recent decline in copper prices through a sound macroeconomic framework and flexible exchange rate. However, the country still requires further economic expansion beyond extracting natural resources, and enhanced knowledge-based contribution to global value chains by implementing productivity-enhancing structural reforms.

Chile's economic reforms, such as trade and investment liberalization and the sound macroeconomic policies, have managed its inflation and smoothed economic cycles, thus mitigating uncertainty and boosting investments. Added progress can be made through economic transformation toward a more knowledge-based and innovative economy, complemented with more firms that can participate and improve their activities in global value chains.

The country being the largest producer of copper in the world, gained substantially from the upsurge in commodity prices and the environment of low global interest rates in the recent commodity supercycle.

The investment growth rose from about 2 percent of GDP in 2002 to almost 7 percent in 2012 due to the capital intensive nature of mining activities. This led to multiplier effects of other sectors especially construction. On the other hand, the opposite side of increasing commodity prices has appeared because of weakening copper prices. The falling copper price is anticipated to remain in the future. The mix of lower copper prices and higher costs has adversely affected mining profitability, thus sharply reducing investment. Household incomes declined as a result of lower terms of trade, and this led to low private consumption. The country's output growth reduced sharply in 2014.

South Africa

For the past few years, South Africa's economy grew weak as a result of low consumer demand, persistently declining business environment, policy uncertainty, and the prolonged drought. However, the country is considered as a regional hub for financial services because of a sophisticated banking system and deep financial markets. Supply-side constraints in the form of electricity shortages, falling commodity prices, and policy uncertainty significantly trended down its growth since 2011.

Furthermore, the country confrontations with many structural hindrances, such as high inflation, limit room for monetary policy support; high public debt constrains public spending; high costs of doing business weaken competition; and political uncertainty affects investment and confidence. Therefore, the country is in need of structural reforms that would enhance its economic potential.

Mexico

Its economy is globally ranked as the world's fifteenth largest economy in terms of GDP, just behind Australia. Over the past thirty years, the country witnessed tremendous structural changes that shifted its economy from an oil-dependent economy up to early 1990s to a manufacturing center in the aftermath of NAFTA in the mid-1990s. Presently, the country is increasingly becoming an international trade hub. Mexico's peso and the competitive advantage rising from its proximity to the U.S. export market, now make it a top global exporter of cars and flat screen TVs, among other products. In 2016, the Mexico's GDP was close to US$1.08 trillion.

However, the country is undergoing a difficult external environment due to weak global trade, investment, productivity and wages, and uncertainty about the future evolution of economic and trade policies in the United States. Mexican related headwinds entail collapsing oil prices, which led to a fall in government revenue as well as energy sector investment, the sharp depreciation of the Mexican peso as a result of tight market expectations of the U.S. Federal Reserve, and increasing global policy uncertainty. The country is anticipated to witness a drop in its economic performance by the end of 2018 because of the above-mentioned difficulties facing its economic activities.

5.3.7 Central Bank Liabilities Today

As shown in Table 5.4, the liabilities to euro area credit institutions took the leading role from the banknotes component in 2016 and 2017, with a slight difference of about £200billion in 2016, growing to a huge margin of about £700billion in 2017. Both banknotes and liabilities to euro area credit institution components accounted for more than 50 percent of the ECB total liabilities in 2016 and 2017.

As at the end of 2016 and 2017, the size of deposits of domestic banks constituted more than half of the SNB total liabilities, followed by equity and banknotes in circulation. This indicates how the composition pattern of the SNB liabilities changed over the past decade (see Table 5.4).

Deposits and banknotes still accounted for the largest share of the RBA liabilities in 2016 and 2017. However, the Australian notes on issue had the highest share in 2016, followed by deposit component. At end of 2017, the deposit component constituted the largest with about 50 percent (see Table 5.4).

More than 90 percent of the Norges Bank liabilities were deposits including government pension fund in 2016 and 2017. Total financial liabilities recorded the second largest share of the aggregate liabilities.

The ECB's banknotes in circulation fell as the Norges Bank's deposit also reduced between 2016 and 2017. The decrease in the ECB's banknotes is influenced by the demand for banknotes among the NCBs in the region. The Norges Bank's policy rate remained at 0.5 percent in 2017, after being slashed by 100 basis points between December 2014 and March 2016 in response to the oil-induced economic slowdown. Expansionary monetary policy was widely considered in 2017 as the country experienced a continued negative output gap, low international interest rate, and 9 percent inflation (below the target). However, rapid house price growth and a high and increasing debt burden for Norwegian households are recognized as the building up of financial imbalances in the country. This was the reason for the reduction in demand for banknotes, which resulted in the fall in banknotes in circulation.

Table 5.4: Liabilities (2017 and 2016)

Country	Name of Bank	Liabilities	2017	2016	Currency	Source
Europe	European Central Bank	Banknotes in circulation	1,170,716.0	1,126,215.0	Euro (million)	European Central Bank website
		Liabilities to euro credit institutions related to monetary policy operations denominated in euro	1,881,596.0	1,313,264.0	Euro (million)	
		Current accounts (covering the minimum reserve system)	1,185,792.0	888,988.0	Euro (million)	
		Deposit facility	695,801.0	424,208.0	Euro (million)	
		Fixed-term deposits	-	-	Euro (million)	
		Fine-tuning reserve operations	-	-	Euro (million)	
		Deposits related to margin calls	2.0	69.0	Euro (million)	
		Other liabilities to euro area credit institutions denominated in euro	20,984.0	9,427.0	Euro (million)	
		Debt certificates issued	-	-	Euro (million)	
		Liabilities to other euro area residents denominated in euro	286,889.0	220,760.0	Euro (million)	
		General government	168,457.0	114,887.0	Euro (million)	

Table 5.4 (continued)

Country	Name of Bank	Liabilities	2017	2016	Currency	Source
		Other liabilities	118,432.0	105,873.0	Euro (million)	
		Liabilities to non-euro area residents denominated in euro	355,381.0	205,678.0	Euro (million)	
		Liabilities to euro area residents denominated in foreign currency	3,830.0	3,644.0	Euro (million)	
		Liabilities to non-euro area residents denominated in foreign currency	11,254.0	9,301.0	Euro (million)	
		Deposits, balances and other liabilities	11,254.0	9,301.0	Euro (million)	
		Liabilities arising from the credit facility under ERM II	-	-	Euro (million)	
		Counterpart of special drawing rights allocated by the IMF	55,218.0	59,236.0	Euro (million)	
		Other liabilities	225,543.0	218,929.0	Euro (million)	
		Revaluation accounts	357,852.0	394,357.0	Euro (million)	
		Capital and reserves	102,298.0	100,601.0	Euro (million)	
		Total Liabilities	4,471,563.0	3,661,439.0	Euro (million)	
Switzerland	Swiss National Bank (SNB)					Swiss National Bank website
		Banknotes in circulation	81,638.9	78,084.4	Chf (million)	
		Sight deposits of domestic banks	470,439.4	468,199.2	Chf (million)	
		Liabilities toward the Confederation	14,754.8	7,229.7	Chf (million)	
		Sight deposits of foreign banks and institutions	54,085.6	24,585.0	Chf (million)	
		Other sight liabilities	34,398.8	30,035.6	Chf (million)	

Table 5.4 (continued)

Country	Name of Bank	Liabilities	2017	2016	Currency	Source
		Liabilities from Swiss franc repo transactions	-	-	Chf (million)	
		SNB debt certificates	-	-	Chf (million)	
		Foreign currency liabilities	45,933.6	49,096.3	Chf (million)	
		Counterpart of special drawing rights (SDR) allocated by the IMF	4,572.7	4,492.8	Chf (million)	
		Other liabilities	314.8	251.6	Chf (million)	
		Equity				
		Provisions for currency reserves	62,771.2	58,121.5	Chf (million)	
		Share capital	25.0	25.0	Chf (million)	
		Distribution reserve	20,000.0	1,904.5	Chf (million)	
		Annual result	54,371.6	24,476.4	Chf (million)	
		Total equity	137,167.8	84,527.4	Chf (million)	
		Total liabilities	843,306.4	746,502.0	Chf (million)	
Australia	Reserve Bank of Australia (RBA)	LIABILITIES				Reserve Bank of Australia website
		Deposits	92,669.0	61,210.0	AUD$ (million)	
		Distribution payable to the Commonwealth	1,286.0	3,222.0	AUD$ (million)	
		Australian banknotes on issue	73,623.0	70,209.0	AUD$ (million)	
		Other liabilities	4,671.0	8,936.0	AUD$ (million)	
		Total Liabilities	172,249.0	143,577.0	AUD$ (million)	
Norway	Norges Bank	FINANCIAL LIABILITIES				Norges Bank website
		Secured borrowing	286.0	154.0	Krones (million)	
		Unsettled trades	6,617.0	14 417	Krones (million)	
		Financial derivatives	10.0	1.0	Krones (million)	
		Other financial liabilities	1,916.0	2,382.0	Krones (million)	

Table 5.4 (continued)

Country	Name of Bank	Liabilities	2017	2016	Currency	Source
		Liabilities to the IMF	59,221.0	56,872.0	Krones (million)	
		Deposits from banks	63,968.0	69,734.0	Krones (million)	
		Deposits from the Treasury	162,386.0	163,790.0	Krones (million)	
		Notes and coins in circulation	48,420.0	45,524.0	Krones (million)	
		Total financial liabilities	342,824.0	352,874.0	Krones (million)	
		Deposits in krone account, Governments Pension Fund Global	8,483,727.0	8, 277,072.0	Krones (million)	
		Other liabilities	15,146.0	15,281.0	Krones (million)	
		TOTAL LIABILITIES	8,841,697.0	8,645,227.0	Krones (million)	
Mexico	Central Bank of Mexico	Liabilities				Central Bank of Mexico website
		Monetary base		1,420,269.0	Dollar (million)	
		Banknotes and coins in circulation		1,419,754.0	Dollar (million)	
		Bank deposits in current account		515.0	Dollar (million)	
		Federal government current account deposits		319,025.0	Dollar (million)	
		Other federal government deposits		8,540.0	Dollar (million)	
		Monetary regulation liabilities		1,258,328.0	Dollar (million)	
		Monetary regulation deposits		1,085,315.0	Dollar (million)	
		Government securities		870,322.0	Dollar (million)	
		Banks		214,993.0	Dollar (million)	
		Monetary regulation bonds		105,050.0	Dollar (million)	
		Other deposits from banks and creditors from repo operations		67,963.0	Dollar (million)	

Table 5.4 (continued)

Country	Name of Bank	Liabilities	2017	2016	Currency	Source
		Deposits from Mexican oil stabilization and development fund		53.0	Dollar (million)	
		International monetary fund		0.0	Dollar (million)	
		Special drawing rights		79,033.0	Dollar (million)	
		Other liabilities		76,877.0	Dollar (million)	
					Dollar (million)	
		Total liabilities		3,162,125.0	Dollar (million)	
South Africa	South Africa Reserve Bank	Liabilities				South Africa Reserve Bank website
		Notes and coin circulation	132,296.7	130,561.6	Rand (million)	
		Deposit accounts	266,820.8	269,690.3	Rand (million)	
		Amounts due to Group companies				
		Foreign deposits	106,655.3	102,083.3	Rand (million)	
		Other liabilities	1,318.2	861.6	Rand (million)	
		South African Reserve Bank debentures	611.3	3,176.4	Rand (million)	
		Forward exchange contract liabilities	3,120.8	1,003.7	Rand (million)	
		Deferred taxation liabilities	40.1	32.8	Rand (million)	
		Post-employment benefits	2,441.9	2,080.5	Rand (million)	
		Gold and Foreign-Exchange Contingency Reserve Account	321,158.2	304,653.1	Rand (million)	
		Total liabilities	744,463.3	814,143.4	Rand (million)	
Chile	Bank of Chile	Foreign liabilities	790,794.1		Dollar (million)	Bank of Chile website
		Reciprocal loan agreements	49.9		Dollar (million)	

Table 5.4 (continued)

Country	Name of Bank	Liabilities	2017	2016	Currency	Source
		Accounts with international organizations	57,681.3		Dollar (million)	
		Special drawing rights (SDR) allocations	733,062.9		Dollar (million)	
		Domestic liabilities	31,298,960.3		Dollar (million)	
		Monetary base	10,342,493.8		Dollar (million)	
		Banknotes and coins in circulation	8,651,831.2		Dollar (million)	
		Deposits from financial institutions (in Chilean pesos)	1,690,662.6		Dollar (million)	
		Deposits and obligations	5,842,324.2		Dollar (million)	
		Deposits and obligations with General Treasury	780,412.4		Dollar (million)	
		Other deposits and obligations	5,061,911.8		Dollar (million)	
		Notes issued by Central Bank of Chile	15,114,142.3		Dollar (million)	
		Central Bank bonds in UF (BCU)	6,777,119.7		Dollar (million)	
		Central Bank bonds in Chilean pesos (BCP)	4,037,484.6		Dollar (million)	
		Central Bank discountable promissory notes (PDBC)	4,206,282.1		Dollar (million)	
		Optional indexed promissory notes payable in coupons (PRC)	66,314.1		Dollar (million)	
		Indexed promissory notes payable in coupons (PRC)	26,930.3		Dollar (million)	
		Other	11.5		Dollar (million)	
		Other liabilities	24,131.6		Dollar (million)	
		Provisions	19,203.8		Dollar (million)	
		Other securities	4,927.8		Dollar (million)	

Table 5.4 (continued)

Country	Name of Bank	Liabilities	2017	2016	Currency	Source
		Net equity	(4,205,881.6)		Dollar (million)	
		Capital	(1,983,898.1)		Dollar (million)	
		Other reserves	10,789.2		Dollar (million)	
		Retained earnings	(2,232,772.7)		Dollar (million)	
		Total liabilities and equity	27,908,004.4		Dollar (million)	

5.3.7.1 Central Bank Liabilities Today : A Case Study of Emerging Economies

The composition pattern of the Bank of Mexico in terms of liabilities remains unchanged before, during, and after the financial crisis, except for the amount of bank deposits in current accounts, which witnessed a significant increase from $1 million in 2008 to $515 million in 2016 (see Table 5.4).

As indicated in Table 5.4, the total liabilities of SARB recorded a decline between 2016 and 2017. This decline was attributed to a significant drop in the SARB's debentures. However, both notes and coins in circulation, and deposit accounts still constituted the largest percent of the total liabilities. A huge decline in the SARB's debentures was driven by its political chaos. South Africa's credit was downgraded to junk by the S&P Global Rating and Fitch Rating in April 2017 after President Jacob Zuma sacked Pravin Gordhan as finance minister. The continued political uncertainty in South Africa showcases the bad image of its securities in the global financial market and makes investors lose their confidence in the country.

In Chile, banknotes and coins in circulation recorded the highest share of the total liabilities reported in Table 5.4 at the end of 2015 and 2016. However, there was a slight decrease in its total liabilities between 2015 and 2016, which was significantly attributed to a fall in Bank of Chile bonds. The privatization of the pension system in 1981 transformed the Chilean economy from being one of Latin America's poorest countries to the richest country in the region. This remarkable achievement was notable when pension funds were utilized in stimulating its nascent capital market. Recently, the country is facing the problem of insufficient savings from the pension scheme because of inconsistent payments and large informal economic settings. This might be linked to the decline in the Bank of Chile's bonds.

Conclusion

In summary, this chapter provides robust insights on the heterogeneous evolution of liability-side components of central bank balance sheets in different economies at different periods (pre-, during, and post-2007–2008 global financial crisis). The next chapter will focus on the asset-side components of central bank balance sheets and how these differ with respect to countries in economic periods.

Questions

1. What is the evolution pattern of liability-side components of central bank balance sheets in advanced countries before, during, and after the 2007–2008 global financial crisis?
2. What is the heterogeneous nature of liability-side components of central bank balance sheets in developing countries pre-, during, and post-2007–2008 era?
3. What are the similarities and differences between the pattern of liability-side composition in advanced economies, and emerging and developing countries?
4. What is the link between the structure of central bank's liabilities and economic growth before, during, and after the 2007–2008 crisis?
5. For each country, what changes took place in their balance sheets from 2007–2008 to 2016? Why?

Chapter 6
Composition of Central Bank Balance Sheet Assets

Central banks obtain assets through purchasing assets or making loans. If a central bank buys an asset, for example, a bond, it makes a payment by creating reserves or currency. This leads to an increase in its assets and liabilities by equal amounts. In the same vein, a central bank creates the new reserves that are lent if it spreads a loan. Banks are often considered as central bank's counterparties, but some central banks accept nonbank counterparties. In a normal period, central banks' assets mainly consist of government bonds, foreign exchange reserves, and loans to banks. Nevertheless, the relative significance of these assets differs substantially across central banks. Before the crisis, changes in the amount of a central bank's asset were usually insignificant and possessed no influence on monetary policy.

Prior to the crisis, the Fed's balance sheet was relatively simple, in which U.S. Treasuries accounted for about 90 percent of its assets as of December 2006. This is almost the same with the quantity of outstanding currency (see Table 6.1).

6.1 Central Bank Assets in Normal Times

As depicted in Table 6.1, Intra-Euro system claims accounted for about 50 percent of the European Central Bank (ECB) assets in 2005 and 2006. The largest component of the SNB assets in 2005 and 2006 was foreign currency investments, followed by gold holdings (see Table 6.1). The Reserve Bank of Australia (RBA) assets were mainly driven by foreign exchange in 2005 and 2006. The foreign exchange component accounted for about 70 percent before the occurrence of the global financial crisis (See Table 6.1).

Prior to the global financial crisis, the asset-side of the Norges Bank balance sheet was significantly composed of investments for the government pension fund. Domestic financial assets accounted for the least share of the entire assets of the Norges Bank (see Table 6.1). As the Fed and the ECB reduced their gold holdings, the Swiss National Bank (SNB) and the RBA increased the amount of gold holdings in foreign reserves. The need for assets to meet liquidity needs in the economy could be the reason for the actions of the Fed and the ECB in terms of gold holdings. In addition, since 1999, the ECB has been a member of the Central Bank Gold Agreement (CBGA) whose purpose is to mitigate the impact of gold sales on the price of gold through imposing a cap on the sales of gold. In line with the CBGA, about 400 tons were sold yearly between 1999 and 2004, and

DOI 10.1515/9781547400577-006

almost 500 tons were sold annually during 2004–2009. This led to the decline of the volume of gold by 33 percent or 246 tons in December 2009, compared to its initial holdings in January 1999. A common reason for selling gold is that it is not interest-bearing. In addition, its storage is associated with significant costs and it is difficult to convert into quick liquidity in the case of liquidity needs. These demerits exceed its advantages, which include a way of diversifying away from currency holdings.

On the other hand, central banks such as the SNB and the RBA attached an important role to holdings in gold. For example, the increasing price of gold mitigated the effect of the depreciating U.S. dollar during 2005 and 2008. Furthermore, it served as a hedge against inflation, and it was considered a safe investment during the crisis era. Gold is anticipated to be broadly acceptable and tradable in quite a liquid market. Both the SNB and the RBA increased their diversifying strategies by holding more gold as a means of providing resilience in case of external shocks.

The Norges Bank felt satisfied with the amount of gold in its foreign reserve portfolio as its gold holdings were the same for both 2005 and 2006. The Norges Bank sold the gold bars in its gold reserves to England in 1940. In addition, it disbursed 33.5 tons of gold bars, which were valued at about US$450 million in the first quarter of 2004. The proceeds from the gold sales have been invested as part of Norge Bank's foreign exchange reserves. Owing to the historically low return on gold, its central bank kept the amount of gold holdings constant in these periods.

Table 6.1: Central banks' assets (2006 and 2005)

Country	Name of Bank	Assets	2006	2005	Currency	Source
USA	Federal Reserves	Gold certificates	11,037.0	11,039.0	Dollar (million)	Federal Reserve's website
		Special drawing rights certificates	2,200.0	2,200.0	Dollar (million)	
		Coin	801.0	686.0	Dollar (million)	
		Items in process of collection	3,486.0	5,930.0	Dollar (million)	
		Loans to depository institutions	67.0	72.0	Dollar (million)	
		Securities purchased under agreements to resell	40,750.0	46,750.0	Dollar (million)	

Table 6.1 (continued)

Country	Name of Bank	Assets	2006	2005	Currency	Source
		U.S. government securities, net	783,619.0	750,202.0	Dollar (million)	
		Investments denominated in foreign currencies	20,482.0	18,928.0	Dollar (million)	
		Accrued interest receivable	6,761.0	5,874.0	Dollar (million)	
		Bank premises and equipment, net	2,376.0	2,252.0	Dollar (million)	
		Other assets	1,785.0	3,394.0	Dollar (million)	
		Total assets	873,364.0	847,327.0	Dollar (million)	
Europe	European Central Bank	Gold and gold receivables	9,929.9	10,064.5	Euro (million)	European Central Bank website
		Claims on noneuro area residents				
		denominated in foreign currency				
		Receivables from the IMF	414.8	170.2	Euro (million)	
		Balances with banks and security investments,			Euro (million)	
		external loans and other external assets	29,313	31,063	Euro (million)	
		Claims on euro area residents	29,728	31,233	Euro (million)	
		denominated in foreign currency	2,774	2,909	Euro (million)	
		Claims on noneuro area residents				
		denominated in euro				
		Balances with banks and security investments and loans	4	13	Euro (million)	

Table 6.1 (continued)

Country	Name of Bank	Assets	2006	2005	Currency	Source
		Other claims on euro area credit institutions denominated in euro	0.034	0.025	Euro (million)	
		Intra-Eurosystem claims				
		Claims related to the allocation of euro banknotes within the Eurosystem	50,259.5	45,216.8	Euro (million)	
		Other claims within the Eurosystem (net)	3,545.9	5,147.0	Euro (million)	
			53,805.3	50,363.8	Euro (million)	
		Other assets			Euro (million)	
		Tangible fixed assets	175.2	175.2	Euro (million)	
		Other financial assets	8,220.3	6,888.5	Euro (million)	
		Off-balance sheet instruments				
		Revaluation differences	29.5	0.0	Euro (million)	
		Accruals and prepaid expenses	1,094.5	679.6	Euro (million)	
		Sundry	5.6	4.4	Euro (million)	
			9,525.1	7,747.7	Euro (million)	
		Total assets	105,766.5	102,331.1	Euro (million)	
Switzer-land	Swiss National Bank (SNB)	Gold holdings	29,190.2	25,066.0	Chf (million)	Swiss National Bank website
		Claims from gold transactions	3,030.3	2,984.2	Chf (million)	
		Foreign currency investments	45,591.9	46,585.5	Chf (million)	
		Reserve position in the IMF	557.3	1,079.8	Chf (million)	
		International payment instruments	330.8	78.9	Chf (million)	

Table 6.1 (continued)

Country	Name of Bank	Assets	2006	2005	Currency	Source
		Monetary assistance loans	236.6	270.2	Chf (million)	
		Claims from Swiss franc repo transactions	27,126.9	26,198.6	Chf (million)	
		Claims against domestic correspondents	5.1	5.3	Chf (million)	
		Swiss franc securities	4,907.6	5,729.1	Chf (million)	
		Banknote stocks	125.0	137.6	Chf (million)	
		Tangible assets	358.5	355.5	Chf (million)	
		Participations	129.6	122.3	Chf (million)	
		Other assets	223.6	375.2	Chf (million)	
		Total assets	111,813.5	108,988.2	Chf (million)	
Australia	Reserve Bank of Australia (RBA)	Cash and cash equivalents	575.0	1,008.0	AUD$ (million)	Reserve Bank of Australia website
		Australian dollar securities	30,306.0	20,899.0	AUD$ (million)	
		Foreign exchange	71,689.0	61,187.0	AUD$ (million)	
		Gold	2,151.0	1,493.0	AUD$ (million)	
		Property, plant, and equipment	329.0	307.0	AUD$ (million)	
		Loans, advances, and other	397.0	377.0	AUD$ (million)	
		Total Assets	105,447.0	85,271.0	AUD$ (million)	
Norway	Norges Bank	FOREIGN FINANCIAL ASSETS				Norges Bank website
kk		Securities and deposits	259,093.0	219,137.0	NOK (million)	
		Lending	90,712.0	94,489.0	NOK (million)	
		Claims on the IMF	4,132.0	4,537.0	NOK (million)	
		Total international reserves	353,937.0	318,276.0	NOK (million)	

Table 6.1 (continued)

Country	Name of Bank	Assets	2006	2005	Currency	Source
		Other foreign assets	146.0	113.0	NOK (million)	
		Total foreign fin. Assets excl. Government Pension Fund—Global	354,083.0	318,276.0	NOK (million)	
		DOMESTIC FINANCIAL AND OTHER ASSETS				
		Lending to banks, etc.	55,647.0	25,404.0	NOK (million)	
		Other domestic assets	2,937.0	1,322.0	NOK (million)	
		Total domestic financial assets	58,584.0	26,726.0	NOK (million)	
		Fixed assets	1,379.0	1,386.0	NOK (million)	
		Gold	291.0	291.0	NOK (million)	
		Total other domestic assets	1,670.0	1,677.0	NOK (million)	
		Total domestic financial and other assets	60,254.0	28,403.0	NOK (million)	
		Total assets excl. Government Pension Fund – Global	414,337.0	346,679.0	NOK (million)	
		Investments for Government Pension Fund – Global	1,782,139.0	1,397,896.0	NOK (million)	
		Total ASSETS	2,196,476.0	1,744,575.0	NOK (million)	
Mexico	Central Bank of Mexico	International reserves	731,725.0	730,253.0	Dollar (million)	Bank of Mexico website
		International assets	825,249.0	788,117.0	Dollar (million)	
		Liabilities to be deducted	(93,524.0)	(57,864.0)	Dollar (million)	
		Credit granted to the federal government	0.0	0.0	Dollar (million)	
		Government securities	0.0	0.0	Dollar (million)	

Table 6.1 (continued)

Country	Name of Bank	Assets	2006	2005	Currency	Source
		Credit granted to financial intermediaries and debtors repo operations	201,387.0	144,484.0	Dollar (million)	
		Credit granted to public entities	63,592.0	61,064.0	Dollar (million)	
		Credit granted to trust funds	17,537.0		Dollar (million)	
		Share in the international financial organizations	7,946.0	7,815.0	Dollar (million)	
		Fixed assets, furniture, and equipment	3,564.0	3,385.0	Dollar (million)	
		Other assets	71,701.0	55,686.0	Dollar (million)	
		Total assets	1,097,452.0	1,002,687.0	Dollar (million)	
South Africa	South African Reserve Bank	Assets				South Africa Reserve Bank website
		Cash and cash equivalents	25.1	18.5	Rand (million)	
		Accommodation to banks	13,233.2	13,475.8	Rand (million)	
		South African Government bonds	9,518.9	7,421.6	Rand (million)	
		Loans and Advances	72.6	60.4	Rand (million)	
		Current taxation prepaid	4.6	89.2	Rand (million)	
		Amount due by subsidiaries	0.0	0.0	Rand (million)	
		Gold and foreign exchange	142,118.6	98,663.3	Rand (million)	
		Inventories	217.9	202.5	Rand (million)	
		Investments	3,872.7	4,211.5	Rand (million)	
		Amount due by South African Government	1,078.7	1,098.6	Rand (million)	

Table 6.1 (continued)

Country	Name of Bank	Assets	2006	2005	Currency	Source
		Gold and foreign exchange Contingency Reserve Account	0.0	4,746.6	Rand (million)	
		Property plant and equipment	1,006.5	1,073.6	Rand (million)	
		Investments in subsidiaries	0.0	0.0	Rand (million)	
		Equity investment in Bank for international settlements	233.3	169.1	Rand (million)	
		Deferred taxation assets	228.0	218.3	Rand (million)	
		Forward exchange contract assets	381.3	1,173.8	Rand (million)	
		Other assets	344.8	830.1	Rand (million)	
		Total Assets	172,336.4	133,453.1	Rand (million)	
Chile	Bank of Chile	Foreign assets	11,293,851.1		Dollar (million)	Bank of Chile website
		Reserve assets	11,151,783.3		Dollar (million)	
		Monetary gold	2,479.3		Dollar (million)	
		special drawing rights (SDR)	31,346.2		Dollar (million)	
		Reserve position in the IMF	64,981.5		Dollar (million)	
		foreign currencies	11,034,682.3		Dollar (million)	
		Other assets	18,294.0		Dollar (million)	
		Other foreign assets	142,067.8		Dollar (million)	
		Shares and contributions to the IDB	105,754.3		Dollar (million)	
		Bank for International Settlements (BIS) shares	36,313.5		Dollar (million)	
		Domestic assets	3,236,066.7		Dollar (million)	

Table 6.1 (continued)

Country	Name of Bank	Assets	2006	2005	Currency	Source
		domestic loans	3,236,066.7		Dollar (million)	
		Loans to state-owned companies	1,323.2		Dollar (million)	
		Loans to Banca del Estado de Chile	120,436.6		Dollar (million)	
		Loans to commercial banks	592,957.6		Dollar (million)	
		Loans to other institutions	566,448.0		Dollar (million)	
		Treasury transfer (Laws 18,267,18,401, and 18,786)	952,741.6		Dollar (million)	
		Loans for subordinated obligations of financial institutions (Laws 18, 401 and 19396)	1,002,159.7		Dollar (million)	
		Other assets	322,818.4		Dollar (million)	
		Bank premises and equipment, net	14,987.1		Dollar (million)	
		Other securities	3,747.6		Dollar (million)	
		U.S. dollars purchased with resell agreement	304,083.7		Dollar (million)	
		Total Assets	14,852,736.2		Dollar (million)	

6.1.1 Central Bank Assets of Emerging Economies

The bulk of the Bank of Mexico's assets were held as international reserves in 2006. Credit granted to financial intermediaries and debtors from repo operations occupied the second position in its asset composition (see Table 6.1). In addition, the Bank of Mexico remained the only central bank among our selected ones that had zero shares of gold in its foreign reserve holdings. This reflects the strong measures put in place to address the issue of liquidity in its financial system. In addition, the Bank of Mexico has been globally accused of not disclosing information about the gold reserves in its balance sheets.

As reported in Table 4.1, the total assets of the South African Reserve Bank were mainly driven by gold and foreign exchange, which accounted for more than 50 percent in 2006. Foreign assets were the largest component of the Bank of Chile's assets, which accounted for more than 70 percent in 2006. The remaining percent was shared between domestic assets and other assets (see Table 6.1).

6.2 Central Bank Assets During the 2007–2008 Crisis

During the period of the crisis, the composition pattern of the ECB assets still remained as they were in 2006. In addition, the largest share of its aggregate assets was attributed to intra-Eurosystem claims with more than 50 percent (see Table 6.2). The ECB balance sheet more than tripled in size between the second quarter of 2007 and the last quarter of 2008 before it declined gradually in 2009 as the special operations matured. In addition, there was an increase in the intra-Eurosystem claims and liabilities denominated in euro. The swap arrangement led to a huge increase in liabilities to non-euro area residents, denominated in euro. The asset-side items of the ECB balance sheet increased because of other smaller operations such as the settlement of the Danish krone and the Swedish krona leg of the swap transactions.

As at the end of 2008, balances from swap transactions took the leading role while foreign currency investments accounted for the third largest component of the SNB assets, after claims from Swiss franc repo transactions (see Table 6.2). This table indicates that securities accounted for the largest share of the RBA assets as at the end of 2008. This implies that the most significant component of the aggregate assets shifted from the foreign exchange to securities in 2008. However, the SNB and the RSA were opposite each other between 2007 and 2008. The SNB's gold holding reduced while the RSA increased the amount of gold holdings in its foreign reserves. This reflects that the SNB expanded the liquidity window in order to absorb the shocks during the global financial crisis.

During the crisis period, the composition pattern of the Norges Bank balance sheets still remained the same as in 2006. At the end of 2008, investments including government pension fund maintained its leading role in the composition (see Table 6.2).

Table 6.2: Central banks' assets (2007 and 2008)

Country	Name of Bank	Assets	2008	2007	Currency	Source
Europe	European Central Bank	Gold and gold receivables	10,663.5	10,280.4	Euro (million)	European Central Bank website
		Claims on non-euro area residents			Euro (million)	
		denominated in foreign currency			Euro (million)	
		Receivables from the IMF	346.7	449.6	Euro (million)	
		Balances with banks and security investments, external loans, and other external assets	41,264.1	28,721.4	Euro (million)	
			41,610.8	29,171.0	Euro (million)	
		Claim on euro area residents denominated in foreign currency	22,225.9	3,868.2	Euro (million)	
		Claims on non-euro area residents denominated in euro			Euro (million)	
		Balance with banks, security investments, and investments and loans	629.3	0.0	Euro (million)	
		Other claims on euro area credit institutions denominated in euro	0.025	0.014	Euro (million)	
		Intra-Eurosystem claims			Euro (million)	
		Claims related to the allocation of euro banknotes within the Eurosystem	61,021.8	54,130.5	Euro (million)	
		Other claims within the Eurosystem (net)	234,095.5	17,241.2	Euro (million)	
			295,117.3	71,371.7	Euro (million)	
		Other assets			Euro (million)	

Table 6.2 (continued)

Country	Name of Bank	Assets	2008	2007	Currency	Source
		Tangible fixed assets	202.7	188.2	Euro (million)	
		Other financial assets	10,351.9	9,678.8	Euro (million)	
		Off-balance sheet instruments revaluation differences	23.5	35.0	Euro (million)	
		Accruals and prepaid	1,806.2	1,365.9	Euro (million)	
		Sundry	1,272.2	69.1	Euro (million)	
			13,656.4	11,337.0	Euro (million)	
		Total asset	383,903.2	126,028.3	Euro (million)	
Switzer-land	Swiss National Bank (SNB)	Gold holdings	27,521.2		Chf (million)	Swiss National Bank website
		Claims from gold transactions	3,340.4		Chf (million)	
		Foreign currency investments	47,428.8		Chf (million)	
		Reserve position in the IMF	724.7		Chf (million)	
		international payment instruments	244.5		Chf (million)	
		Monetary assistance loans	326.3		Chf (million)	
		Claims from U.S. dollar repo transactions	11,670.9		Chf (million)	
		Balances from swap transaction against Swiss francs	50,421.4		Chf (million)	
		Claims from Swiss franc repo transactions	50,320.6		Chf (million)	
		Clams against domestic correspondents	11.1		Chf (million)	
		Swiss franc securities	3,596.7		Chf (million)	

Table 6.2 (continued)

Country	Name of Bank	Assets	2008	2007	Currency	Source
		Stabilization fund investments	16,227.1		Chf (million)	
		Banknote stocks	136.5		Chf (million)	
		Tangible assets	382.8		Chf (million)	
		Participations	147.8		Chf (million)	
		Other assets	3,407.7		Chf (million)	
		Total assets	215,908.5		Chf (million)	
Australia	Reserve Bank of Australia (RBA)	Cash and cash equivalents	862.0	586.0	AUD$(million)	Reserve Bank of Australia website
		Australian dollar securities	54,702.0	34,955.0	AUD$(million)	
		Foreign exchange	42,505.0	93,538.0	AUD$(million)	
		Gold	2,509.0	2,001.0	AUD$(million)	
		Property, plant and equipment	456.0	421.0	AUD$(million)	
		Loan, advances, and other	438.0	393.0	AUD$(million)	
		Total Assets	101,472.0	131,894.0	AUD$(million)	
Norway	Norges Bank	FOREIGN FINANCIAL ASSETS				Norges Bank website
		Equities	69,974.0	88,498.0	NOK (million)	
		Bonds and other fixed income instruments	195,624.0	174,031.0	NOK(million)	
		Deposits in foreign banks	36,970.0	3,899.0	NOK (million)	
		Lending	49,036.0	97,302.0	NOK (million)	
		Claims on the IMF	5,699.0	3,099.0	NOK (million)	
		Total international reserves	357,303.0	366,829.0	NOK(million)	
		Other assets in foreign currency	172.0	154.0	NOK(million)	
		Other assets in NOK	55,807.0	0.0	NOK(million)	
		Total other foreign assets	55,979.0	154.0	NOK(million)	

Table 6.2 (continued)

Country	Name of Bank	Assets	2008	2007	Currency	Source
		Total foreign assets excl Government Pension Fund – Global	413,282.0	366,983.0	NOK(million)	
		DOMESTIC FINAN-CIAL AND OTHER ASSESTS			NOK(million)	
		Lending to bank, etc.	80,158.0	75,627.0	NOK(million)	
		Other assets in foreign currency	57,585.0	0.0	NOK(million)	
		Other assets in NOK	2,359.0	1,834.0	NOK(million)	
		Total domestic financial assets	140,102.0	77,461.0	NOK(million)	
		Fixed assets	1,568.0	1,444.0	NOK(million)	
		Gold	291.0	291.0	NOK(million)	
		Total other domestic assets	1,859.0	1,735.0	NOK(million)	
		Total domestic financial and other assets	141,961.0	79,196.0	NOK(million)	
		Total assets excl. Government Pension Fund - Global	555,243	446,179	NOK(million)	
		Investments, Government Pension - Global	2,273,289.0	2,016,955.0	NOK(million)	
		Total Assets	2,828,532.0	2,463,134.0	NOK(million)	
Mexico	Central Bank of Mexico	International reserves	1,181,863.0		Dollar (million)	Central Bank of Mexico website
		International assets	1,318,260.0		Dollar (million)	
		Liabilities	(136,397.0)		Dollar (million)	
		Credit granted to the federal government	0.0		Dollar (million)	
		Government securities	145,672.0		Dollar (million)	
		Government securities	0.0		Dollar (million)	

Table 6.2 (continued)

Country	Name of Bank	Assets	2008	2007	Currency	Source
		IPAB securities	145,672.0		Dollar (million)	
		Credit granted to financial intermediaries and debtors from repo operations	171,380.0		Dollar (million)	
		Credit granted to public entities	0.0		Dollar (million)	
		Credit granted to trust funds	12,526.0		Dollar (million)	
		Shares in international financial institutions	10,168.0		Dollar (million)	
		Fixed asset, furnishing and equipment	3,876.0		Dollar (million)	
		Other assets	18,847.0		Dollar (million)	
		Total assets	1,544,332.0		Dollar (million)	
South Africa	South African Reserve Bank	Cash and Cash equivalents	77.1	23.6	Rand (million)	South Africa Reserve Bank website
		Accommodation to banks	10,935.4	15,053.4	Rand (million)	
		South African Government bonds	8,280.0	8,918.1	Rand (million)	
		Loans and advances	72.3	73.2	Rand (million)	
		Current taxation prepaid	1.7	6.2	Rand (million)	
		Amounts due by subsidiaries	0.0	0.0	Rand (million)	
		Gold and foreign exchange	277,887.7	192,421.8	Rand (million)	
		inventories	375.3	291.8	Rand (million)	
		Investments	6,835.8	2,881.6	Rand (million)	
		Amounts due by the South African Government	984.0	1,035.1	Rand (million)	
		Property, plant and equipment	1,087.7	1,047.3	Rand (million)	

Table 6.2 (continued)

Country	Name of Bank	Assets	2008	2007	Currency	Source
		Investment in subsidiaries	0.0	0.0	Rand (million)	
		Equity investment in Bank for international Settlements	348.4	287.3	Rand (million)	
		Deferred taxation assets	282.8	242.4	Rand (million)	
		Forward exchange contract assets	16.1	37.1	Rand (million)	
		Other assets	491.8	406.0	Rand (million)	
		Total assets	307,676.2	222,725.0	Rand (million)	
Chile	Bank of Chile	Foreign assets	14,575,229.6	8,508,562.6	Dollar (million)	Bank of Chile website
		Reserve assets	14,422,065.4	8,384,368.1	Dollar (million)	
		Monetary gold	4,295.5	2,688.2	Dollar (million)	
		Special drawing rights (SDR)	35,134.6	26,483.5	Dollar (million)	
		Reserve position in the IMF	103,214.7	43,830.6	Dollar (million)	
		Correspondent banks abroad	24,669.2		Dollar (million)	
		Investments in foreign currency	14,203,468.1	8,277,839.8	Dollar (million)	
		Instruments at fair value with effect on net income	10,801,377.6		Dollar (million)	
		Available- for sale securities	0.0		Dollar (million)	
		Held - to maturity securities	3,402,090.5		Dollar (million)	
		Reciprocal loan agreements	51,002.3		Dollar (million)	
		Other assets	281.0	33,526.0	Dollar (million)	
		Other foreign assets	153,164.2	124,194.5	Dollar (million)	
		Shares and contributions to IDB	113,156.3	91,281.3	Dollar (million)	
		Shares Bank for International Settlements (BIS)	40,007.9	32,913.2	Dollar (million)	
		Domestic assets	2,807,140.6	2,412,778.4	Dollar (million)	

Table 6.2 (continued)

Country	Name of Bank	Assets	2008	2007	Currency	Source
		Domestic loans	936,235.0	2,412,778.4	Dollar (million)	
		Loans to state-owned companies		1,033.5	Dollar (million)	
		Loans to banks and financial institutions	936,235.0		Dollar (million)	
		Loans to commercial banks		569,927.7	Dollar (million)	
		Loans to Banca del Estado de Chile		0.0	Dollar (million)	
		Operations Under Specific Legal Regulation	1,870,905.6		Dollar (million)	
		General Treasury transfers (Laws 18,267 and 18 401)	238,833.5	292,389.3	Dollar (million)	
		Loan for subordinated liabilities of financial institution (Law18, 401 and 19,396)	967,451.8	956,888.5	Dollar (million)	
		Loans to other institutions		592,539.4	Dollar (million)	
		Sinap Liquidation Law 18,900	663,579.5		Dollar (million)	
		Securities receivable Corfo Law 18,401	1,040.8		Dollar (million)	
		Other assets	645,000.3	19,123.1	Dollar (million)	
		Premises and equipment	44,736.3	15,223.1	Dollar (million)	
		Other securities	5,579.1	3,900.0	Dollar (million)	
		Temporary assets	194.6		Dollar (million)	
		Repurchase agreements	594,490.3	0.0	Dollar (million)	
		Total Assets	18,027,370.5	10,940,464.1	Dollar (million)	

6.2.1 Central Bank Assets of Developing and Emerging Economies during the 2007–2008 Crisis

In the period of the financial crisis, international reserves still accounted for the largest portion of the Bank of Mexico's total assets. Government securities, with a value of zero in 2006, took the third position after credit granted to financial intermediaries and debtors from repo operations (see Table 6.2). As of March 31, 2008, almost 70 percent of the South African Reserve Bank assets were in the form of gold and foreign exchange. Gold still maintained the position up to 2008 (see Table 6.2). As of the end of 2008, almost 70 percent of the Bank of Chile's assets were in the form of foreign assets. Foreign assets maintained the leading role up to 2009 (see Table 6.2). Both South Africa and Chile moved in the same direction by diversifying their foreign reserves through a rise in the amount of gold holdings. These strategies were implemented to serve as a hedge against negative effects arising from the global financial crisis.

6.3 Central Bank Assets Today

A decade after the global financial crisis, securities of euro area residents took the lion share of the ECB total assets. More than half of the ECB assets in 2016 and 2017 were held in forms of securities of euro area residents. This implies that the structure of the ECB significantly changed from that of 2006, 2007, and 2008 (see Table 6.3). As the Fed commenced bond purchases in 2008, the ECB waited until January 22, 2015 to implement the same program. The ECB's quantitative easing (QE) focused on mitigating financial stress through the following:

– A reduction in interest rates and a negative deposit rate.
– It set up a targeted long-term operation in order to increase incentives for banks to lend.
– It bought bonds from weaker economies like Italy, Spain, and Portugal, and backed up the stronger economies of Germany and France through the asset purchase plan (APP). Items purchased include government bonds, asset-backed securities, and corporate bonds.

Despite the low yields and stability in the present Eurozone, its balance sheet has significantly expanded from about 384 billion euro in 2008 to almost 5 trillion euro in 2017. The ECB's balance size is likely to continue to expand in the near term because of its continuing asset purchase program. It might end this program when the ECB feels it has attained a point required to reduce its balance sheet.

The recent available data show that foreign currency investments accounted for almost 90 percent of the SNB total assets in 2016 and 2017 as balances from swap transactions were cleared out in these periods. Gold holdings were the second largest component as reported in Table 6.3. In late 2014, the SNB intervened in the foreign exchange market in order to protect the currency ceiling through accumulation of more reserves and expansion of its balance sheets. In December 2014, foreign currency reserves increased to about 7 percent of the gross domestic product (GDP) because of interventions. Owing to the presence of divergence in monetary policy between the United States and euro area, this posed a challenge to the sustainability of the exchange rate ceiling. This resulted in the abandonment of the Franc ceiling in January 2015. At the same time, the SNB reduced its rate further imposing 0.75 percent on all deposits above a specific exemption threshold. The threshold was twenty times the minimum reserve requirement for domestic banks and was adjusted in relation to the amount of cash held. A threshold of Chf 10 million was placed on other account holders.

This expansionary policy is suitable for long term-very low or negative inflation, but it poses a challenge to pension funds in meeting their legal target returns on portfolios. In addition, this might lead to low-quality investment in other assets. This would lead to a situation where individuals and institutions hold cash instead of bank deposits (a "rush to cash"). As the Swiss removed their exchange rate ceiling in January 2015, its domestic currency appreciated intensively against the euro but then reached about 1.05, which recorded a 12.5 percent appreciation. The value of the franc against the euro has fallen since September 2015 because of a decline in the volatility of the exchange rate market. This lowered safe haven effects, and the interest rate differential effect became pronounced.

At the end of 2016 and 2017, Australian dollar investments constituted the largest components of the RBA assets, followed by foreign currency investments. These two components had about 95 percent of the total assets of the RBA (see Table 6.3). The inflation rate in Australia has been low and its interest rate is higher than in the United States or the euro area. This makes the monetary stimulus consistent with the RBA's medium-term inflation target band of 2 to 3 percent. The present supportive stance of monetary policy remains effective especially in the absence of inflationary pressures. Nevertheless, accommodative policy might pose a risk of increasingly distorting financial markets, and particularly house prices, which have risen to very high levels. The normalization of rates is required but the timing and pace will be subject to developments in growth, employment, inflation, and the housing market.

As at the end of 2017, the structure of the Norges Bank balance sheet assets did not change in terms of its composition. Investments that include government pension funds accounted for the largest percentage at about 80 percent in 2016 and 2017 (see Table 6.3). The country is in a very strong position to mitigate risks and shocks because of flexible monetary policy with a floating exchange rate that mixes with the wealth fund and fiscal framework. These measures reduce exposure to oil-price-related and other risks. Its flexible inflation-targeting regime provides a good track record in achieving low and stable inflation. Its policy rate has been reduced in recent months, as of September 2015, the policy rate was 0.75 percent. Inflation is temporarily enhanced by currency depreciation but is driven by remaining economic slack. The Norges Bank wiped out gold holding in order to increase its level of liquidity.

Table 6.3: Central bank assets (2017 and 2016)

Country	Name of Bank	Assets	2017	2016	Currency	Source
Europe	European Central Bank	Gold and gold receivable	376,300.0	382,061.0	Euro (million)	European Central Bank website
		Claims on noneuro area residents denominated I foreign currency	296,217.0	327,859.0	Euro (million)	
		Receivable from the IMF	70,214.0	78,752.0	Euro (million)	
		Balance with banks and security investments, external loans, and other external assets	226,002.0	249,107.0	Euro (million)	
		Claims on euro area residents denominated in foreign currency	38,058.0	30,719.0	Euro (million)	
		Claims on noneuro area residents denominated in euro	19,364.0	19,082.0	Euro (million)	
		Balances with banks, security investment and loans	19,364.0	19,082.0	Euro (million)	
		Claims arising from the credit facility under EMR 11	0.0	0.0	Euro (million)	

Table 6.3 (continued)

Country	Name of Bank	Assets	2017	2016	Currency	Source
		Lending to euro area credit institutions related to monetary policy operations denominated in euro	764,310.0	595,873.0	Euro (million)	
		Main refinancing operations	3,372.0	39,131.0	Euro (million)	
		Longer-term refinancing operations	760,639.0	556,570.0	Euro (million)	
		Fine-turning reverse operation	0.0	0.0	Euro (million)	
		Structural reverse operations	0.0	0.0	Euro (million)	
		Marginal landing facility	299.0	172.0	Euro (million)	
		Credits related to margin calls	0.0	0.0	Euro (million)	
		Other claims on euro area residents denominated in euro	37,563.0	69,134.0	Euro (million)	
		Securities of euro area residents denominated in euro	2,660,726.0	1,974,866.0	Euro (million)	
		Securities held for monetary policy purposes	2,386,012.0	1,653,995.0	Euro (million)	
		Other securities	274,714.0	320,870.0	Euro (million)	
		General government debt denominated in euro	254,010.0	235,384.0	Euro (million)	
		Total Asset	4,471,563.0	3,661,439.0	Euro (million)	
Switzerland	Swiss National Bank (SNB)	Gold holding	42,494.0	39,400.3	Chf (million)	Swiss National Bank website
		Foreign currency investments	790,124.8	696,104.2	Chf (million)	
		Reserve position in the IMF	871.3	1,341.2	Chf (million)	

Table 6.3 (continued)

Country	Name of Bank	Assets	2017	2016	Currency	Source
		International payment instruments	4,495.5	4,406.2	Chf (million)	
		Monetary assistance loan	210.3	155.4	Chf (million)	
		Claims from Swiss franc repo transactions	-	-	Chf (million)	
		Swiss franc securities	3,956.2	3,997.6	Chf (million)	
		Tangible assets	396.3	375.1	Chf (million)	
		Participations	156.9	137.2	Chf (million)	
		Other assets	601.1	584.8	Chf (million)	
		Total assets	843,306.4	746,502.0	Chf (million)	
Australia	Reserve Bank of Australia (RBA)	Cash and cash equivalents	221.0	367.0	AUD$ (million)	Reserve Bank of Australia website
		Australian dollar investments	104,769.0	88,500.0	AUD$ (million)	
		Foreign currency investments	83,577.0	72,879.0	AUD$ (million)	
		Gold	4,147.0	4,567.0	AUD$ (million)	
		Property, plant, and equipment	741.0	640.0	AUD$ (million)	
		Other assets	557.0	536.0	AUD$ (million)	
		Total Assets	194,012.0	167,489.0	AUD$ (million)	
Norway	Norges Bank	Financial Assets				
		Deposits in banks	8,533.0	2,048.0	NOK (million)	Norges Bank website
		Secured lending	25,559.0	42,242.0	NOK (million)	
		Unsettled trades	2,046.0	3,109.0	NOK (million)	
		Equities	173,403.0	173,403.0	NOK (million)	
		Equities lent	10,584.0	8,536.0	NOK (million)	
		Bonds	299,357.0	283,716.0	NOK (million)	
		Financial derivatives	2.0	7.0	NOK (million)	
		Claims on the IMF	67,965.0	65,059.0	NOK (million)	

Table 6.3 (continued)

Country	Name of Bank	Assets	2017	2016	Currency	Source
		Lending to banks	250.0	-	NOK (million)	
		Other financial assets	5,707.0	6,035.0	NOK (million)	
		Total financial assets	593,406.0	584,105.0	NOK (million)	
		Investments, Government Pension Fund Global	8,483,727.0	8,277,072.0	NOK (million)	
		Nonfinancial assets	2,563.0	2,804.0	NOK (million)	
		Total Assets	9,079,696.0	8,863,981.0	NOK (million)	
Mexico	Central Bank of Mexico	International reserves		3,640,181.0	Dollar (million)	Central Bank of Mexico website
		International assets		3,670,769.0	Dollar (million)	
		Liabilities to be deducted		(30,588.0)	Dollar (million)	
		Credit granted to the federal government		0.0	Dollar (million)	
		Government securities		0.0	Dollar (million)	
		Credit granted to banks and debtors from repo operations		203,240.0	Dollar (million)	
		Participation in international financial institutions		15,150.0	Dollar (million)	
		Fixed assets, furnishings, and equipment		3,725.0	Dollar (million)	
		Other assets		14,986.0	Dollar (million)	
		Total assets		3,877,282.0	Dollar (million)	
South Africa	South African Reserve Bank	Cash and cash equivalents	25,675.8	5,947.9	Rand (million)	South African Reserve Bank website

Table 6.3 (continued)

Country	Name of Bank	Assets	2017	2016	Currency	Source
		Amounts due to group companies	-	-	Rand (million)	
		Accommodation to banks	59,685.1	53,509.9	Rand (million)	
		Investments	3,734.8	27,042.3	Rand (million)	
		Other assets	700.5	643.5	Rand (million)	
		Gold and foreign - exchange	617,783.1	688,403.1	Rand (million)	
		Inventories	585.2	467.1	Rand (million)	
		Forward exchange contract assets	317.1	498.0	Rand (million)	
		Loans and advance	27,657.1	27,359.6	Rand (million)	
		Current taxation prepaid	4.9	0.0	Rand (million)	
		South African government bonds	8,153.4	7,931.7	Rand (million)	
		Equity investment in bank for international settlements (BIS)	470.6	542.4	Rand (million)	
		Investment in subsidiaries	-	-	Rand (million)	
		Investment in associate	4,445.8	5,002.3	Rand (million)	
		Property, plant, and equipment	2,814.4	2,643.4	Rand (million)	
		Intangible assets	479.9	528.7	Rand (million)	
		Deferred taxation assets	1,365.0	1,913.4	Rand (million)	
		Total assets	753,872.7	822,433.2	Rand (million)	
Chile	Bank of Chile	Foreign assets		27,181,581.1	Dollar (million)	Bank of Chile website
		Reserve assets		27,021,006.9	Dollar (million)	
		Monetary gold		6,070.8	Dollar (million)	
		Special drawing rights (SDR)		485,453.8	Dollar (million)	

Table 6.3 (continued)

Country	Name of Bank	Assets	2017	2016	Currency	Source
		Reset position in the international monetary fund (IMF)		143,497.2	Dollar (million)	
		Correspondent banks abroad		683,756.5	Dollar (million)	
		Investments in foreign currency		25,691,282.3	Dollar (million)	
		Securities recorded at fair value through earning		18,322,931.3	Dollar (million)	
		Held - for sale securities		3,085,235.9	Dollar (million)	
		Held to maturity securities		4,283,115.1	Dollar (million)	
		Reciprocal loan agreements		10,014.5	Dollar (million)	
		Other assets		931.8	Dollar (million)	
		Other foreign assets		160,574.2	Dollar (million)	
		Shares of and contribution to the inter-American Development Bank (IDB)		122,849.2	Dollar (million)	
		Shares of bank for international settlements (BIS)		37,725.0	Dollar (million)	
		Domestic assets		667,452.8	Dollar (million)	
		Domestic loans		12,501.8	Dollar (million)	
		Loans to banks and financial institutions		12,501.8	Dollar (million)	
		Transactions under specific legal regulations		654,951.0	Dollar (million)	
		General Treasury transfers Law 18,401		299,945.0	Dollar (million)	
		Loan for subordinated liabilities of financial institutions (Laws 18, 401 and 19396)		355,006.0	Dollar (million)	
		Other assets		58,970.5	Dollar (million)	

Country	Name of Bank	Assets	2017	2016	Currency	Source
		Property, equipment, and intangible assets		41,605.6	Dollar (million)	
		Other securities		14,101.2	Dollar (million)	
		Transition assets		3,263.7	Dollar (million)	
		Total assets		27,908,004.4	Dollar (million)	

6.3.1 Central Bank Assets of Emerging Economies Today

As at the end of 2016, international reserves as well as credit granted to banks and debtors from repo operation were the major components of the Bank of Mexico's assets. In addition, the value of government securities returned to zero as it was prior to the financial crisis (see Table 6.3).

With reference to Table 6.3, the gold and foreign-exchange component still dominated the structure of the South Africa Reserve Bank's (SARB's) assets in 2016 and 2017. Despite changes in the value of assets and its components, the configuration of the asset compositions remained unchanged before, during, and after the global financial crisis.

The country's inflation rose from 4.6 percent in 2015 to 6.4 percent in 2016 due to currency depreciation and the drought-related rise in domestic food prices. From the domestic view, the confidence level in the economy was shaken given changes in the political environment. Private investment could further be constrained by a rise in political tension. From the global perspective, the local currency is highly sensitive to U.S. interest rates, thus increasing its exposure. Furthermore, with the United Kingdom being its largest European trading partner, the country's imports and financial flows may be affected by uncertainty about Brexit.

The monetary policy operation in South Africa takes place in a difficult environment of high inflation and low growth. Inflation exceeded the reserve bank's target band (3–6%) throughout 2016. This was a result of the delayed exchange rate pass-through following the substantial depreciation of the rand throughout 2015. A long-lasting drought further created pressure on agricultural prices but in 2016 there was a huge fall in prices, which pushed the headline inflation down into the target band. Stable core inflation was witnessed throughout 2016 but at the upper limit of the target band.

The reserve bank maintained the repurchase rate at 7 percent since March 2016 and reduced it by 25 base points in 2017. With a long-term fall in inflation, monetary policy would have room for adopting accommodative measures. On the other hand, if the rand value falls as U.S. monetary policy continues to tighten, this would impose pressure on inflation. The country's stock market exhibits more volatility than many other emerging countries due to the fact that its currency is mainly driven by external factors such as U.S. monetary policy and national policy uncertainty.

As reported in Table 6.3, foreign assets still dominated the structure of the Bank of Chile's assets in 2015 and 2016. This suggests an unchanged element in the compositions of its assets over time. Chile's central bank increased its interest rates from 3 to 3.25 percent in mid-October 2015 due to the headline inflation above the policy target. However, further increases in interest rates might not be effective because the recent inflation has been substantially attached to exchange rate depreciation. Slow domestic and external activity as well as a recent fall in commodity prices indicate the likely chance of a reduction in the price pressures. Nevertheless, if expectations are continuously above the target, this might require some further monetary tightening.

The country had a current account surplus because of fiscal rules, which allowed the fiscal surplus to be saved in the sovereign wealth fund during much of the commodity boom. Its fiscal surplus increased from 2 percent in 2004 to over 7 percent of GDP in 2007, encouraging the country to keep more than 10 percent of GDP in its sovereign wealth fund. Then the surplus turned to deficits due to the countercyclical response to the 2009 global financial crisis, reconstruction spending related to the 2010 earthquake and tsunami, and the rise in production costs in mining. However, the government was able to respond counter-cyclically to the 2014 slowdown in activity, as well as sustain aggregate demand because of the near absence of net debt.

However, central banks in small open countries may have a large share of foreign reserves on their balance sheets as depicted in Figure 6.1. The reason can be historically traced as follows:

In the time of a fixed exchange rate regime and restricted capital flows, central banks held huge amounts of foreign reserves as a means of funding imports and making the exchange rate regime credible. However, with free capital flows and floating exchange rates, central banks sometimes intervene in foreign exchange markets and require foreign reserves to accomplish this. Additionally, in the era of financial instability, reserves can be explored to serve central bank customers such as the government, and to mitigate risk of instability in financial systems that heavily relied on foreign currency funding. The relevance of these aims will be based on each country's thirst for interventions and the unhedged vulnerability of its financial system to exchange rate risk. Reserve holdings are valuable in the situation of financial stress, when the central banks' exposure to exchange rate risk that could be higher than the interest rate risk attached to holding government bonds. For instance, the Norges Bank held 86 percent of its assets in the form of foreign reserves, with the exclusion of the sovereign wealth fund as at end of 2006, compared to the Fed whose foreign exchange reserve accounted for 4 percent of its assets by the end of 2006.

In addition, loans to banks can be a significant asset of central banks. This usually occurs when the central bank has few securities as assets, compared to the quantity of its liabilities, especially currency. On the other hand, central banks with huge securities against the currency can provide sizable lending to the banking sector. The loans are critical to create reserves, which can enhance interbank payments. In the case of low supply of reserves, central bank lending to banks can provide reserves to boost payments among banks. In December 2006, more than 50 percent of the Bank of England (BoE) assets were loans to banks in the form of repos, while about 40 percent of the ECB assets were loans, as illustrated in Figure 6.1. Loans and repos accounted for only 4 percent of the Fed assets at that period.

In some situations, a huge share of bank loans on the central bank's balance sheet may be a signal of undeveloped money markets. This requires the central bank to provide direct liquidity to its banks instead of redistributing the liquidity among them through the money market.

During normal situations, the composition of central bank balance sheets can significantly differ across countries. Every central bank can issue two major forms of money, currency, and reserves as liabilities, but the relative magnitude of these items can vary considerably.

In addition, some central banks issue deposits to the government and provide term liabilities, while others do not have this privilege. Generally, assets comprise government bonds, foreign reserves, and loans to banks in different proportions, and also with wide variation across central banks.

A significant invention that is not as well known to many people, is *financial contracts*. Finance performs two simple roles. It serves as an economic time machine that helps savers transport current surplus income into the future or provides borrowers access to future earnings now. In addition, it can be considered as a safety net protecting against floods, fires, or illness.

In reference to these two kinds of service, an effective financial system ensures stability in a period of financial crisis, and makes an uncertain world more predictable. Additionally, finance acts as an engine of growth when investors are searching for people and companies with the best ideas.

However, finance has negative sides. For instance, the crisis of 2008 created a legacy of unemployment and debt. Therefore, it is worth investigating whether correct measures are explored to enhance the benefits of finance, and to eliminate its problems.

Historically, the commencement of America's first crash in 1792 and the recent global financial crisis in 2007/2008 tend to provide financial innovation. The first issue then is that financial institutions such as central banks, deposit insurance, and stock exchanges were ill-designed in these periods. This contributed to the problematic nature of the second phase of finance history. The response to the crises in the second phase commenced with blame.

6.4 Asset-Side Composition and Economic Growth Nexus

6.4.1 Asset-Growth Nexus before the 2007–2008 Crisis

As explained in the previous sections in terms of economic growth rate in the concerned countries, there were significant variations in the structure of central banks' assets. For instance, 50 percent of ECB's assets were made up of intra-Euro system claims while its counterparts, SNB and RSA, were mainly driven by foreign currency before 2007. In this period, investment for government pension fund accounted for the bulk of the Norges Bank.

In emerging countries like Mexico, South Africa, and Chile, their central banks' assets mainly consisted of foreign reserves. In the case of South Africa, its assets were driven by both gold and foreign exchange. This might be a factor that triggered the improvements in those countries between 2005 and 2006 (see Figure 6.1). For instance, Chile's central bank assets were 70 percent driven by the foreign assets before the financial crisis. This could be the reason why the country experienced the highest growth rate.

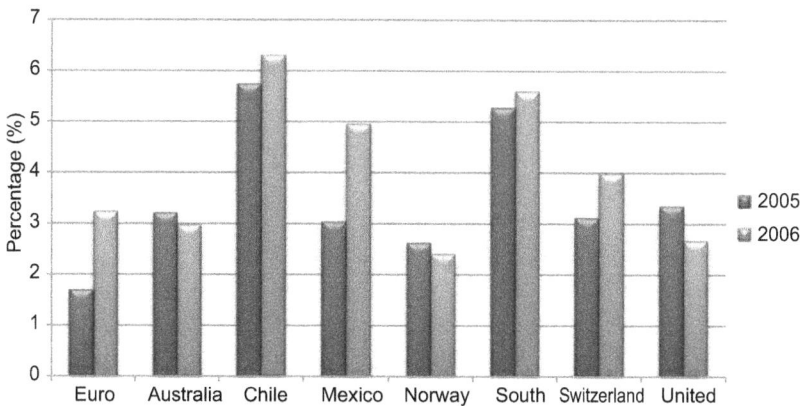

Source: World Bank World Development Indicator (WDI) 2017.
Figure 6.1: Pre-2007–2008 GDP Growth Rate

6.4.2 Asset-Growth Nexus during the 2007–2008 Crisis

During the 2007–2008 crisis, the pattern of central banks' assets changed in countries like Switzerland and Australia. Balances from swap transactions led the SNB assets list, while securities accounted for the largest share in the RBA assets. The composition of the RBA assets in the same period was able to prevent a drastic fall in the economic growth of Australia compared to its counterparts (see Figure 6.2). All the emerging economies in Figure 6.2 witnessed a sharp fall in their economic growth rate as the overall composition of their central bank assets witnessed changes. This implies that the pattern of asset composition played a critical role in influencing the economic growth rate in the periods. Appropriate asset compositions are sufficient conditions for improving an economy as it observed for the case of the SNB and the RBA.

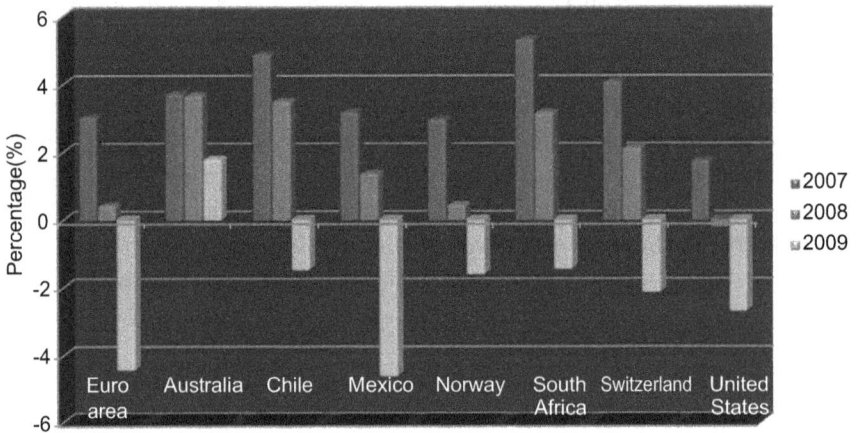

Source: World Bank Development Indicator (WDI) 2017.
Figure 6.2: GDP growth rate during the 2007–2008 crisis

6.4.3 Asset-Growth Nexus after the 2007–2008 Crisis

Between 2015 and 2016, all the concerned economies in Figure 6.3, excluding Australia witnessed a decline in their economic performance, but their economies still grew positively. The pattern of Australia's central bank assets might be an important reason for the improvement in the country's economic growth. Australian dollar investments constituted the largest components of the RBA assets, followed by foreign currency investments.

In the case of emerging economies, South Africa witnessed the most significant reduction in its economic performance. This might be as a result of maintaining the asset-side composition in which gold and foreign exchange accounted for the largest share. Other emerging economies also witnessed a sharp drop in their economic performance because of maintaining the same asset-side composition during these periods. This indicates that the amount of the central bank assets are a necessary condition for stimulating the economy while compositions of these assets provide sufficient conditions.

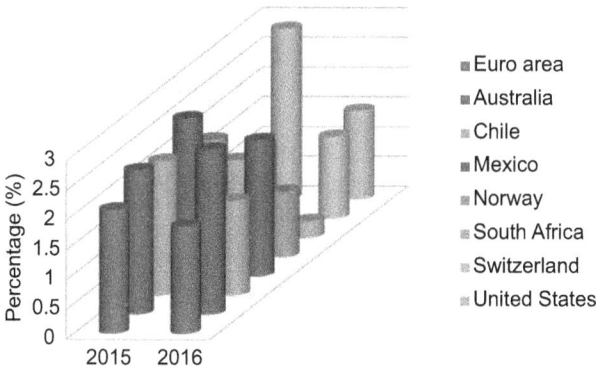

Source: World Bank World Development Indicator (WDI) 2017.

Figure 6.3: GDP growth rate after the 2007–2008 crisis

6.5 The Evolution of Central Bank Balance Sheets in the Future

There has been a dramatic change in central bank balance sheets over a decade ago. Many factors are responsible for these changes which are expected to be continually evolving in the future. The three key drivers of these changes in the future are as follows:

a. Central Bank Digital Currency (CBDC): There is a future expectation that a central bank will be an issuer of digital currency. Since digital currency is an electronic form of money used by the public, the central bank is responsible for issuing this. However, this needs not be a cryptocurrency.

At present, the only electronic form of central bank money is reserves. The reserves exist with the physical form, which is known as banknotes. Access to these forms is restricted to only a select number of financial institutions. With the era of digital currency, the central bank would potentially have another instrument that can be used to influence its monetary policy. This will happen as the increased potential flexibility of digital currency enables both the quantity and/or the interest rate of the digital currency to be adjusted.

However in a situation where the increase in digital currency is not balanced by a decline in the issuance of banknotes, the issuance of any significant amount would result in a substantial rise in liabilities for the central bank, demanding them to purchase more assets. Part of these assets would be government bonds, even though many central banks have already acquired a very huge quantity of these bonds after the 2007–2009 global financial crisis (such as Federal Reserve). Consequently, they may decide not to have more in order to prevent distress in the bond markets. In addition, it might be due to political concerns about monetary financing or insufficient government bonds in circulation.

Quite a lot of discussions have been focused on how central bank digital currency would significantly change payment systems as well as the whole financial system. The impacts on the asset-side component of central bank balance sheets are of great concern.

b. Equity as a policy instrument: Another possible development occurs when central banks explore equity in more creative ways in order to implement policy. Currently, central bank equity is considered as a "loss-absorbing buffer" rather than a tool to implement policy. For instance with QE, central banks create new reserves in order to purchase financial assets from the private sector. Nevertheless, central banks could attain the same objective through bookkeeping channels by issuing central bank shares in return for private sector assets. These shares are not the same as the conventional ones in a listed company because they would not exercise voting rights on the activities of the central bank.

The benefit of utilizing equity to purchase private sector assets is that the central bank would boost its capital base at a period when it is exposed to more risk.

c. Helicopter money or helicopter drop;[1] This measure could be implemented by a central bank to boost economic activities. The measure can take many forms in achieving the purpose, but most proposals anticipate the use of money to monetize fiscal policy basically by creating money for the government to either spend or distribute to people. In addition to the concern of central bank autonomy, helicopter money could lead to a substantial change in the balance sheet of the central bank. For example, implementation of

---

[1] Helicopter money is a hypothetical unconventional tool of monetary policy that involves printing huge sums of money and distributing it to the public in order to boost the economy.

helicopter money through the buying of a perpetual zero-coupon government bond issued particularly for this purpose would significantly change the central bank balance sheet. As these bonds can not be sold (unlike the case of QE), thus they would provide a commitment to never relax the policy, which poses a larger influence on the economy. Most economists have argued that helicopter drops create more problems than their benefits. This means that its adverse consequences in the form of high inflation rates might outweigh its benefits in the form of economic growth rate.

In summary, the relevance of the central bank balance sheet will still be identified in the future. The data-driven illustrations of responses of central bank balance sheets to the 2007–2008 global financial crisis provide in-depth insights toward computation of central bank balance sheet ratios that will be discussed in the subsequent chapters.

Questions

1. What is the evolution pattern of asset-side components of central bank balance sheets in advanced countries before, during, and after the 2007–2008 global financial crisis?
2. What is the heterogeneous nature of asset-side components of central bank balance sheets in developing countries pre-, during, and post-2007–2008 era?
3. What are the similarities and differences between the pattern of asset-side composition in advanced economies and emerging and developing countries?
4. What are the conditions for stimulating an economy through the asset-side of central bank balance sheets?

Chapter 7
Financial Ratios of the Central Bank Balance Sheet

Two main aspects of central bank balance sheet financial ratios are particularly useful. First, they assist users in analyzing the ability of the central bank to safeguard the value of a currency, for example, in the foreign-exchange market. Second, financial ratios reveal possible limitations in the central bank's position, and highlight potential problems such as insolvency; ratios can act as an early warning system and press authorities into action to strengthen or recapitalize the central bank. These ratios allow the quality of money and the health of the central bank to be measured in a somewhat objective manner.

The absence of homogenous data makes international comparisons of accounting statements difficult. International balance sheet comparisons are difficult due to variations in accounting traditions and standards from country to country. Banks are not as transparent when reporting financial accounts relative to other firms, resulting in disagreement and uncertainty about their asset and liability values.

The introduction of international financial reporting standards (IFRS) encourages a better comparison of balance sheets internationally and across different industries. Strength, liquidity, and equity ratios are required to analyze the financial stability of a central bank.

7.1 International Strength

Th international strength ratio measures the potential ability to defend the external value of a currency (i.e., the foreign exchange rate). The defense potential ratio is the ratio of the foreign-exchange reserves (excluding gold, if applicable) to the monetary base.

This indicates the percentage of monetary liabilities that are supported with foreign reserves available to be utilized to defend the currency on the foreign-exchange market. Sales of foreign reserves on the open market and buying domestic currency can back the value of the currency in times of crisis or speculative attacks.

$$\textit{Defense potential ratio (\%)} = \textit{foreign reserves} \big/ \textit{monetary base}$$

Quick question: What is the defense potential ratio for your country or region's central bank balance sheets using data in Appendix 1.1?

DOI 10.1515/9781547400577-007

7.2 External Strength Ratio

The external strength ratio measurement is the ratio of the central bank's foreign-exchange reserves as a proportion of total world foreign-exchange reserves, that is, the total of foreign-exchange reserves held by all central banks of the world:

$$External\ strength\ ratio\ (\%) = foreign\ reserves/total\ world\ foreign\ reserves$$

The higher the proportion of total world foreign exchange reserves that a central bank possesses, the greater its potential will be to defend the currency globally. This implies a higher degree of external strength as the central bank controls a higher share of available reserves vis-à-vis other monetary authorities. In addition, it may show the past strength of a currency area to stimulate exports (and hence accumulate foreign currency as the central bank sells domestic currency to facilitate cross-border transactions), improving the quality of money by raising trade-based demand. If a currency area is competitive, it is easier to generate foreign-exchange reserves that can be utilized to safeguard the currency.

A central bank that unilaterally allows its currency supply to be purchased by foreign central banks will witness a fall in its external strength ratio (this result was observed throughout the Bretton Woods era, and the culmination of this loss of external strength put an end to the gold exchange standard in 1971). This occurs as global currency reserves increase through expansionary monetary policy while its own foreign-exchange holdings do not.

The quality of domestic money can fall, even without any direct action on the part of domestic authorities. The large U.S. dollar foreign exchange reserves held by certain central banks (e.g., Japan and China) create a potential danger for the U.S. dollar, as either economy could sell large amounts of their dollar holdings, leading to depreciation of the American currency. This means that a central bank can defend its currency more effectively against such speculative actions if its external strength ratio improves.

On the other hand, the external strength ratio is also important for a country whose currency is not a global reserve currency. The higher the dollar reserves of the central bank of Nigeria in terms of the world dollar reserves, the stronger its ability to safeguard its own currency from speculative attacks and lessen exchange rate volatility.

Quick question: What is the stance of your country or region's central bank balance sheet in terms of external strength ratio using Appendix 1.1 data?

7.3 External Impact Ratio

The external impact ratio can be defined as the foreign reserves of a country divided by the overall daily trading volume in foreign-exchange markets of those reserves.

$$External\ impact\ ratio\ (\%) = {foreign\ reserves}/{foreign-reserve\ daily\ trading\ volume}$$

The dollar reserves of a central bank divided by the total daily trading volume in the foreign exchange market is an important external impact determinant. It shows the ability to influence the exchange rate in the market as a whole. Traditionally, the widespread global use of and demand for the U.S. dollar has led to its low external impact factor, while there is a high external impact factor for gold and other less frequently traded currencies. Low external impact factor figures show that greater volume of a currency can be traded with insignificant impact on the current exchange rate, hence contributing to stabilizing a currency against speculative attacks.

A greater portion of liquid and high quality assets in the central bank's reserves indicates a higher quality of money. Gold and high quality currencies are commonly regarded as liquid due to very low credit risk. High quality government bonds like U.S treasury bills exhibit a very large and liquid market, and a central bank can sell large amounts of these bonds with insignificant losses resulting from increased bid-ask spreads (a situation that is unlikely to hold true for thinly traded currencies in little global demand). This, combined with an extremely low credit risk, makes U.S. T-Bills an example of high quality reserve assets that can be liquidated in short notice in the case of a domestic economic emergency.

Quick question: What are the calculations of the external impact ratio for central bank balance sheets of your interest?

7.4 Liquidity Ratios I, II, and III

The more liquid an asset is, the lower the costs a central bank will incur when selling the asset in large volumes. In the event of a domestic economic or financial crisis, liquid assets are utilized to back a faltering currency. A greater liquidity ratio implies a lower share of illiquid assets held in reserve. Illiquid assets pose a problem as it is difficult to sell such assets without suffering losses on a broad bid-ask spread, and they are more difficult to sell in panic conditions as there may not be a willing buyer or market. A greater proportion of illiquid assets implies a lower liquidity ratio. Thus, the quality of money will be lowered as the assets backing the money can not be readily mobilized to support its strength during a time of crisis.

Gold was historically the asset that authorities liquidated during an economic or banking crisis. Thus, gold was the dominant world currency until the early twentieth century. Gold experienced a high volume of sales without negative bid-ask spreads due to high demand and a wide market; it is especially popular during times of crisis as a hedge against inflation. In addition, gold possesses no credit risk and debt unlike other financial assets.

7.4.1 Liquidity Ratio I

The liquidity ratio I is the percentage of assets that can be sold without incurring debt. Generally, this is utilized to measure gold as a proportion of central bank assets.

$$Liquidity\ ratio\ I\ (\%) = {}^{gold}\!\big/\!_{monetary\ base}$$

7.4.2 Liquidity Ratio II

Liquidity ratio II is the percentage of gold and foreign-exchange reserves in terms of total assets. Foreign exchange reserves are usually very liquid because of large daily trading volumes. Their value is more volatile compared to gold and can exhibit credit risk, implying that their value can theoretically decline to zero in a period of crisis. Gold reserves restrict the ability of the central bank to put pressure on the price of gold, but central banks are able to devalue their own currency to virtually zero by inflationary policies.

$$Liquidity\ ratio\ II\ (\%) = {}^{gold+foreign\ reserves}\!\big/\!_{monetary\ base}$$

7.4.3 Liquidity Ratio III

Liquidity Ratio III refers to the sum of high quality government bonds with a low default risk (like AAA rated bonds), gold and foreign reserves expressed in terms of total assets.

$$Liquidity\ ratio\ III\ (\%) = {}^{gold+foreign\ reserves+government\ bonds}\!\big/\!_{monetary\ base}$$

High quality government bonds are usually liquid even in periods of crisis. Unfavorable markets may even encourage some capital flight in order to safely increase their demand. Their value is supported by the taxation power of government as well as the performance of the economy. An excessive issuance of the bonds leads to a fall in their value. The quality of money is worsened by government deficit spending as a result of the challenge of higher future taxes or debt monetization, as interest payments become more burdensome and difficult to service.

Government bonds are likely to become illiquid if the government is not creditworthy. This is particularly notable in times of economic crisis. For instance, the recapitalization of the Icelandic central bank, complemented with an issuance of government bonds, did not guarantee the increase in the quality of money needed to save the banking system from its financial crisis. Also, the government's taxation effectiveness was not adequate for its aims to create liquid assets to support the currency.

Quick question: What are the similarities and differences between the three liquidity ratios for your country or region based on the data in Appendix 1.1?

7.5 Equity Ratio

Equity ratio shows the central bank's leverage. A higher equity ratio translates to a more conservative situation (i.e., less leverage) and an increased quality of money.

$$Equity\ ratio\ (\%) = {}^{equity}\!/_{total\ assets}$$

Potential losses on the asset component of the balance sheet can be moderated by available equity, and therefore lessens the likelihood that a central bank will need to recapitalize. Recapizalization can contribute to a rise in debt or loss of independence, which has further adverse effects on the quality of money.

Quick question: What is your country or region's central bank's leverage using the data in Appendix 1.1?

Questions

1. How are financial ratios used in testing the financial stability of central banks?
2. What are the calculations of each of these ratios in relation to any central bank and interpret the outcomes?
3. Based on the results obtained in question 2, what policies or future actions can you recommend?

Chapter 8
Central Bank Operations

Changes in some components of the central bank's balance sheet influence the amount of resources available to the banking system. Although central banks have limited direct influence over commercial banking operations, central banks can change the volume of reserves held by commercial banks. This is done through central bank operations. A record is made on the asset side of the central bank if the operation provides reserves to commercial banks, while an operation that results in a reduction in the quantity of commercial bank reserves is reflected on its liability side. This chapter explains central bank operations and various policy instruments that support central banking operations.

8.1 Types of Central Bank Operations

8.1.1 Supply Liquidity

Operations relating to the supply of liquidity to the market are classified as *active* and *passive* types. An example of an active type of liquidity supply is open market operations, while standing facilities (monetary instruments of the Eurosystem, which banks are able to use daily on their own initiative) and bilateral operations (currency swap deals between two central banks) are examples of passive types. The maturity of these operations ranges from the overnight repo of securities to the outright buying of long-term assets.

8.1.2 Absorb Excess Liquidity

In the case of surplus liquidity, central banks decide whether to accept excess liquidity or to absorb excess liquidity. The central bank has various maturity instruments that can be used to restore equilibrium into the market if it accepts the surplus of liquidity. The balance is established when market prices are in line with policy. This reflects the shortest-term operations to balance liquidity absorption.

If the central bank moves toward a shortage of liquidity through longer maturity operations where the amount of liquidity exceeds the magnitude of the liquidity surplus, this creates a shortage. This shortage is resolved through short maturity liquidity providing operations. This implies the short term operations will normalize liquidity.

DOI 10.1515/9781547400577-008

8.1.3 Asset Securities

A new asset is established on the central bank's balance sheet when a central bank lends to a commercial bank. It is very rare for this type of lending to be unsecured. Central banks obtain collateral to safeguard themselves against credit and market risks. The new asset on the central bank's balance sheet is the collateral taken in return for the provision of reserves.

The choices of collateral in mitigating risks significantly affect the functioning of the central bank and the entire economy. The impact on the central bank is reflected on its income and exposure to credit and market risks, while economy-wide impacts are on portfolio balance and liquidity. These effects are illustrated in Figure 8.1.

Illustrations of how a central bank operates its reserves are shown in Figures 8.1 and 8.2.

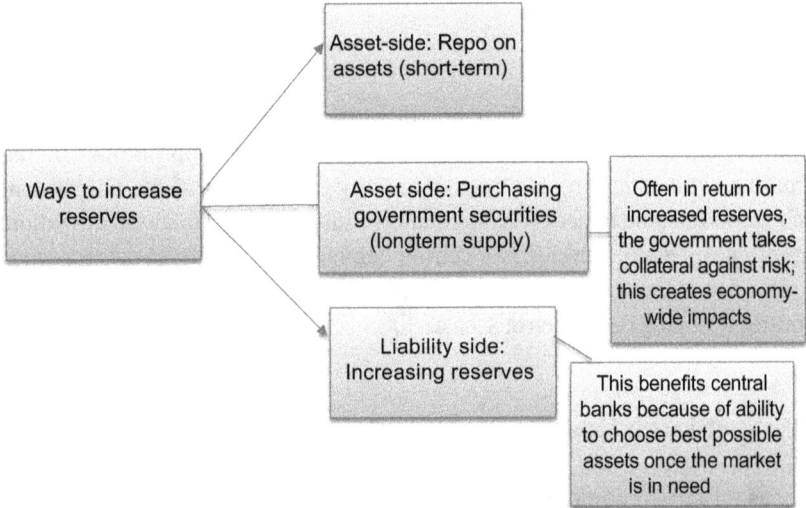

Figure 8.1: Central bank methods of increasing reserves

When a central bank absorbs liquidity from the market there is no impact on the asset side of the balance sheet. On the liability side the operation coverts commercial bank reserves into other liabilities. However if a central bank absorbs by providing collateral, it sells assets issued by another issuer. Then the commercial bank will hold that asset as collateral instead. The decision to provide collateral to the commercial banks or leave them with an unsecured claim on the central bank is not made for risk reasons but wider market functioning reasons.

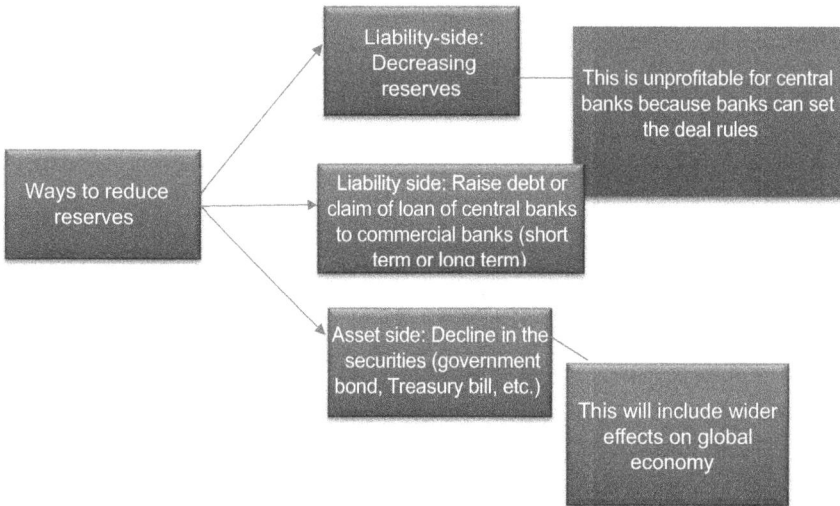

Figure 8.2: Central bank methods of reducing reserves

The choices of collateral used to mitigate risks significantly affect the functioning of the central bank and the entire economy. The impact on the central bank is reflected in its income and exposure to credit and market risks, while economy-wide impacts are apparent in liquidity and the portfolio balance. These effects are presented in Tables 8.1 and 8.2.

Table 8.1: Balance-sheet effects of different central bank operations and collateral choices

	Repo of government bond	Repo of private sector assets	Outright purchase of short-term maturity government bonds	Outright purchase of long-term maturity government bonds
Income	Positive effect in the period of supporting bank notes and unremunerated reserves	Positive effect in the period of backing banknotes and unremunerated reserves	Positive effect in the period of backing banknotes and unremunerated reserves	Positive effect in the period of backing banknotes and unremunerated reserves
	No effect in the time of backing remunerated reserves	Likely positive effect in the time of supporting remunerated reserves, depending on price charged for collateral taken	Small effect in the time of supporting remunerated reserves if term premia (risk) is positive	Likely large effect in the time of supporting remunerated reserves if term premia (risk) is positive
Market risk	Small	Modest, depending on the collateral taken	Possibly modest	Possibly significant
Credit risk	none	Modest, depending on the collateral taken	None	None
Chun[1] risk	High, rises as term of repo declines	Modest, depending on the collateral taken	None	None
Liquidity	High	Based on the liquidity of the underlying assets	modest, at extremes (very difficult) could be used in repo if required	Lower, at extremes (very difficult) could be applied in repo if required

---

1 Chun is the name of a professor at McDonough School of Business who estimated conditional Value-at-Risk and average Value-at-Risk using statistical techniques.

Table 8.2: Economy-wide impacts of central bank money operations and collateral choices

	Repo of government bond	Repo of private sector assets	Outright purchase of short-term maturity government bonds	Outright purchase of long-term maturity government bonds
Economic impact	Minimal	Effect will rise as substitutability of collateral and reserves falls	Some limited portfolio renormalizing outcomes	Huge portfolio rebalancing impacts
		Possible effects on supply of assets	Possible effects on supply of assets	
Liquidity	High	Significant, depending on liquidity of under-lying assets	Modest	Modest

Source: BIS (2018).

8.1.4 Off Balance Swap

Not every operation the central bank conducts will necessarily appear on its balance sheet. For example, during the global financial crisis that began in 2007 the Bank of England created a facility known as the Special Liquidity Scheme (SLS). The SLS was designed to acquire illiquid, legacy mortgage-backed securities from commercial banks and swap them for liquid treasury bonds created by the UK Debt Management Office with the aim of reducing commercial bank funding costs. As these transactions were a pure collateral swap, they did not appear on the Bank of England's balance sheet.

8.2 Central Bank Policy Instruments

8.2.1 Open Market Operations

Open market operations (OMO) are a type of monetary policy instrument that involves the purchasing and selling of government securities from or to the public and banks. This operation affects the reserve stock of banks, government securities yields, and the lending rate. The central bank reduces the flow of credit by selling government securities, and increases credit flows through buying government securities from the public and banks. By engaging in OMO, monetary authorities can ensure the effectiveness of bank rate policies and ensure the stability of the government securities market. Achieving the demand for base money at the target interest rate is accomplished by purchasing and selling government securities or financial instruments. The implementation of OMO is monitored in line with monetary targets such as inflation, interest rates, or exchange rates.

OMO are mostly conducted through an electronic channel as most money presently exists in the form of electronic records rather than in paper form. These operations are executed by electronically increasing or decreasing (crediting or debiting) the amount of base money that a bank possesses in its reserve account at the central bank. Hence, this operation does not require minting new currency, but it might require that the central bank print currency if the member bank needs banknotes in exchange for the fall in its electronic balance.

In the situation where demand for base money rises, the central bank has to act in order to maintain the short-term interest rate by raising the supply of base money. The central bank purchases a financial asset, such as government bonds, in the open market. Payment of these assets is settled by transferring the seller's bank reserves in the form of base money crediting the seller's account. This leads to an increase in the total amount of base money in the economy. Conversely, if the central bank sells these assets, the volume of base money owned by the buyer's bank decreases the amount of base money.

8.2.2 Reserve Requirements

Laws require that a certain portion of deposits held by banking (or other depository) institutions be held in reserve, in the form of very safe, secure assets. Over time, the reasons for mandating these regulatory requirements have changed. During the initial years, reserve requirements were designed or formulated to ensure the liquidity of bank notes and deposits, especially during periods of financial distress. The continuous financial panics despite the presence of reserve requirements made it obvious that reserve requirements were ineffective as a guarantor of liquidity.

The establishment of the Federal Reserve System as a lender of last resort reduced the regulatory importance of reserve requirements. Reserve requirements have since been considered as an auxiliary instrument to enforce the impact of OMOs and discount policy on the whole monetary and credit system in order to achieve the objectives of the Federal Reserve System. The decision exhibits significant implications for the effectiveness of its fundamental tool, OMOs.

During the early 1980s, OMOs were implemented to ensure fairly precise, short-term control of narrowly defined money (M1) while the aim of reserve requirements was to bolster the effectiveness of this control in order to ensure a relatively stable, contemporaneous connection between reserves and M1 deposits. The instrument ensures that desired reserve market conditions are attained by influencing the supply of reserves. Thus, reserve requirements are implemented to safeguard potentially disruptive fluctuations in the money market.

Costs to the private sector are attached to the implementation of reserve requirements. Requiring that depositories keep a certain fraction of their deposits in the form of cash in their vaults or in the form of non-interest bearing balances at the central bank imposes costs on the private sector based on the amount of forgone interest on these reserves—at least on the portion of reserves that banks only hold as a result of legal mandates (and not for customer needs). As the level of reserve requirements increases, the cost imposed on the private sector increases. However, higher levels of reserve requirements might smooth the implementation of monetary policy and mitigate fluctuations in the reserves market.

Central banks like the Federal Reserve address this policy dilemma through paying interest on required reserves or at least on the components of these reserves. This approach effectively eliminates much of the cost of reserve requirements while still ensuring stability in demand for reserves required for the effective running of OMOs and the reserves market.

However, the implications of this approach affect Treasury revenue. Paying interest on required balances implies a decline in net earnings, thus the Treasury's revenues would fall as well. By mitigating the cost of reserve requirements, one government-mandated obstacle to deposit-taking and lending through the banking system might be resolved.

8.2.2.1 Regulations for Reserve Requirements

Taking a case from the Federal Reserve in the United States, all depository institutions (including thrift institutions and credit unions) are required to keep reserves against transaction deposits, which entail demand deposits, negotiable orders of withdrawal accounts, and other highly liquid funds. These reserves can either be in the form of currency (vault cash) or balances at the Federal Reserve. Variations in the percentage of transaction deposits can occur based on the ranges stipulated by law. In addition, requirements can be placed on non-transaction accounts based on specified limits. The required reserve ratio for non-transaction accounts is zero, and for transaction deposits it is about 10 percent.

These required reserves are met through holding vault cash in order to satisfy the liquidity needs of their customers. These depository institutions see this as essentially costless. However, nearly 3,000 depositories now hold vault cash balances that are inadequate to satisfy the entire reserve requirement. In order to address this issue, these institutions have to keep deposits called required reserve balances at the Federal Reserve.

Keeping idle and non-interest bearing balances at a central bank is basically equivalent to taxing these institutions in an amount equivalent to the interest they could have realized on the balances if there are no reserve requirements. Therefore, forgone interest or "reserve tax" directly affects only the depository system and its customers, but no other sections of the financial system. This establishes an artificial incentive for depositors and borrowers to engage in transactions outside the depository system. Invariably, these credit flows adversely influence the efficiency of resource allocations specifically through the relative price of transaction accounts at depositories. The reserve tax may encourage a smaller level of transaction services below the appropriate level of transaction activity for the functioning of the economy.

Who bears the burden of the reserve tax is very difficult to determine. This is influenced by the degree of competitive pressure in the market for deposits and loans, and the attached sensitivities of borrowers, lenders, and depositories to changes in prices and interest rates. It is worth noting that depositories and their shareholders pass at least some of these costs to their customers in the form of lower deposit rates and higher loan rates. For instance, in a case of compensating-balance arrangements where customers maintain non-interest bearing deposits as compensation for bank services, the customers bear the burden of the reserve tax by holding additional balances. In the same vein, some borrowers—for example, small and medium-sized businesses—have few avenues beside the depository system; these firms may finally pay part of the reserve tax through higher costs of credit.

8.2.3 Discount Rate

The discount rate refers to the interest rate asked of commercial banks and other depository institutions for loans they receive from the central bank. Commercial banks often react in relation to changes in the discount rate through changes in their prime lending rate. The discount rate is an instrument of discount policy utilized to influence the flow of money and credit in a desired direction. For example, people's borrowing decisions are affected by the interest rate levied on their borrowing. Thus, a rise in the discount rate is a signal to reduce credit expansion by increasing the burden attached to loans. Owing to this, people are discouraged from new borrowing.

8.2.4 Money Market Investor Funding Facility

The Federal Reserve created a credit facility known as the Money Market Investor Funding Facility (MMIFF) in 2008. This credit facility is aimed at supporting private sector initiatives to stimulate liquidity in money market funds. The MMIFF is a short-term measure designed to respond to the then current illiquidity in the market for specific money market instruments, as well as to mitigate the risk of forced sales of portfolio instruments at discounts from amortized cost with the aim of meeting unexpected redemptions. A large rise in redemptions was recorded after the collapse of Lehman Brothers and the subsequent "breaking of the buck" (occurs when the money market fund's investment income does not cover operating expenses or investment losses) of several Reserve Funds. In response to these events, the maturity of the portfolio holdings had been significantly shortened. The decision made money market funds an unattractive prospect for financial institutions and businesses that depend on longer-term commercial paper to satisfy their funding obligations to finance inventory, payroll, and other obligations. The MMIFF mainly focuses on encouraging money market funds to invest in long-term matured money market instruments through the provision of a willing buyer (the Special Purpose Vehicles) of those instruments.

8.2.4.1 Who Can Be Involved in the MMIFF?

At present, the involvement in the MMIFF is restricted to open-end management investment companies registered with the Securities and Exchange Commission (SEC). Over time, these restrictions may loosen to allow other types of money market investors.

8.2.4.2 Operations of the MMIFF

J.P. Morgan Securities Inc. (JPMSI) would create special purpose vehicles (SPVs) to buy eligible assets from money market funds at amortized costs. Each SPV will buy only debt instruments issued by ten designated financial institutions. Since there are five SPVs, this implies that debt instruments that originate from fifty different financial institutions are legally allowed to be sold through SPVs. The attributes of these institutions are unclear, and the selection of these institutions is based on the largest issuers of highly rated short-term liabilities held by money market funds as well as geographic diversification and short-term debt-rating.

A money market fund that sells eligible assets to a SPV will receive 90 percent of the buying price in cash and the remaining percentage in commercial paper notes from the SPV. The maturity of the commercial paper notes will be the same as the maturity of the eligible assets that SPV purchases with the rating of at least A-1/P-1/F-1 by two or more nationally recognized statistical rating organizations (NRSROs), which are credit rating agencies.

8.2.4.3 Risks Associated with the MMIFF

Since some percentage of the eligible assets sold would be paid in commercial paper notes, the money market fund is exposed to risk through these holdings. For example, in the case of default of an eligible asset held by a SPV, the SPV must terminate all asset purchases and payments on outstanding commercial paper notes. Money realized from the maturation of the eligible assets kept by the SPV is utilized to settle with the Federal Reserve while only remaining cash would be used to repay principal and interest on the money market funds. This implies that the default of an eligible asset sold by a money market fund could adversely affect the commercial paper notes received by another money market fund in relation to the sale of an eligible asset.

8.2.5 Term Auction Facility

Some central banks, including the Federal Reserve, created a short-term measure known as Term Auction Facility (TAF) with the purpose of lending funds directly to depository institutions for a fixed term of twenty-eight or thirty-five days. The TAF was established partly due to a low volume of discount window borrowing, despite persistent stress in interbank lending markets, and partly because of a perceived stigma attached to such borrowings. Furthermore, most discount window loans operate as overnight loans despite encouraging loans up to thirty days. The TAF provides an unidentified source of term funds to remove the stigma linked to discount window borrowing. It accepts any collateral stipulated for discount window loans. However, differences exist between the TAF and the discount window program. Conventional discount window loans are based on interest rates given by the Federal Reserve with no restriction on the total volume of loans that can be extended on any given date. On the other hand, under the TAF, the Federal Reserve states the dollar amount of funds it will lend at each auction in advance, and an auction determines the interest rate charged on loans. For instance, the Federal Reserve offered an auction of US$20billion with a twenty-eight-day term on December 17, 2017, and about US$61.553 billion was received as total bids. The bids with the highest interest rates were accepted until the full US$20 billion had been allocated. At the end, all successful bids were funded at the lowest accepted bid rate of 4.65 percent. Difficulties in determining the effects of the auction are attributed to seasonal patterns, expectations of future monetary policy actions, and other factors affecting interest rates and financial market conditions (Allen et al., 2015).

8.2.6 Commercial Paper Funding Facility

Commercial banks and other institutions utilize the commercial paper market to secure short-term external funding.

8.2.6.1 Types of Commercial Paper

There are two broad types of commercial paper, namely unsecured and asset-backed paper.

1. Unsecured commercial paper: This comprises promissory notes issued by financial or non-financial institutions with a fixed maturity ranging between 1 and 270 days, except if the paper is issued with the option of an extendable maturity. This type of commercial paper is not supported by collateral, which provides a key role for credit rating of the originating institution in determining the cost of issuance.

2. Asset-backed commercial paper (ABCP): This is a secured type of commercial paper as it is collateralized by other financial assets. Historically, senior tranches of asset-backed securities (ABS) are considered as collateral for ABCP. Therefore, ABCP is a financial instrument that often provides maturity transformation. The fundamental loans or mortgages in the ABS are characterized by a maturity period of five to thirty years, but the maturity period of ABCP ranges between 1 and 270 days (see Figure 8.3).

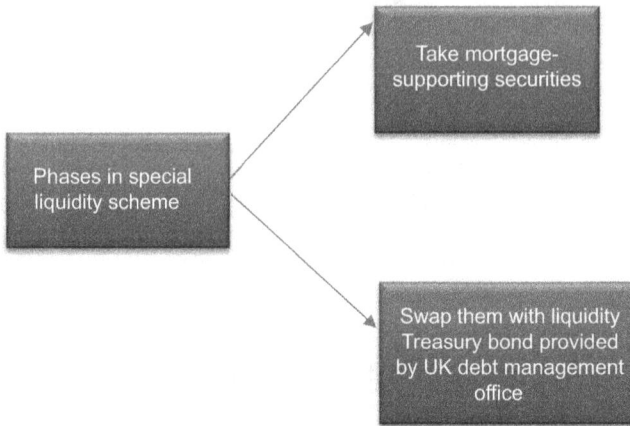

Figure 8.3: Off balance sheet transaction

Before issuing ABCP, institutions sell their assets to a bankruptcy SPV. The SPV then issues the ABCP; the creditworthiness of the ABCP is supported by the assets in the vehicle as well as by the backup credit lines of the sponsoring institution. The assets of the SPV do not belong to the sponsor's pool of assets if the sponsoring institution enters bankruptcy (Adrian et al., 2011).

Trading of all commercial paper takes place in the over-the-counter (OTC) market, where the money market deals with security, and broker-dealers and banks render both underwriting and market-making services. For example, the Depository Trust Company (DTC) is responsible for clearing and settling commercial paper in the United States (see Figures 8.4 and Figure 8.5). The importance of commercial paper is that it provides institutions with direct access to the money market. Figure 8.6 is graph of the total US commercial paper outstanding over time.

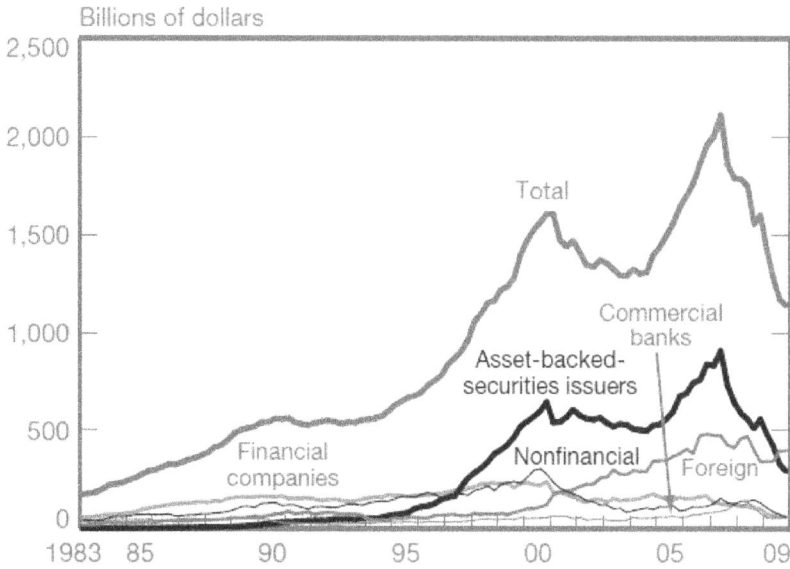

Source: Board of Governors of the Federal Reserve System.

Figure 8.4: Commercial paper issuers in the United States

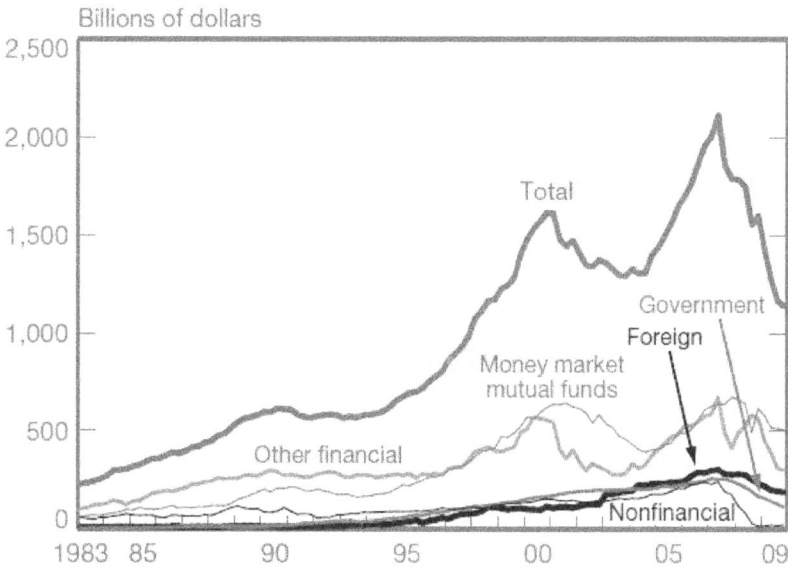

Source: Board of Governors of the Federal Reserve System.

Figure 8.5: Commercial paper holdings in the United States

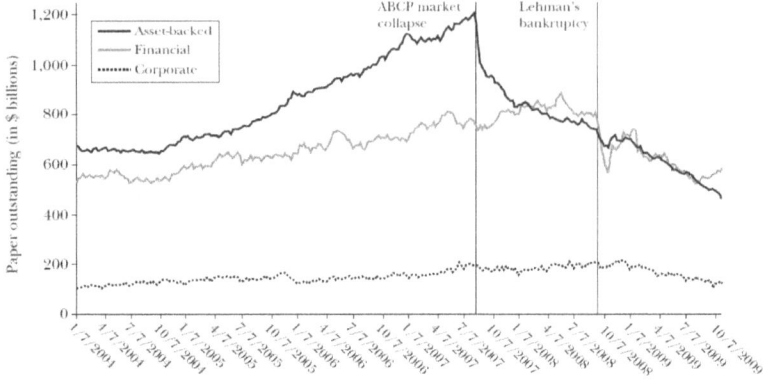

Note: Figure 1 shows the weekly commercial paper outstanding. The asset-based commercial paper (ABCP) market collapse was August 9, 2007. Lehman's bankruptcy was September 15, 2008. *Source:* Author's analysis based on Federal Reserve Board data.

Figure 8.6: Commercial paper outstanding in the United States

8.2.7 Primary Dealer Credit Facility

The Primary Dealer Credit Facility (PDCF) was established in the United States on March 16, 2018, when the Federal Reserve Board approved the PDCF request from the Federal Reserve Bank of New York. The PDCF welcomes primary dealers (banks and securities broker-dealers who are involved in the trading of U.S. government securities and other securities as well as market participants including the Federal Reserve Bank of New York) to borrow from the New York Fed on a collateralization basis during periods of market stress. In addition, the facility is designed to reduce liquidity pressures in the wider repo market.

The PDCF was designed to mitigate the funding challenges primary dealers face under uncertain market conditions by providing a backstop facility, which offers overnight loans against a fairly wide range of collateral. Its broad aim is to support the repo market in functioning efficiently during periods of negative liquidity spirals, when a credit risk is increasing and lending against many types of securities has stalled.

In practice, it allows time for dealers to arrange other financing for their assets either by increasing equity or selling assets at a time which would not hinder the markets and reduce security prices. It is similar to the Fed's discount window (a backstop source of liquidity for depository institutions during market disruptions) in many aspects.

8.2.8 Recap of Policy Instruments

Policy instruments used by central banks to address the impact of external factors on domestic financial systems are broadly classified into two categories: *conventional* and *unconventional* policy instruments. Conventional policy instruments center on amending interest rates and engaging in foreign exchange market intervention. Unconventional policy instruments can be categorized into three actions (financial impact of capital inflows, balance sheet policies, and fiscal and quasi-fiscal measures)

The first category focuses on addressing the financial implications of capital inflows. The second category focuses on balance sheet policies, while the third category utilizes fiscal and quasi-fiscal measures to resolve the domestic consequences of foreign intervention (alternative central bank policy instruments Dubravko Mihaljek and Agne Subelyte 2017). The main rationale supporting the use of unconventional policy instruments is as follows:

1. They are fairly straightforward
2. Changes in the role of central banks arise from the global financial crisis of 2007–2010

Questions

1. How do central banks operate?
2. What are some types of central bank operations?
3. What are the implications of central bank operations?
4. What are the categories of central bank policy instruments?
5. What are some examples of conventional and unconventional policy tools?

Chapter 9
Real Business Cycles

The modern theory of business cycles originated from policy actions taken to address the Great Depression. While Keynesian economic models originally gained credibility and traction among economists after its central tenets (reduction in interest rates, government investment in infrastructure) were successful in tackling the Great Depression, the bouts of stagflation experienced during the 1970s, the absence of microeconomic theories, and inability of Keynesian models to predict policy changes challenged the assumptions of Keynesian economics and dented its popularity as an ethos to tackle economic downturns. The shortcomings of Keynesian theories of business cycles led to the development of the real business cycle (RBC) model. Rather than focusing on changes in aggregate demand, the RBC model provides a more sophisticated understanding that looks at the importance of changes in the aggregate supply curve, and how this interacts with changes in aggregate demand.

The RBC model postulates that most changes in real short-term and long-term aggregate output are determined by changes in technology, a phenomenon usually referred to as "technology shocks" as well as other factors. According to the model, the growth rate of real gross domestic product (GDP) increases in line with significant technological advances, and declines when the technology improves slowly (moves at a normative pace). Thus, as productivity declines, the real GDP growth rate turns negative, which is the actual sign of a business downturn or recession.

The RBC model was introduced to bridge the gaps observed in the Keynesian model, especially in regard to microeconomic aspects. Key questions the RBC model attempts to answer are: what causes economic (positive) fluctuations, and what can be done to reduce the depths of economic downturns?

This chapter will provide more insights on RBCs as well as how these cycles relate to central bank balance sheets. In addition, the chapter will end with a mathematical look that is based on the utility function perspective in relation to the RBC.

9.1 The RBC Model

RBC is the combination of the neoclassical model (the model relates the supply-demand situations to individual rationality) and the ability to maximize utility or profit with the phenomenon of supply shocks in order to conclude whether market

DOI 10.1515/9781547400577-009

economies are fundamentally stable or unstable. The RBC approach states that the internal mechanisms of market economies are stable, but that there are exogenous shocks or disturbances that disrupt normal economic activity. The RBC is a real model because it accommodates the role of money or nominal variables in its model. The inclusion of the neoclassical model in the RBC model makes the first welfare theorem[1] (states that in the presence of idealized conditions, any competitive equilibrium results in a Pareto efficient allocation of resources) hold. The link with central bank balance sheets and real business theory is established through the financial system. The central bank balance sheet is designed to ensure that the financial system is stable, and that the financial system is an integral part of the whole economic system. The state of the financial system can influence the different phases of RBCs, and vice versa.

9.1.1 Features of RBC Models

The RBC models could be built using an agent-based technique. This technique is based on the following assumptions:
1. Uses a representative agent model, in which there is a representative household and firm.
2. It assumes that the agents are homogenous and there are no aggregation problems.
3. The agents optimize their explicit objective functions given resource and technology constraints.
4. Exogenous disturbances or shocks to productivity are the responsible factors for the cycle.
5. Intertemporal substitution of leisure triggers productivity outcomes. As productivity rises, the opportunity cost of leisure increases and thus leads to a rise in employment.
6. The RBC model assumes rational expectations for all agents.
7. There is continual equilibrium in all markets.
8. All markets are perfectly competitive.
9. There is perfect information in all markets.

---

1 While the second welfare theorem postulates that any efficient allocation can be sustainable by a competitive equilibrium.

Traditional Business Cycle Theory

In the traditional theory, output trend $\overline{Y}_t$ changes smoothly over time, $\overline{Y}_t = \infty + \beta t$. Cycles are perceived as deviations from trends, that is, $Y_t - \overline{Y}_t$.

RBC Theory

Under the RBC theory, cycles can be explained with the assumption of $\overline{Y}_t$ evolving based on a random walk, that is, $\overline{Y}_t = \beta + \overline{Y}_{t-1} + u_t$. In this condition, much of the movements in Y_t are a result of movements in Y_t rather than in trend deviations $Y_t - \overline{Y}_t$, which combines the growth and business cycle theory.

The RBC theory attempts to explain business cycles through the classical model. Demand equates to supply in every market implying a general equilibrium. The fundamental principle of this approach is that microeconomic theory states that markets are at equilibrium, so there is need to use general equilibrium theory to understand the economy.

9.1.2 Basic Economic Factors

Exogenous economic factors that influence the general equilibrium allocation of resources are:
a. Consumer preferences
b. Technology
c. Resource stock

These factors affect all real variables such as real quantities, relative prices, real wages, and the real interest rate.

9.1.3 Fluctuations in the Business Cycle

Fluctuations in basic economic factors lead to variations in the business cycle. Equilibrium quantities, as well as relative prices, change as a result of changes in these factors. These situations are graphically explained in the next subsection.

9.1.4 Boom and Recession

If changes in the fundamental factors (consumer preferences, technology, resources) lead to a rise in employment and product, this expansion is known as a boom. On the other hand, when changes in the fundamentals result in a reduction in employment and product for two or more consecutive periods, this contraction is tagged as a recession.

Example 9.1

A change in consumer preferences might lead to a contraction of output and employment. It has been argued that European perspectives of work versus leisure time has changed placing greater emphasis on leisure; this change in attitudes is reflected in a larger number of employees choosing to work part-time rather than opting for full-time employment. Thus, they work less, and the aggregate product is lower. While this may be true, economists consider this impact as a long-term structural change, rather than a short-term cyclical issue that can explain fluctuations in the business cycle.

Example 9.2

A fall in resource stock might lead to a contraction of output. Specifically, a rise in the global price of oil decreases profitability, thus output may reduce. The decline in real wages makes workers reduce the supply of labor as leisure becomes a more attractive substitute. As illustrated in Figure 9.1, LRAS denotes the long-run aggregate supply; LRAD is the long-term aggregate demand; Y represents the aggregate output in the economy, while L and K are labor and capital, respectively. A decrease in resource endowment would lead to a shift in aggregate supply from $LRAS_1$ to $LRAS_2$ with no effect on aggregate demand. Thus, it causes a fall in aggregate output and a rise in price level.

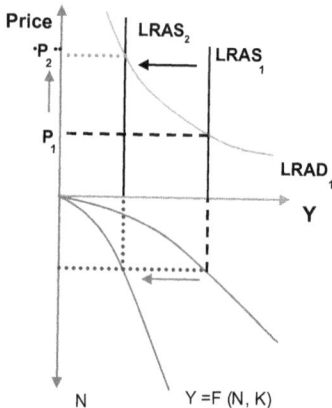

Figure 9.1: Impact of a fall in resource stock on aggregate output

Example 9.3

Supporters of the RBC theory often attribute business cycle fluctuations to the rate of technological change. Rapid technological change results in economic expansion, while slow technological change leads to economic contraction.

With rapid technological change, the production possibility curve shifts outward, implying more production of aggregate goods and services. Techno-logical change increases the marginal product of both capital and labor, while keeping the amount of capital or the number of labor hours constant. This will lead to a rise in real wages and the real interest rate, so the supply of labor increases, increasing employment. As illustrated in Figure 9.2, LRAS denotes the long-run aggregate supply; LRAD is the long-term aggregate demand; Y represents the aggregate output in the economy, while L and K are labor and capital, respectively. An improvement in technology would lead to a shift in aggregate supply from $LRAS_1$ to $LRAS_2$ with no effect on aggregate demand. Thus, it causes an increase in aggregate output and a fall in price level. The opposite case is shown in Figure 9.3.

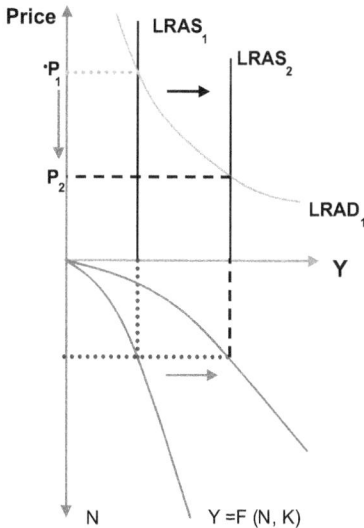

Figure 9.2: Impact of positive technology shock on aggregate output

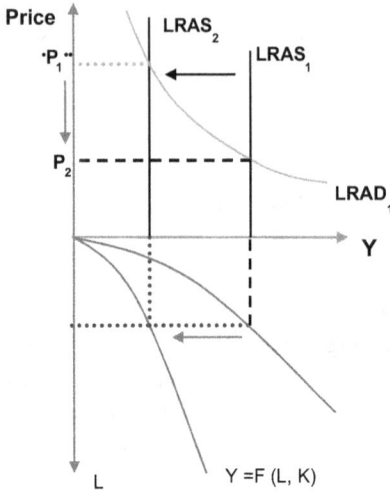

Figure 9.3: Impact of negative technology shock on aggregate output

General Criticisms of RBCs

RBC theory has been generally criticized with regard to the following:

– The business cycles fail to work in real economic situations.
– Technology shocks pose industry-specific impacts rather than economy-wide impacts.
– The assumption of a voluntary response by workers as a reaction to changes in real wages does not hold in the real labor market, where the supply curve of workers is very steep.

Econometric Problems of RBC Models

To model the RBC phenomenon, the following econometric concerns are manifested:

1. RBC models commonly apply the Hodrick-Prescott (HP) filter approach to carry out their decomposition series into growth and business cycle components: The HP filter is used to obtain the potential output or GDP, which will be deducted from the actual GDP in order to capture the various periods of RBCs.
2. The model eliminates some relevant time series information during the decomposition phase (King and Rebelo, 1993).
3. The HP can convey incorrect information about data patterns (generating random data with a random number generator).

4. The RBC models fail to provide explanations for economy-wide disturbances.
5. There is no objective method to test how well these models explain business cycles.
6. The presence of weak explanations to explore the effects of reality through time.
7. The RBC can not explain recessions due to its inability to capture economy-wide disturbances.

Example 9.4
If money is neutral, as product rises in an expansionary period, the price level has to fall.

9.2 Concept of RBCs Applied to Economic Policy

The aggregate output of any economy experiences fluctuations. These fluctuations might be above or below potential output. During economic booms, actual output is usually at or above its potential output. However, actual output declines below its potential during economic downturns. The ups and downs in GDP are commonly known as business cycles. These capture how close current output is to the economy's potential output.

An output gap is the difference between actual output and potential output. Put differently, it is a deviation from the potential output.

Potential output and the output gap are important because they provide guidance for calibration of short-term macroeconomic policies. In addition, short-term policies that determine the aggregate demand depend on output gap estimates. These estimates guide policy makers in dealing with long-term structural issues. For instance, a sluggish GDP growth rate in the medium term indicates the need for policy makers to implement structural reforms in the long term.

The following factors capture the case when actual output exceeds potential output (i.e., in the case of a positive output gap):
- Strong growth in aggregate demand
- The economy is at full employment
- Capacity utilization exceeds its full level
- Increasing upward pressure on prices and inflation

For the case of a negative output gap, the symptoms include: idle resources, low levels of employment, low capacity utilization, and a consequent fall in inflation.

Important Features of Business Cycles

The basic features of business cycles are well known and many are summarized below:

a. Cycles vary a lot in amplitude and duration.
b. Output movements in many sectors display a high degree of coherence. This indicates that sectoral outputs move in the same direction with the pattern of business cycles.
c. Investment and the production of durable goods are much more volatile than output.
d. Consumption of non-durable goods is less volatile than output.
e. The velocity of money is countercyclical in most countries. This means that the velocity of money moves in an opposite direction with aggregate output.
f. The relationship of monetary aggregates (money supply) and output is highly variable.
g. Long-term interest rates are less volatile than short-term interest rates.
h. Short-term interest rates are almost always positively correlated with output.
i. Long-term interest rates have a negative or zero correlation with output.
j. Price levels are pro-cyclical meaning that the price level and economic activities follow the same pattern.
k. Employment is as variable as output, and positively correlated.
l. Productivity is less volatile than output.

9.3 Techniques of Estimating RBCs

It is critically important to understand potential output and output gaps in order to formulate coherent macroeconomic policies. However, these concepts can be difficult to observe, which can lead to making policy decisions that are ineffective or even counter-productive.

The way in which economists evaluate the potential output and output gaps has changed over the past few decades. Originally, potential output was computed by applying mechanistic linear trends or relatively "inert" production functions. This approach failed to incorporate large supply side shocks and their related inflationary pressures. Errors in identifying economic trends resulting from over-optimistic estimates of potential output probably stimulated over-expansionary macroeconomic policies during the 1970s and the 1980s.

Since these eras, efforts have been made to improve the conceptualization and estimation methods of potential output. An enhanced understanding of these methods is expected to support policy makers for better macroeconomic policies, but fails to provide strong evidence of such an effect. In some continents like Europe, many policy failures have been attributed to other factors, such as insufficient fiscal consolidation and the absence of structural reforms during cycles of strong economic growth. This led to the ineffectiveness of both the Stability and Growth Pact and the Lisbon Strategy. These difficulties can be attached to political failure to act on existing information. However, new techniques to estimate potential output have aided in the effectiveness of policy decisions in relation to the size of potential growth.

It is important to present the strengths and limitations of the different techniques used to estimate potential output.

Different Techniques of Estimating Potential Output

Different techniques that provide estimates of potential output should support a better means of cross-checking diagnostics. However, these methods often produce different answers, thus leading to ongoing debates regarding the selection of the best techniques. Diversity in methods used for estimating potential output might also encourage optimal specialization for certain purposes. For instance, a simple stochastic filter may be more cost effective for historical analysis than its counterparts, which are appropriate for forward-looking and long-term structural analysis. The requirements to conduct a simple stochastic filter involve a simple method and software that can be applied to the existing historical data. However, forward looking analysis requires more sophisticated software which is more expensive.

9.4 Methods to Estimate Potential Output and Output Gaps

It is critical to observe whether the different measures of output gaps produce the same description of cycles. In the remainder of the chapter we will present several techniques used for estimation. The goal in doing so is to give you a general sense of how the techniques work and not a complete discussion which would be quite extensive.

There are four broad approaches used to estimate potential output and output gaps. These are as follows:

Statistical techniques for estimating potential output

9.4.1 Trending Methods

This method consists of linear trend and split trend techniques.

9.4.1.1 Linear Trend

This is the simplest method of computing potential output. Under the linear trend technique, the trend component of output is a linear function of time. Hence, it applies a linear regression of the log of real GDP on a constant and a time trend. Its equation is expressed as:

$$\ln Y_t = \alpha + \beta t + e_t \qquad 9.1$$

Where is α constant, t denotes time, and β is the regression coefficient of the time trend.

This technique is built by assuming that GDP can be decomposed into a deterministic trend and a cyclical component. Potential output is captured by the trend components $(\alpha + \beta t)$. The approach can not allow for any supply shocks to the system, thus implying a constant potential output growth rate (estimated slope). In addition, the resulting gaps might not often be stationary as the stochastic (disturbance) trend is not totally eliminated. Owing to this, the linear trend is biased in estimating an output gap by partially allocating trend components into the cyclical component.

9.4.1.2 Split Time Trend

Under the split trend technique, the trend output is computed as a linear trend during each cycle. The cycle is considered as the period between peaks in economic growth:

$$\ln Y_t = \alpha + \sum_j^n \beta_i t_i + e_t \qquad 9.2$$

Equation 9.2 allows estimated trend growth to change between cycles but not within each cycle. The approach is conceptually straightforward, but in practice, it is difficult to determine the peaks of economic growth. Output gaps exhibit symmetric patterns over each complete cycle.

9.4.2 Univariate Filters Method

These methods include HP, Baxter-King filter, Beveridge Nelson decomposition, and the Kalman filter.

9.4.2.1 HP Filter

This method obtains a trend component by taking the difference between a good fit to the actual series and the degree of smoothness of the trend series. Formally, it minimizes the objective function as below:

$$Min \sum_{t=1}^{T}(lnY_t - lnY_t^*)^2 + \lambda \sum_{t=1}^{T-1}[(lnY_{t+1}^* - lnY_t^*) - (lnY_t^* - lnY_{t-1}^*)]^2 \qquad 9.3$$

Where Y_t represents actual output, Y_t^* is trend output, and λ denotes the Lagrange multiplier.

λ determines the smoothness of the resulting trend, and its appropriate value is based on the relative size of the variances of the shocks to permanent and transitory components to output (Hodrick and Prescott,1997). At the initial stage, the value of HP is set to 1,600 (a default value or standard value) in order to assess the relative size of shocks to the GDP of advanced economies like the United States. A low value of λ will generate a trend that follows observed output very closely, while a high value of λ minimizes the sensitivity of the trend to short-term fluctuations in actual output. In the case of a very large , the filter will converge to the linear time trend method, with a linear time trend near the mean growth rate of real GDP over the sample. λ affects the outcome length of the cycles. A λ of 100 for yearly data provides cycles for fifteen to sixteen years, whereas a λ value of 10 is equivalent to cycles not exceeding eight years.

The HP filter is not an appropriate estimate of potential output because it is suboptimal at the end point. It also fits a trend through all the observations of real GDP ignoring the presence of any structural breaks.

Table 9.1: Estimates of Nigeria's potential output and output gap using linear trend and HP methods

Years	Total Real GDP	Potential GDP_Trend	Output Gap_Trend	Potential Gap_HP	Output Gap_HP
1981	15,258.00	17694.72	−2436.72	14025.75	1232.25
1982	14,985.08	17678.91	−2693.83	14290.39	694.69
1983	13,849.73	17610.03	−3760.31	14567.35	−717.63
1984	13,779.26	17605.58	−3826.33	14875.90	−1096.65
1985	14,953.91	17677.08	−2723.17	15228.14	−274.23
1986	15,237.99	17693.57	−2455.59	15625.19	−387.20
1987	15,263.93	17695.06	−2431.14	16065.43	−801.50
1988	16,215.37	17748.15	−1532.78	16543.39	−328.02
1989	17,294.68	17804.90	−510.23	17045.55	249.13
1990	19,305.63	17902.20	1403.43	17555.13	1750.50
1991	19,199.06	17897.29	1301.77	18057.85	1141.21
1992	19,620.19	17916.54	1703.65	18556.91	1063.28
1993	19,927.99	17930.36	1997.63	19066.94	861.05
1994	19,979.12	17932.64	2046.49	19613.20	365.92
1995	20,353.20	17949.13	2404.08	20229.56	123.64
1996	21,177.92	17984.48	3193.44	20953.55	224.37
1997	21,789.10	18009.85	3779.25	21823.93	−34.83
1998	22,332.87	18031.86	4301.01	22881.71	−548.85
1999	22,449.41	18036.51	4412.90	24167.55	−1718.14
2000	23,688.28	18084.57	5603.71	25716.63	−2028.35
2001	25,267.54	18142.49	7125.05	27546.92	−2279.38
2002	28,957.71	18265.43	10692.28	29656.15	−698.44
2003	31,709.45	18347.76	13361.69	32019.21	−309.77
2004	35,020.55	18438.26	16582.28	34604.05	416.50
2005	37,474.95	18500.25	18974.70	37375.49	99.46
2006	39,995.50	18560.00	21435.50	40302.52	−307.02
2007	42,922.41	18625.06	24297.35	43355.14	−432.74
2008	46,012.52	18689.32	27323.20	46500.28	−487.76
2009	49,856.10	18763.75	31092.35	49700.51	155.59
2010	54,612.26	18848.65	35763.62	52913.56	1698.71
2011	57,511.04	18897.00	38614.04	56098.69	1412.35
2012	59,929.89	18935.61	40994.28	59232.17	697.72
2013	63,218.72	18985.80	44232.92	62304.38	914.34
2014	67,152.79	19042.67	48110.12	65312.68	1840.10
2015	69,023.93	19068.61	49955.32	68263.57	760.36
2016	67,931.24	19053.55	48877.69	71181.95	−3250.71

Source: GDP data obtained from CBN Statistical Bulletin (2017).

9.4.2.2 Baxter-King Filter

This filter is a band pass method (a method that passes frequencies within a certain range and rejects frequencies outside that range) developed by Baxter and King (1995) based on the idea that business cycles are considered as fluctuations with a certain frequency. The approach is defined as a linear filter, which eliminates very slow moving ("trend") components and very high frequency ("irregular") components, while intermediate trends are retained as "business cycle" components. During the application of the filter, the critical frequency band to be allocated to the cycle must be determined exogenously.

Similar to the HP filter, the Baxter-King filter presents finite order, two-sided and symmetric moving averages that can eliminate stochastic trends. Its advantages include flexibility and ease of changing the filter construction when the frequency changes. However, it is calculated by a moving average with no value for recent quarters.

9.4.2.3 Beveridge Nelson Decomposition

Beveridge and Nelson (1981) identified some assumptions in order to extract trends and cycles from a given time series. They assumed that the trend can be modelled as a random walk, and trend and cycle shocks are perfectly inversely correlated. This places restrictions on the trend cycles and the cycle to identify the decomposition trend/cycle.

In order to compute the output gap, the actual GDP series is transformed into a stationary series. Then, an ARMA[2] (autoregressive moving average) model is estimated and applied to forecast the series over a horizon s. The output gap for each period of the sample is expressed as follows:

$$C_t = E_t(\Delta y_{t+s} + \Delta y_{t+s-1} + \cdots + \Delta y_{t+1}) - s\hat{\alpha} \quad 9.4$$

Where $\hat{\alpha}$ denotes the constant of the estimated ARMA model.

This decomposition places a very unique functional form on the trend component and assumes that both trend and cycle are affected by the same disturbances. The approach is a backward filter with no end-point problem. However, it can create very noisy cycles and establish some negative correlation between the cycle and actual GDP growth.

---

2 The ARMA model is a tool for understanding and predicting future values in this series.

9.4.2.4 Kalman Filter
Under the Kalman filter approach, the unobserved component model is based on the assumption that macroeconomic time series incorporates trend cycle and erratic components, which are difficult to observe directly. The components can be obtained by placing adequate restrictions on the trend and the cycle process. For example, the log of real GDP is assumed as follows:

$$y_t = y_t^p + z_t \qquad\qquad 9.5$$

Where y_t^p is the permanent component and z_t represents the cyclical component; the two components are not correlated with each other.

The permanent component can be regarded as an estimate of potential GDP while the transitory component depicts an estimate of the output gap. The equation of permanent output is expressed as:

$$y_t = y_{t-1}^p + \mu_{t-1} + \eta_t \qquad\qquad 9.6$$

$$\mu_t = \mu_{t-1} + \zeta_t \qquad\qquad 9.7$$

Where η_t and ζ_t capture orthogonal white noise.

9.4.3 Multivariate Filters

This method consists of using the Hodrick Prescott (hereafter HPMV), Beveridge Nelson decomposition, and Kalman filter tools.

9.4.3.1 Multivariate Hodrick Prescott (HPMV)
The HPMV was initiated by Laxton and Teltow (1992). Under HPMV, potential output reduces to a weighted average of the deviation of output from potential output, changes in the potential rate of growth and errors in the three conditioning structural relationships: A Phillips curve, an Okun's Law and a relation between capacity and output gaps.

Potential output is hence referred to as the series that minimizes the loss function below:

$$Min \sum_{t=1}^{T}(lnY_t - lnY_t^*)^2 + \lambda\sum_{t=1}^{T-1}[(lnY_{t+1}^* - lnY_t^*) - (lnY_t^* - lnY_{t-1}^*)]^2 + \sum_{t=1}^{T}\beta_t\varepsilon_{\pi,t}^2 + \sum_{t=1}^{T}\mu_t\varepsilon_{U,t}^2 + \sum_{t=1}^{T}\psi_t\varepsilon_{CU,t}^2 \qquad 9.8$$

Where $\varepsilon_{\pi,t}{}^2, \varepsilon_{U,t}{}^2, \varepsilon_{CU,t}{}^2$ represents the residual of a price Phillips curve of an Okun relationship and of a link between capacity utilization and output gap, respectively.

Assigning weights to the various components in the loss function needs to be resolved through empirical studies.

9.4.3.2 Multivariate Beveridge Nelson Decomposition

This technique was developed by Forni and Reichlin (1998). Under this approach, there is the assumption that the trend is a random walk, and is driven by stochastic shocks. Stochastic shock is considered to be a linear combination of new fluctuations in GDP and other variables, which include relevant information used to determine long-term GDP. For instance, a change in output correlated with a change in employment would imply a supply side shock and hence a change in potential output. Alternatively, if the change in output is associated with a change in consumption, this would indicate a demand-side shock. This method regards potential output as the level of output that is attained after all transitory dynamics have established equilibrium. In addition, it provides a transitory component whose relevance rises with the number of series utilized. Therefore, the features of the trend are highly sensitive to the additional variables employed.

9.4.3.3 Multivariate Kalman Filter

This method is the extension of its univariate technique through including additional equations such as a Phillips curve. The potential output is assumed to exhibit a random pattern, while inflation is associated with past inflation and the lagged output gap. There is a reduced form of the aggregate demand equation that links the output gap to its own lag and interest rate. There are many specifications of multivariate Kalman filter models. The merits of the model depend on a correct specification of the additional equations.

9.4.4 Production Function Approaches

The production function technique often utilizes a Cobb-Douglas technology with labor and capital as inputs. With the assumption that technical progress is Harrold neutral (it is labor-related technology), the production function can be specified as follows:

$$Y_t = (TFP_t N_t)^{\alpha} K_t^{(1-\alpha)} \qquad\qquad 9.9$$

Where Y_t denotes actual output, *TFP* is total factor productivity, N represents employment and K is capital. α and $\alpha - 1$ are the labor share and capital share, respectively. The values of α range between 0 and 1.

As TFP is not observable, it is often estimated as the Solow residual, that is, deducting the contribution of capital and labor to actual GDP. The TFP is expressed in log form of Equation 9.9 as:

$$tfp_t = \frac{1}{\alpha(y_t - (1-\alpha)k_t)} - n_t \qquad 9.10$$

The potential output series is then estimated by substituting trend variables in the production function, along with actual capital.

$$Y_t^* = (TFP_t^* N_t^*)^{\alpha} K_t^{(1-\alpha)} \qquad 9.11$$

With N_t^* defined as $N_t^* = hrs_{t}^* pop_t pr_t^* (1 - u_t^*)$
Where $hrs_{t,}^*$ represents an index of trend hours
Pop denotes population at working age
Pr* is the trend participation rate
U* represents the trend unemployment rate

Detrending techniques are not applied to the capital stock series because the maximum potential contribution of capital is captured by the full utilization of the existing capital in the economy.

9.4.4.1 Key Shortcomings of the Production Function Method
The production function method has been identified with the following disadvantages:
a. The choice of specifying the production function is open to discussion.
b. It employs capital stock data, which is of poor quality.
c. Different assumptions of the trend components give very different estimates of the level of potential output.

9.4.4.2 Other Production Function Methods
Other production function methods include a full structural model, production function with exogenous trends, and structural vector autoregressive (VAR).

9.4.4.2.1 Full Structural Model

Under the full structural model, a macroeconomic model is explored to endogenously recompute all the inputs of the production function. All the star-variables in Equation 9.11 (above) are estimated endogenously using the macroeconomic model.

9.4.4.2.2 Production Function with Exogenous Trends

This technique determines all the inputs of the production function exogenously using uni- or multivariate filters.

9.4.4.2.3 Structural VAR

The SVAR was developed by Blanchard and Quah (1989). This estimates potential output and the output gap based on structural assumptions related to the nature of economic disturbances. The SVAR model utilizes information from the labor market (employment) and capacity utilization to decompose actual output into a permanent trend component (supply) and a temporary cyclical component (demand). The trend is considered as a measure of potential output and the cycle as a measure of the output gap.

As the first step of the estimation process, relationships are determined by regressing each of the three variables in the system on their own lags and the lags of other variables. The reduced form disturbances are composites of the supply and demand disturbances that influence potential output and the output gap, respectively. To capture these structural shocks, a minimal set of identifying restrictions is placed on the system. The key identifying restrictions are that demand-side shocks do not influence long-term output while supply shocks do. The restrictions are placed on the long-term dynamics of the variables. As the structural shocks are recovered, the variables of the system are specified as the sum of current and previous realization of these shocks.

The disadvantage of the SVAR method is that it is sensitive to the identifying assumptions, which are not testable.

Output gap measures are commonly assessed in relation to other indicators in order to check whether the different techniques produce the same picture of the business cycles. In many situations, the output gaps are compared with capacity utilization or survey data. Another issue is whether estimated output gaps can explain past inflation developments. Figure 9.4 presents potential output for the Latin American and Caribbean regions. As shown in the Figure 9.4, the actual GDP growth is attributed to potential GDP growth and business cycles. The bottom of the contribution bar captures the share of potential growth while the lighter top part indicates the share of the business cycle in relation to actual

GDP growth. The contribution from South America's business cycles accounted for the largest among the concerned regions for the period covered. On the other hand, the contribution of potential growth in the Caribbean region constituted the largest among its counterparts.

Percent

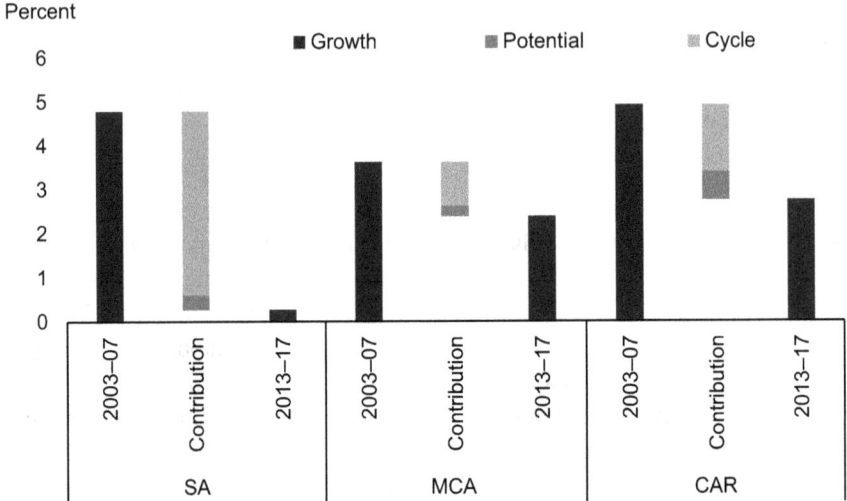

Notes: Simple GDP averages during year spans of annual GDP-weighted averages. Potential growth is measured using the production function approach. SA = South America, MCA = Mexico and Central America, and CAR = the Caribbean. SA includes eight economies (Argentina, Brazil, Chile, Colombia, Ecuador, Paraguay, Peru, and Uruguay), MCA includes five economies (Costa Rica, Guatemala, Honduras, Mexico, and Panama), and CAR includes three economies (Antigua and Barbuda, Dominican Republic, and Jamaica).
Sources: Penn World Tables, World Bank.
Figure 9.4: Contribution of potential growth and business cycle to actual growth

Table 9.2 indicates how real potential GDP growth changes across countries and over time. This provides a snapshot in terms of the speed of the convergence in the long run.

Table 9.2: Average real potential GDP growth (in percent)

	1998-02	2003-07	2008-12	2013-17	2018-22
United States	1.9	1.5	1.1	1.3	1.7
Japan	0.8	0.5	0.5	1.0	1.4
Euro area	1.8	1.1	0.5	0.7	1.3
Germany	1.1	0.9	1.3	1.2	1.3
France	1.7	0.9	0.5	0.9	1.5
Italy	1.4	0.3	-0.5	-0.3	1.0
United Kingdom	2.7	1.7	0.5	1.4	1.9
Canada	2.3	1.3	0.7	0.9	1.1
Australia	2.2	1.8	1.3	1.7	2.2
Austria	2.0	1.4	1.3	1.2	1.3
Belgium	2.0	1.2	0.3	0.6	1.3
Chile	3.1	3.1	3.3	3.1	3.7
Czech Republic	3.3	3.4	1.1	1.9	3.6
Denmark	1.8	1.0	0.2	0.5	1.1
Estonia	5.7	5.0	1.8	3.1	3.3
Finland	3.4	2.0	0.0	0.4	1.8
Greece	3.3	1.8	-1.4	0.1	3.0
Hungary	3.8	2.8	0.4	1.6	2.5
Iceland	2.6	2.9	0.7	0.6	1.3
Ireland	5.1	2.5	0.8	1.3	2.2
Israel	2.0	1.4	1.6	1.9	1.5
Korea	4.5	3.7	3.2	3.0	2.9
Luxembourg	3.3	2.0	0.8	0.7	1.2
Mexico	1.5	1.1	1.1	1.8	1.9
Netherlands	2.1	1.4	0.6	0.6	1.6
New Zealand	2.2	1.7	0.7	1.6	1.9
Norway	2.6	2.3	1.1	1.2	1.3
Poland	4.2	4.3	3.4	3.0	2.9
Portugal	2.3	0.7	0.1	0.2	0.7
Slovak Republic	4.0	5.4	2.4	2.7	3.4
Slovenia	3.4	2.9	0.4	0.7	1.7
Spain	2.7	1.4	0.1	0.2	0.7
Sweden	2.8	1.9	1.0	1.4	2.2
Switzerland	1.3	1.4	0.7	1.0	1.5
Turkey	1.7	2.7	3.3	2.9	3.1
China	8.7	9.9	8.8	6.8	5.1
India	4.5	5.8	6.0	4.9	5.0

Source: OECD Economic Outlook 96 database and the extension of potential real GDP growth projections based on the methodology described in Johansson et al. (2013).

9.4.5 Criteria for Evaluating Different Methods of Estimating Potential Output

Potential output and output gaps are widely explored economic policy-making processes. As potential output is not observable, it must be estimated with the use of available macroeconomic data. Therefore, this subsection assesses the methods discussed above in relation to international criteria that are specifically important to policy makers.

It is critical to note that there is no single correct ranking of criteria that can be used to examine different policy issues, based on potential output and output gaps. However, the objectives of the user—as well as the relevant horizon—influence the prioritization of these criteria. For example, a user whose focus is on recent developments and short-term forecasts would have a strong interest in the output gap measures at the end point of the sample. Conversely, a user whose concern is long-term trends will be interested in estimating some subsamples, which exclude the latest observations (Cotis et al., 2018).

An individual who focuses on international comparisons will place more weight on applicability across countries, whereas a user focusing on a single country may emphasize greater richness in economic content.

These criteria are categorized into two main areas; core requirements that are concerned with the universal features of a method, or user specific requirements whose criteria are focused on specific purposes required to estimate potential output and output gaps.

Core requirements are discussed in the following subsections.

9.4.5.1 Consistency Between Economic Expectations and the Fundamental Assumptions of the Method

Expected result may depend on economic theory or stylized facts. A relevant approach must be in line with economic theory. A technique that provides stationary cycles might be appropriate. Expected outcomes may also need to consider the statistical features of potential output, its fluctuations, or the length of the cycle.

9.4.5.2 Accountability and Transparency

The policy maker has to utilize variables that have been computed in a transparent way in order to support its policy choices. Similarly, other users should be transparent when providing a rationale supporting the method utilized to make their forecast. Without any constraints, other actors can easily replicate the estimates.

Transparency also provides the possibility of an equal treatment of countries, which can be important in the context of international investigations. Therefore, a key property for a method is that all fundamental assumptions stated during estimation are obviously identified and justified.

9.4.5.3 Data Availability and Consistency

It is critical that data updates do not include very large and unwarranted revisions in estimates in order to ensure the credibility of the method employed. An approach that provides very large revisions will be regarded as uncertain or methodically flawed. Based on this, a method that generates estimates consistent over time without too much sensitivity to the sample period of estimation will be accommodated. Specifically, the accuracy of estimates to the last observations of the sample—which may be significantly revised when new information is available—need not be too high.

9.4.5.4 Precision of the Estimates

The ability of a method to present precise information is necessary, as this information assists in determining what weight or importance is assigned to the estimates relative to other information available in the process of making policies. In addition, it is substantially relevant to differentiate between the end point (considered as the main importance for policy makers) and the rest of the sample.

User Specific Requirements

The following conditions must be met to apply different approaches:

- A user whose focus is on international comparisons has to obtain regular reports to monitor the economy. Thus, such a user will explore a method which is easy to update. Based on this, the amount and nature of information required to implement the method is of paramount importance. If a method needs a very large set of long time series data, it will be more difficult to apply the method. In addition, a method that depends on information, which exists only with a long lag will not be useful in a number of contexts. This criterion will be relevant to users whose interest is in countries which still lack reliable data.
- As most policy makers have an interest in what will influence future economic developments, estimates of the output gap at the end of the sample have more weight than estimates at the middle of the sample. Based on this, more attention is placed on addressing the end-point problems associated with a number of methods. For this reason, an important requirement is good end-of-sample performance. In addition, it is necessary that the method encourages the policy maker to identify any permanent structural changes such as a decline in the level of potential, and to provide adequate responses to these changes. Policy makers who are more concerned with the expected future values of the output gap will require more than just an estimated gap at the end of the historical sample (Cotis et al., 2018).
- In order to overcome the end-point problem, a method that extends the sample with forecasts has been utilized. However, this method is not helpful as it implies substituting a transparent method aimed to support the forecaster with the forecaster's non-transparent (more subjective) judgment. This approach led to an over-estimation of potential output in European coun-

tries. Therefore, forecasting future estimates has to be based on variables and assumptions that can be extended from past data. This may often imply a need for economic context in approaches if forecasted estimates are to be credible.

A Simple RBC Model

As RBC models are linked with neo-classical theory, the RBC model is expressed in line with the following utility function conditions:

Step 1: Utility function

$$U_t = \max E_t \left[\sum_{j=0}^{\infty} \beta^j u(c_{t+j} l_{t+j}) \right], 0 < \beta < 1$$

Step 2: Aggregate output function

$$y_t = z_t f(k_t, n_t), z_t \sim iid(0, \sigma_z^2) \text{ f is CRS (constant return to scale)}$$

Step 3: Capital (k) function

$$k_{t+1} = (1 - \delta)k_t + i_t$$

Step 4: Aggregate income function

$$y_t = c_t + i_t$$

Step 5: Labor (n) function

$$n_t + I_t = 1$$

First Solution Recipes: First Order Conditions
Step 6

$$u_1(c_t, I_t) - \lambda_t = 0$$

Step 7

$$u_2(c_t, I_t) - \lambda_t z_t f(k_t, n_t) = 0$$

Step 8

$$-\lambda_t + E_t \beta \lambda_{t+1}[z_t f(k_t, n_t) - (1 - \delta)] = 0$$

Step 9

$$c_t + k_{t+1} = z_t f(k_t, n_t) + ((1 - \delta)k_t$$

With the assumptions of $\delta = 1$, log-linear utility, and Cobb-Douglas production; z_t, c_t, and k_{t+1} can be estimated

Second Solution Recipes

The utility function allows income and substitution effects of a wage change to offset each other.

Step 1: Therefore, employment is constant
Step 2:

$$c_t = [1 - (1-\alpha)\beta]z_t n^\alpha k_t^{1-\alpha}$$

Step 3:

$$k_{t+1} = (1-\alpha)\beta n^\alpha k_t^{1-\alpha}$$

Where $z_t f(\cdot) = z_t n^\alpha k_t^{1-\alpha}$

It is important to note that shocks influence consumption, as well as capital stock. Therefore, they have long-term impacts.

Questions

1. What do you understand about the concept of business cycles?
2. What are the theories of business cycles?
3. What are the fundamental economic factors that affect business cycles?
4. What are the different approaches to compute the output gap?

Chapter 10
Central Bank Balance Sheets
and Real Business Cycles

The government of any country attempts to use monetary and fiscal policy to prevent a decline in aggregate output. However, it is difficult to use countercyclical monetary policy when money is neutral. Countercyclical fiscal policy is possible through an increase in government spending (or a decrease in government tax) when aggregate production is declining. However, the policy might be irrelevant because the general equilibrium allocation of resources is Pareto efficient. The use of countercyclical policy to resolve a fall in output is not optimal.

10.1 Linkages between Central Bank Balance Sheets and Real Business Cycles

A firm's past performance and potential future performance is reflected in its balance sheet. Analyzing the strengths and weaknesses of an organization's balance sheet provides stakeholders with relevant insights as to the current and future financial well-being of the business under consideration. Making financial data for publicly listed corporations transparent and freely available encourages the analysis of balance sheets in a cost-effective manner. In addition, the availability of data in open sources allows analysts to reach a collective conclusion about the health of a firm while minimizing information asymmetry.

A key objective of balance sheet analysis focuses on identifying the strengths and weaknesses of a given firm. Although many books and academic papers have been written on the subject of balance sheet analysis, there have been few texts that aim to enhance our understanding of how to analyze the balance sheets of central banking institutions. This book attempts to bridge this gap and provides a comprehensive application of balance sheet analysis to central banks across different regions of the world.

The insights obtained from analyzing a central bank's balance sheet are relevant on a macroeconomic level, rather than at the firm specific level in the case of a corporation's balance sheet. For instance, the analysis of a central bank balance sheet captures fluctuations in assets, which boost currency unlike its counterpart, the firm, that shows economic value. Aggregate economic values are reflected in the balance sheet of the monetary authority. In addition, central bank assets influence the ability to achieve monetary policy goals effectively

DOI 10.1515/9781547400577-010

using different measures like open market operations, reserve requirements, and discount rates. The analysis of central bank balance sheets is gaining more attention as most central banks have started to favor monetary policy decisions that involve compositional shifts in their assets. The limitations of conventional monetary policy are observed as many developed economies have become bound by near-zero interest rates. In order to address such limitations, central banks have sought to leverage their balance sheets to affect change through unconventional monetary policies. For example, the Federal Reserve implemented significant compositional changes and balance sheet expansions from late 2008 to 2014 through quantitative easing. The issue of central bank asset holdings has also received more attention in recent times due to the increasing heterogeneity of such holdings; historically, central bank assets were comparatively more homogenous, mainly consisting of short-term government bonds.

The analysis of central bank balance sheets is particularly relevant when we understand the relationship between the quality and quantity of central bank assets and liability values. In order to achieve this comprehension, this chapter explores theoretical and instrumental approaches used in both economics and business management.

10.1.1 Monetary Policies and Business Cycles

As real output fluctuates around an increasing trend, economists turn their focus to increasing the trend, and reducing volatility around this trend. This section of the chapter focuses on how policy makers can leverage their balance sheet position to reduce fluctuations around the trend.

In the early twentieth century, the central focus of monetary policy was predominately the gold standard. The outcome of this focus was that price stability was achieved in the long run, but there was significant economic fluctuation in the short run. This stance was reappraised following the Great Depression, which led to the use of fiscal policy as an instrument to smooth the fluctuations in output.

Later, monetary policy emerged as countercyclical to fiscal policy, and monetary policy failures began to surface. As the 2007–2008 Global Financial Crisis took its grip on world economies, a lot of central banks moved to other unconventional forms of monetary policy known as quantitative easing (QE). QE is considered an unconventional monetary policy form as it involves large purchases of government bonds of long maturities funded by interest-paying reserves. In addition, many central banks went further by purchasing non-government issued securities and/or providing lending based on a wide set of long-term collateral.

10.1.1.1 Argument in Favor of Unconventional Policies in Normal Situations

a. Unconventional policies are more important tools for both wealth effects and investment decisions. Wealth effect occurs when the value of stock portfolios increases as a result of escalating stock prices. This makes investors more comfortable and secure about their wealth, thus leading to more spending. On the other hand, an investment decision is a decision made by investors or top level management in relation to the amount of funds to be deployed in investment opportunities. In the same vein, central banks need to decide how to allocate their financial resources to different asset types.
b. Their usage enables practitioners and academics to obtain a deeper understanding of how these unconventional policies will affect an economy in the short and long run as well as making accurate predictions in relation to these policies.
c. They have to be operationalized at least for the near term in order to manage risks.

10.1.1.2 Arguments Against Unconventional Policies in Normal Situations

a. They are less well-understood than conventional policies so they may be implemented poorly.
b. They should only be explored when conventional policy has attained its limits, for instance, when interest rates have reached the zero lower bound.
c. They do not work efficiently in some normal cases as they fail to boost private credit expansion.
d. There is an absence of transparency surrounding unconventional policies and their implementation.
e. They are quasi-fiscal operations that can cause losses and damage the autonomy of the central bank, especially if such policy actions require the approval of partisan political bodies.
f. Further increasing the size of the central bank balance sheets may hinder future central bank interventions.

10.1.2 Identifying an Acceptable Range of Values

Owing to the subjective nature of the quality of money, objective thresholds would not accommodate the situation of hyperinflation or devaluation. These ratios are objective determinants for the quality of money, but they also affect the subjective assessment of the currency. It is difficult to establish a deterministic relationship in the case of a fiat currency system where the currency value is totally attached to trust.

Other ratios that analyze repurchase agreements or discount activities can be considered in the calculation of appropriate adjustments for each individual central bank. The quality of the collateral for repurchase agreements as well as discount activities are also relevant to the quality of money. Such considerations include the volume of direct credits to financial institutions, the quality of guarantees and the potential for creditor haircuts(a percentage reduction of amounts that will be repaid to creditors). Loans provided by the central bank to the banking system are commonly considered as illiquid assets that cannot be recalled and used to defend the currency. These loans have greater credit risks when compared to government bonds. Using securities of dubious quality in the form of loan collateral at the expense of government debt reduces the quality of money. The use of a collateral ratio in terms of definition and applications makes the objective difficult to achieve.

An adjusted equity ratio may be required to create transparency because central bank balance sheets may include hidden reserves or burdens. This can be calculated using a revaluation reserve without affecting the central bank income statement. For instance, the Federal Reserve has gold reserves of 8,134 tons valued at the historical price of US$42.44 per troy ounce, but its current market value is nearly thirty times higher. As with private sector balance sheets, central bank balance sheets may not indicate impending write-downs of impaired assets. In this event, the central bank's balance sheet may appear more favorable than its actual position.

10.1.3 Asset Transparency

In order to ensure asset transparency, the exact quality of accepted guarantees and collateral is important. In addition, the naming of debtors enhances transparency. For instance, there were complaints of opacity leveled at the Federal Reserve's Term Auction Facility (TAF) initiated at the outset of the financial crisis due to failure to disclose the identity of the users of such programs and the quality of the collateral used.

The heterogeneity of central bank balance sheets due to the absence of a standard set of reporting guidelines is another factor responsible for a lack of transparency. Adopting the method of setting standard practices in corporate organizations to central bank balance sheets would improve transparency and comparability.

10.2 Impact Evaluation of Central Bank Balance Sheets on Economic Environment

The magnitude and structure of central bank balance sheets provides useful insights regarding policy risks that may arise as the outcome of certain policies. Central bank balance sheets also indicate potential disequilibrium in the macro-economy and financial system, irrespective of the specific policies influencing the burgeoning balance sheets. The disequilibrium might be a result of a gap between the financial sector's balance sheets and its counterpart's balance sheet. In other words, the magnitude and structure of a central bank balance sheet provides a valuable bird's eye view of growing risks across the financial system, but paying narrow attention to the marginal influence of central bank actions on a policy-by-policy basis may lead to the wrong conclusions. Fundamentally, there is correlation between inflation risk and the central bank balance sheet size, but it is important to include judgments regarding financial stability risks in this analysis. An increase in size of a central bank's balance sheet provides a signal of risks in the economy, as well as a relevant input for formulating exit strategies from current policies.

The concerns that surround an increase in the size of central bank balance sheets arise from three types of risk. These risks are inflation risk, financial stability risk, and credibility and independence risk.

Inflation risk: There is a positive correlation between the rapid expansion of central bank balance sheets and the growth of monetary aggregates. This extra liquidity in the economy is intended to serve as a financial stimulus, but can also translate into higher inflation due to the growth in the money supply (ceteris paribus). This inflationary outcome can be minimized if central banks sterilize foreign exchange purchases by removing reserves from the financial system. This method has been employed by Asian central banks to control inflation, despite the huge accumulation of foreign reserve assets.

It is critical to note that central banks in some Asian economies have achieved strong price stability credibility over the past two decades. This credibility assists in meeting inflation targets, despite the accompaniment of broad money and credit growth with foreign intervention trends. Based on these observations, large growth in central bank balance sheets does not always translate into significantly higher inflation rates.

Financial stability risk: An increasing rate of foreign reserve accumulation is likely to exceed domestic investment in the region in the short run. In the event that the economies of Europe and the United States underperform, depreciation of the USD or EUR or appreciation pressures on Asian exchange rates may cause less short-term investment.

Credibility and independence risk: Over time, the massive accumulation of foreign reserve assets at the central bank will generally lead to a rise in "lazy assets" on the books of private sector banks. In an environment of high global risk aversion since the 2007/2008 financial crisis, banks are comfortable with holding these lazy assets, despite their minimal returns. As the global economy commences its recovery, these banks are triggered to sell or leverage these highly liquid securities on their balance sheets in the form of loans. This action is in line with the relationship between credit and foreign reserves in the past. Monetary policy actions, as well as macroprudential tools, are used to offset risk-taking channels. If the rise in lending is significant and the central bank response lags this trend, the credit expansion has the potential to be a "credit boom gone bad," with well-identified adverse consequences for economic and financial stability.

10.2.1 Central Bank Balance Sheets and Debt Management

In developed economies, central banks have taken a passive role in the management of sovereign debt; in their stead, new agencies were established with the mandate of managing sovereign debt (Turner, 2011). In addition, debt managers were generally given the task of minimizing the expected cost of government funding over the medium to long term while ensuring prudent risk management practices. However, emerging market economies still allow central banks to perform a substantial role in enhancing deep and liquid financial markets, particularly the market for government bonds, due to the nascent state of the economy's financial system. Concomitantly, the Reserve Bank of India has retained some functions pertaining to government debt management.

As a consequence of expanding balance sheets, many central banks have felt the need to expand bill issues as part of sterilization operations. The outstanding stock of central bank paper now accounts for over 10 percent of GDP in some Asian economies; the average maturity of these issues is still relatively short, though this average maturity timeframe increased from 2010–2011 (Mehrotra, 2012). These T-bill issues assist in suppressing surplus liquidity for longer periods, which is especially crucial in a situation of strong capital inflows. These trends pose a high probability of conflict between debt managers and central banks. As the central banks of major developed economies implemented large-scale asset purchase programs, longer-term interest rates fell. These central banks now hold substantial amounts of outstanding government debt—from 10 to 20 percent of domestic government debt outstanding. This measure was adopted to stimulate the economy (at the zero lower bound of nominal interest rate) by reducing the cost of long-term borrowing, making long-term government borrowing programs appear increasingly attractive. If debt managers were to issue more long-term debt in an attempt to minimize financing costs, this may conflict with the goals of the central bank (i.e., this action might adversely affect the cost of borrowing in the economy).

Government debt management choices may act as a constraint if developed economies choose to ease monetary policy in the future. This will be true as the concern for the cost of short-term debt financing continues to escalate concurrently with new large-scale asset purchase programs. Similarly for emerging market economies, this would happen if there is a need to finance the large and growing stock of foreign reserve assets.

The above possibilities suggest the need for debt managers and central banks to coordinate on policy actions. Potential tensions can be managed by understanding the motives and policy goals of each party. In addition, it is critically important that markets share this understanding. Helpful actions can include stable and predictable issuance, with issuance calendars announced well in advance of auctions and with central banks spreading their purchases over a range of maturities to prevent squeezes in specific market segments. For emerging markets, central banks may require the authorities to lengthen the maturity of their central bank bill issuance and to provide incentives for local and foreign investors to hold longer maturities, an approach the Bank Indonesia has been following in recent years.

10.2.2 Modeling Challenges Confronting Central Bank Balance Sheets

In recent times, macroeconomic literature has become increasingly interested in modeling the behavior of central bank balance sheets to aid monetary policymaking and assist the general understanding of balance sheet trends. Prior to this, central bank balance sheets were considered to be of minor importance. The financial crisis in the West, as well as the build-up of foreign exchange official reserves in Asia, are among the events that have highlighted the relevance of closing the gap between theory and practice.

The standard model employed in most policy analysis can be reduced to three central relationships: (1) a Phillips curve that links inflation to inflation expectations and output; (2) an IS curve that connects output to real interest rates; and (3) a Taylor rule that expresses monetary policy in terms of deviations between macroeconomic variables, typically inflation and output and their targets.

$$\pi_t = f(\pi_{t-1}^e, y_{t-1}) \tag{1}$$

$$y_t = g(i_{t-1}, -\pi_{t-1}^e) \tag{2}$$

$$i_t = h(\pi_{t-1} - \pi^*, y_{t-1} - y_{t-1}^*) \tag{3}$$

The model may be complicated in many realistic channels in the absence of fundamental changes. For instance, for an open economy, exchange rates are included in all of the equations: in the Phillips curve (to accommodate the pass-through from exchange rates to inflation); in the IS curve (to reflect the connection between external demand and exchange rates); and in the Taylor rule (to encourage a policy response to exchange rate movements). However, the model is still fundamentally characterized by a three-equation reduced form.

What is the role of central bank balance sheets in this model? Traditionally, there has not been a role for central bank balance sheet variables in the model. Most of the benchmark macroeconomic models utilized in recent years do not have a role for central bank balance sheets or even for the information that they contain.

From a realistic point of view, until recent events, sidelining central bank balance sheets was a reasonable simplification for most developed countries. Prior to the global financial crisis, the focus of monetary policy was to set short-term interest rates and offer signals about the likely future path of policy rates. There was less variability in the size and composition of central bank balance sheets, and the balance sheets were treated as a straightforward reflection of generally stable policy action.

In recent times, a better understanding of the role of central bank balance sheets in policy analysis may have alerted authorities to potential risks inherent in the economy. For instance, in the lead-up to the Asian financial crisis, many domestic currencies in the emerging region were overvalued, resulting in a fall in foreign currency assets on central bank balance sheets as foreign exchange intervention was utilized to strengthen the value of these currencies. The anticipation of currency depreciation as a result of the loss of foreign currency assets triggered currency crises in many economies. The current condition of emerging Asian economies is a reflection of this, with the rapid accumulation of foreign currency assets expanding central bank balance sheets because of measures taken to avoid exchange rate appreciation.

Recent events in developed economies pose a further challenge to the established model. Central bank balance sheets have been growing exponentially, largely triggered by the purchases of domestic currency assets. There is also a change in the composition of balance sheets due to extraordinary policy actions aimed to boost the economy and offset the recessionary effects of deleveraging within the private sector.

Examining the effects of such policies, with consideration of the macro-economic risks and policy challenges that large balance sheets might create, demands new analytical frameworks that differ from the canonical model in forms that provide a meaningful role for central balance sheets.

The key to incorporating the significance of central bank balance sheets in models is to ensure that changes in balance sheets are not automatically cancelled by the decisions of other actors in the economy. A key assumption that underlies the perspective that balance sheets are irrelevant is that the balance sheets of taxpayers, governments, and central banks are intertwined, since taxpayers are residual claimants on public sector wealth—or equivalently, residual players of public sector liabilities. Wallace (1981) pointed out that variations in the official sector's balance sheet will not influence the risk-return profile of households or change balanced financial-asset prices when markets are not perfectly competitive. Effectively, optimal decision making by residual-claimant taxpayers/investors will lead to variations in private sector balance sheets that exactly cancel the effects of changes in the government sector.

Challenges that would overturn the assumptions of Wallace's result are many, which include: eliminating perfect substitutability between different types of assets; assuming that actors in the private sector are confronted by leverage constraints; and modeling possible connections between monetary policy and fiscal policy.

10.2.2.1 Theoretical Studies

For the central bank balance sheet irrelevance theory to hold, different types of assets have to be perfectly substitutable at the margin. Eggertsson and Woodford (2003) have found that if private agents have a liquidity preference for central bank monetary liabilities, for instance, the size and composition of central bank balance sheets will have equilibrium effects. They concluded that such a liquidity preference is likely to be particularly important when interest rates are limited by a zero lower bound. The case of their argument can be considered as a special case of portfolio balance theory (see Branson and Henderson, 1985). Portfolio balance theory believes in imperfect substitutability of domestic and foreign bonds in the portfolios of private investors as a result of frictions in financial markets. Owing to this, financial markets are inefficient, and investors will prefer some assets over others; thus these models are sometimes called 'preferred habitat' models. Changes in the asset and or liability composition of the central bank balance sheet will then imply changes in the private sector balance sheet that may determine the private sector decisions to spend, save and invest. In this framework, central bank foreign exchange sterilization interventions have significant real effects on the economy.

Another challenge to the irrelevance assertion can be made by accepting that actors face leverage constraints, as suggested in Bernanke, Gertler, and Gilchrist (1999) and Woodford (2011). A key assumption that supports the unimportance of central bank asset purchases is that investors are unconstrained in the buying of individual assets. However, constraints to asset purchases may hinder investors from fully cancelling changes to the balance sheet of the central bank.

Several works have examined how targeted central bank lending may have significant real effects when private investors face leverage constraints. For instance, Curdia and Woodford (2011) built a model with heterogeneous consumers, in which borrowers may have less than full access to the pool of private savings. In line with their model, they concluded that the level of direct central bank lending to credit-constrained private sector borrowers can improve societal welfare.

Ashcraft, Garleanu, and Pederson (2011) developed a model in which only a fraction of bank assets are considered as collateral. Central bank lending, which requires lower collateral "haircuts," can relax credit conditions efficiently by lending at lower margins. Reis (2009) explained a model whereby financial intermediation, as well as information costs, may reduce the funding for profitable investment projects when central bank balance sheets expand.

Chadha, Corrado, and Meaning (2012) built a model based on two effective leverage constraints. First, households confront a leverage constraint in terms of the level of their collateral, and second, banks face a leverage constraint because of required reserve ratios. They concluded that these constraints indicate there is a crucial role to be played by asset purchase programs as a useful policy tool for improving economic welfare.

Cook and Yetman (2012) investigated the effects of a central bank's accumulation of foreign exchange reserves in an open economy, given leverage constraints. To them, foreign exchange reserves are financed through the sale of central bank paper to the banking system. In the absence of leverage limitations, real allocations of private sector agents would remain unchanged in order to achieve foreign exchange interventions. However in leverage constraints, the acquisitions of foreign assets crowd out investment at the expense of long-run growth. Thus, it leads to huge current account imbalances.

A final approach to identify a role for central bank balance sheets is to model the interconnections between inflation and fiscal policy. Durre and Pill (2010) provide evidence by developing a model based on the fiscal theory of the price levels (Woodford, 1995), wherein the path for prices can be ultimately determined by fiscal policy. This is based on the assumption that if governments ignore their intertemporal budget constraints, fiscal considerations will push prices away from equilibrium. Durre and Pill (2010) indicate that credit policies, which are quasi-fiscal in nature, may be applied by a central bank to achieve price stability goals.

There are varying stances on the best means to incorporate central bank balance sheets into policy analysis. However, existing measures postulate the likely shape of coming analytical frameworks. In addition, different techniques to showcase a role for central bank balance sheets are likely to be more suitable for specific situations. For instance, the portfolio balance technique is the most appropriate method for evaluating the relevance of policies aimed at adjusting the balance sheet of financial systems in order to boost some sectors, as with "Operation Twist"[1]. With historical data, it is possible to assess the degree of substitutability of different assets, and thus the degree of stimulus to the macroeconomy from a given change in the central bank's balance sheet.

Models incorporating binding leverage constraints allow for a careful analysis of the extent to which expansion of the central bank balance sheet will cancel the contraction of private sector balance sheets, and also provide a way of evaluating the entire economy by analyzing the trade-offs created by central bank balance sheet expansion.

In conclusion, models entailing clear connections between fiscal and monetary policy may be helpful for assessing balance sheet expansions in countries battling with fiscal distress (Buiter, 2002).

On the whole, most economists believe that central bank balance sheets may perform a crucial role in a given economy and reveal relevant information about monetary policy, despite canonical macroeconomic models having little to no role for central bank balance sheet variables.

Questions

1. What are arguments against and in favor of unconventional monetary policies in normal conditions?
2. What is potential output?
3. What is the output gap?
4. What are the different approaches used to compute potential output and explain the advantages and disadvantages of each approach?

---

1 This is a program of qualitative easing utilized by the Federal Reserve, and it happens whenever the Fed uses the proceeds of its sales from Treasury bills to purchase long-term Treasury.

Chapter 11
Conclusion

The hard economic blow arising from the global financial crisis pushed central banks to adopt unconventional monetary policy tools. These tools were initially utilized to prevent deeper financial destabilization and bankruptcy of solvent-but-illiquid private sector balance sheets, and subsequently to address economic stagnation and deflation risks. Central banks such as the U.S. Federal Reserve Bank (Fed) and the Bank of England embarked upon huge asset purchasing programs, buying government securities as well as private securities from markets, consequently creating bank reserves on their liabilities side.

This book has provided an overview of how central bank balance sheets function in relation to the real business cycle. In addition, it presents a framework for analyzing the composition of central bank balance sheets. Large variations in the structure of balance sheets are observed across regions and countries. The observed data reveals the evolution of balance sheet compositions since the global financial crisis. Also, the response to the initial crisis in 2007–2009 was similar across a number of economies, whose central banks responded to the crisis by accumulating more foreign assets in order to support financial stability. In contrast, the arrangement of central bank balance sheets has differed significantly from 2009 onward.

In Chapter 1, the book explained the role of central bank balance sheets in designing and understanding the policies needed to support an economic recovery in the post-financial crisis years. It asserts that a deeper comprehension of changes to the central bank balance sheet can lead to more effective policymaking. We support this assertion by highlighting the challenges and controversies faced by central banks in the past and present when implementing policies, and analyze the links between these policies, the central bank balance sheet, and the consequences of these policies at a macroeconomic level.

Chapter 2 presented conceptual definitions involved in gaining a better understanding of the central bank balance sheet size and its composition. Furthermore, it provided a simplified framework to examine the dynamic pattern of central bank balance sheet composition in a conceptual manner. Misconceptions regarding the central bank balance sheet components are explored and discussed in Chapter 3 of the book. However, it must be noted that there are no unified standards that dictate how often a central bank balance sheet should be disclosed to the public, how the sheet should be formatted, or which items are to be included on the balance sheet.

DOI 10.1515/9781547400577-011

With the empirical data obtained from the International Monetary Fund's International Financial Statistics and provided by central banks, the book analyzes central bank balance sheet size and composition from 2005 to August 2017 across advanced economies and emerging market economies. The analyses are performed commensurate with Christiaan Pattipeilohy's (2016) simplified framework.

Interactions between central bank balance sheets and the macroeconomic environment are discussed extensively in Chapter 9. The chapter identifies various measures of computing potential output, and broadly classifies them into two categories: univariate and multivariate. Both linear trend techniques and HP filter techniques are utilized to compute potential gross domestic product.

Questions Left Unanswered: Areas for Future Research

Despite the links established between central bank balance sheets, monetary policy goals, and macroeconomic performance, there is still a need to further understand the underlying causes of differences in balance sheet composition. In addition, the relative weight of both structural and policy-related factors requires more attention from policy makers, academic researchers, and financial sector experts. Other future determinants such as monetary policy strategies (inflation-targeting, exchange-rate targeting), the structure of the financial system (bank- or market-based), and the sources of the legal system (civil or common law) deserve further exploration. It is widely accepted that a reciprocal link is found between the design and operational framework of monetary policy and central bank balance sheets.

Variations in the composition of central bank balance sheets arising from the onset of the global financial crisis lead us to question why some economies are more affected by shocks than others. The asymmetric effects could arise because some central banks have less resilience or expertise to deal with this than other central banks. A deeper understanding of the balance sheet can give policy makers a better idea of how much leeway the central bank has in implementing certain strategies, and could allow policy makers to explore more unconventional monetary responses if the balance sheet has enough slack to allow such strategies without exacerbating negative economic conditions.

As the book empirically reveals substantial differences across central bank balance sheets, especially in the aspect of asset composition, this poses a challenge in attempting to examine the effectiveness of central bank balance sheet policies. Follow-up policy research could investigate to what extent differences in the design of balance sheet policies influence the variations in the macroeconomic and financial effects of balance sheet policies. In addition, policy research that examines the consequences of other types of innovations in the composition of central bank balance sheets would be an interesting field of inquiry.

Policy Debates

As indicated above, the degree to which central banks are exposed to risk significantly relies on the design of the central bank balance sheet, and therefore is contingent upon future balance sheet policies. Central banks in certain economies may be more or less exposed to different types of risk; for instance, exchange risk is attached to foreign exchange holders while credit risk is linked to private sector holders. The need to identify which risks are regarded more or less critical in a certain economy is crucial to avoid implementing misguided and ineffective policies.

The link between monetary policy and other policies is another debate discussed in this book, especially in regard to public debt management. For instance, the holding of government bonds by central banks requires an increased coordination between fiscal and monetary authorities.

The implications of unconventional short-term monetary policies (such as quantitative easing) have been presented in this book. Since programs (such as TARP) that "bail out" financial institutions can be extremely unpopular or politically controversial, it is necessary that monetary authorities closely monitor the use of injected liquidity, plan an exhaustive exit strategy once it has been identified that unconventional policies have achieved their goals, and explore ways to reduce morally hazardous behavior in the future.

Appendix I
Central Bank Balance Sheets of Different Countries

The original central bank balance sheets of different countries are provided below to observe variations in terms of asset-side items and liability-side items. In addition, it provides information on how patterns of reporting balance sheets are varied across countries and regions.

Asia Region

Malaysia's Central Bank Balance Sheets for the Month of February 2018

Assets	RM
Gold and Foreign Exchange and Other Reserves including SDR	419,549,797,551 *
Malaysian Government Papers	4,463,229,458
Deposits with Financial Institutions	5,598,818,970
Loans and Advances	7,493,903,885
Land and Buildings	4,179,614,080
Other Assets	9,516,489,885
	450,801,853,829

Capital and Liabilities	RM
Paid-Up Capital	100,000,000
Reserves	137,234,486,113
Currency in Circulation	108,303,399,938
Deposits by:	
Financial Institutions	167,881,909,188
Federal Government	11,105,958,177
Others	1,112,181,442
Bank Negara Papers	12,992,576,427
Allocation of Special Drawing Rights	7,759,395,868
Other Liabilities	4,311,946,676
	450,801,853,829

Source: Central Bank of Malaysia

DOI 10.1515/9781547400577-012

Monetary Authority of Singapore

As at 31 March in $ millions	Note	2017	2016
CAPITAL AND RESERVES			
Issued and Paid-up Capital	10	25,000	25,000
General Reserve Fund	11	19,908	6,396
Currency Fund Reserves	12	8,040	9,418
		52,948	40,814

Represented by:

	Note	2017	2016
ASSETS			
Cash and Bank Balances		853	861
Singapore Dollar Securities	13	9,518	8,661
Foreign Financial Assets	14	373,936	361,150
Gold		296	285
Other Assets	15	10,003	13,974
Property and Other Fixed Assets	16	189	190
		394,795	385,121

Less:

	Note	2017	2016
LIABILITIES			
Currency in Circulation		44,019	39,339
Deposits of Financial Institutions	17	25,027	26,823
MAS Bills	18	87,870	77,982
Foreign Financial Liabilities	14	11,613	19,972
Provisions and Other Liabilities	18	76,238	54,892
Amounts Due to Singapore Government	19	97,080	125,299
		341,847	344,307
NET ASSETS OF THE AUTHORITY		52,948	40,814

Africa Region

Nigeria's Central Bank Balance Sheets for the Month of November 2017

Date		11/30/2017
Gold		19009
Convertible Currency		12010447867
IMF Gold Tranche		22623
Special Drawing Rights		631681317
Total External Reserve		12642170816
Federal Govt Sect.		1667227008
Other Securities		4330538381
Rediscount & Advance		1906224520
Other Assets		4229102626
Fixed Assets		459108596
	Total Assets	**25234371947**
Capital Subscribed		5000000
General reserve		220068958
Other Reserves		40764187
Total Capitalisation		265833145
Currency in Circulation		1896585425
Government Deposits		904622429
Bankers Deposit		3568164797
Other Deposits		16128321448
Subtotal Liabilities		20601108674
Other Liabilities		2470844703
	Total Equity and Liabilities	**25234371947**

Source: Central Bank of Nigeria

South America

Central Reserve Bank of Peru

CENTRAL RESERVE BANK OF PERU

STATEMENTS OF FINANCIAL POSITION
As of December 31, 2015 and 2014

	Notes	2015 (S/ 000)	2014 (S/ 000)
ASSETS			
GROSS INTERNATIONAL RESERVES:			
Cash in foreign currency		170,699	149,244
Deposits in foreign Banks	4	68,576,820	40,575,042
Deposits in foreign institutions	5	2,544,531	2,321,112
Securities from international institutions	6	131,177,712	135,369,689
Gold	7	4,023,913	3,933,998
Contributions to international institutions	8	2,907,637	2,758,586
Other available assets	21(d) and (e)	316,663	765,851
		209,717,975	185,873,522
OTHER ASSETS ABROAD:			
Contributions in local currency to IMF	8 (b)	2,069,904	1,723,101
Other assets abroad	12 (c)	68,160	59,620
		2,138,064	1,782,721
DOMESTIC CREDIT:	9		
To banks		30,491,916	9,770,572
To the public sector		2,856,443	2,027,914
To other entities and funds		45,717	87,831
To the private sector		9	9
To financial companies		-	117,786
		33,394,085	12,004,112
PROPERTY, FURNITURE AND EQUIPMENT, NET:	10	158,005	155,038
OTHER ASSETS	11	1,942,637	1,723,935
TOTAL ASSETS		**247,350,766**	**201,539,328**
OFF-BALANCE SHEET ACCOUNTS	21	139,478,624	118,870,624

The accompanying notes are an integral part of these statements.

	Notes	2015	2014
		(S/ 000)	(S/ 000)
LIABILITIES AND NET EQUITY			
RESERVE LIABILITIES	21(d) and (e)	177,471	133,069
OTHER LIABILITIES ABROAD:			
Equivalent of the contribution in local currency to IMF	8 (b)	2,069,689	1,723,101
Other liabilities abroad	12	2,950,029	2,699,238
		5,019,718	4,422,339
STERILIZED STOCK:			
Outstanding securities issued	13	22,544,000	17,911,320
Deposits in local currency	14	32,256,053	38,537,142
		54,800,053	56,448,462
MONETARY BASE:	15		
Currency in circulation		48,890,028	47,543,004
Deposits in local currency		2,401,455	6,321,944
		51,291,483	53,864,948
DEPOSITS IN FOREIGN CURRENCY	16	93,595,612	73,343,923
OTHER LIABILITIES	17	32,330,381	10,920,176
TOTAL LIABILITIES		237,214,718	199,132,917
NET EQUITY	18		
Capital		1,182,750	1,182,750
Fair value reserve		(1,614,827)	(1,297,271)
Retained earnings		915,890	(716,336)
CAPITAL, RESERVES AND RETAINED EARNINGS		483,813	(830,857)
Readjustment for valuation article N°89 – Organic Act	18 (e)	9,652,235	3,237,268
TOTAL NET EQUITY		10,136,048	2,406,411
TOTAL LIABILITIES AND NET EQUITY		**247,350,766**	**201,539,328**
OFF-BALANCE SHEET ACCOUNTS	21	139,478,624	118,870,624

Brazil

BANCO CENTRAL DO BRASIL
CONDENSED INTERIM BALANCE SHEET (as at June 30, 2007)
In Thousands of Reais

ASSETS	Notes	Jun 30, 2007	Dec 31, 2006 (Restated)	LIABILITIES	Notes	Jun 30, 2007	Dec 31, 2006 (Republicado)
ASSETS IN FOREIGN CURRENCIES		313,897,642	200,980,845	LIABILITIES IN FOREIGN CURRENCIES		29,373,986	18,901,263
Cash and Cash Equivalents		11,979,448	10,566,592	Items in the Course of Collection		10,116,150	4,956,147
Time Deposits Placed with Financial Institutions	6	36,224,842	28,009,886	Deposits Received from Financial Institutions		520	577
Financial Assets Purchased Under Agreements to Resel	7	9,029,890	1,900,113	Financial Assets Sold Under Agreements to Repurchase	7	9,029,569	1,499,992
Derivatives		9,449	37,640	Derivatives		2,321	40,729
Debt Securities	8	246,248,132	149,424,976	Loans Payable		1,219,942	1,497,009
Credits Receivables		52,178	71,262	Deposits Received from International Financial Organizations		8,978,993	9,940,621
Gold		1,419,055	1,526,867	Other		27,491	87,178
Investments in International Financial Organizations		8,934,031	9,843,509	LIABILITIES IN LOCAL CURRENCY		575,968,729	432,860,944
Other		608	-	Items in the Course of Collection		768,663	1,076,320
ASSETS IN LOCAL CURRENCY		382,192,041	343,871,835	Deposits Received from Financial Institutions		126,792,894	118,438,665
Deposits		594,783	609,950	Financial Assets Sold Under Agreements to Repurchase	7	156,960,624	77,871,622
Financial Assets Purchased Under Agreements to Resel	7	-	504,501	Derivatives		1,140	121,601
Derivatives		157,712	1,640	Payables to the Federal Government		282,211,406	226,456,910
Debt Securities Issued by the Federal Government		323,658,940	303,860,298	Accounts Payable	11	2,289,061	2,180,309
Receivables from the Federal Government		31,877,336	14,322,275	Deposits Received from International Financial Organizations		26,757	26,973
Credits Receivable	9	23,110,518	21,815,930	Provisions	12	6,905,902	6,778,856
Property, Plant and Equipment		788,577	765,684	Other		22,292	21,798
Other	10	2,204,075	2,171,557	CURRENCY IN CIRCULATION	13	77,487,205	88,824,753
				NET EQUITY		13,260,163	8,065,730
				Income Reserve		1,606,019	4,662,369
				Revaluation Reserve		482,153	485,584
				Gains (Losses) Recognized Directly in Equity		8,595,635	4,090,432
				Changes in Accounting Policies - Process of Adopting IFRSs		-	1,906,017
				Transition adjustments to IFRSs		-	(4,962,367)
				Retained Earnings		2,576,356	1,883,715
TOTAL		696,089,683	544,852,680	TOTAL		696,089,683	544,852,680

Chile

ANNUAL REPORT 2013 FINANCIAL STATEMENTS OF THE CENTRAL BANK OF CHILE

STATEMENTS OF FINANCIAL POSITION AS OF 31 DECEMBER 2013 AND 2012
(Ch$ million)

Assets	Note	2013	2012
Foreign assets		21,653,585.9	30,052,478.3
Reserve assets	11	21,523,320.5	19,933,433.5
Monetary gold		5,050.3	6,290.6
Special drawing rights (SDR)		600,805.7	579,847.7
Reserve position in the IMF	12	335,578.0	331,087.3
Correspondent banks abroad		10,011.6	9,953.3
Investments in foreign currency		20,501,943.4	18,967,149.6
Securities at fair value through profit or loss		18,144,375.8	16,783,042.3
Held-to-maturity securities		2,357,567.6	2,184,107.3
Reciprocal loan agreements		69,397.1	38,819.6
Other assets		434.4	285.4
Other foreign assets		130,345.4	119,044.8
Shares of and contributions to the Inter American Development Bank (IDB)		96,425.1	88,111.1
Shares of Bank for International Settlements (BIS)		33,920.3	30,933.7
Domestic assets		1,853,189.6	3,002,363.3
Domestic loans	13	256.9	1,110,964.2
Loans to banks and financial institutions		256.9	1,110,964.2
Transactions under specific legal regulations	14	1,852,932.7	1,891,399.0
General Treasury transfers (Laws 18,267 and 18,401)		265,355.6	260,018.7
Loan for subordinated liabilities of financial institutions (Laws 18,401 and 19,396)		649,521.0	754,321.6
Sinap Liquidation Law 18,900		938,056.1	877,058.7
Other assets		53,866.3	45,002.8
Premises, equipment and intangible assets	15	36,476.5	38,386.8
Other securities		16,073.9	6,146.7
Transition assets		1,316.0	469.3
Total assets		**23,560,622.3**	**23,099,844.3**

Accompanying notes from 1 to 29 are an integral part of these financial statements.

STATEMENTS OF FINANCIAL POSITION, CONTINUED AS OF 31 DECEMBER, 2013 AND 2012
(Ch$ million)

Liabilities	Note	2013	2012
Foreign liabilities	16	710,092.8	656,457.2
Reciprocal loan agreements		4,629.7	13,253.0
Accounts with international organizations		46,455.0	42,254.1
Special drawing rights (SDR) allocations		659,008.1	600,950.1
Domestic liabilities		26,651,957.3	26,903,859.3
Monetary base	17	8,754,473.9	7,890,603.7
Banknotes and coins in circulation		6,917,607.4	6,195,118.2
Deposits from financial institutions (in Chilean pesos)		1,139,731.0	965,242.2
Deposits for technical reserve		697,135.5	730,243.3
Deposits and obligations	18	4,864,461.1	6,108,201.1
Deposits and obligations with General Treasury		384,665.8	694,763.0
Other deposits and obligations		4,479,795.3	5,413,438.1
Documents issued by Central Bank of Chile	19	13,033,022.2	12,905,054.5
Central Bank of Chile bonds in UF (BCU)		7,830,132.7	8,535,033.2
Central Bank of Chile bonds in Chilean pesos (BCP)		4,080,623.4	3,905,683.5
Central Bank of Chile discountable promissory notes (PDBC)		925,319.1	–
Optional indexed coupons (CERO) in UF		135,669.2	230,094.7
Indexed promissory notes payable in coupons (PRC)		61,256.7	234,221.9
Other		21.1	21.1
Other liabilities	20	18,880.6	18,777.3
Provisions		18,502.7	18,365.6
Other securities		377.9	411.7
Net equity	21	(3,820,308.1)	(4,479,240.5)
Capital		(4,478,737.6)	(2,355,778.8)
Valuation accounts		(713.0)	(511.9)
Surplus (deficit) for the year		659,142.3	(2,122,858.8)
Total liabilities and equity		**23,560,622.3**	**23,099,844.3**

Accompanying notes from 1 to 29 are an integral part of these financial statements.

Argentina

Summary Balance of Assets and Liabilities
- In thousands of $ -

	15-Mar-18
ASSETS	
INTERNATIONAL RESERVES	
GOLD, CURRENCY, DEPOSITS TO BE REALIZED AND OTHERS	1,255,528,135
- Gold (net of allowances)	47,148,335
- Foreign Currency	750,227,373
- Deposits to be realized in foreign currency	469,478,367
- Derivatives over International Reserves	-11,326,937
- Multilateral Credit Agreements	997
GOVERNMENT SECURITIES	1,384,408,062
CENTRAL BANK HOLDINGS	
- Securities issued under Foreign Legislation	938,070
- Securities issued under Argentine Legislation	1,384,272,124
1990 National Treasury Consolidated Bond	4,655,458
- Nontransferable Bills from the National Treasury	987,511,874
Others	395,958,118
LESS:	
Adjustment for accrual on 1990 Consolidated Bond	3,853,326
- Allowances for impairment of Government Securities	802,132
REPO SECURITIES WITH THE FINANCIAL SYSTEM	0
- Securities received on Reverse Repo	0
- Securities received on Crossed Reverse Repo	0
TEMPORARY ADVANCES TO THE ARGENTINE GOVERNMENT	495,530,000
- Payments to International Agencies and payments in foreign currency	
- Other applications	
LOANS TO THE ARGENTINE FINANCIAL SYSTEM	405,093
- Financial Institutions	980,933
LESS:	
- Loan loss allowance	575,840

CONTRIBUTIONS TO INTERNATIONAL AGENCIES ON BEHALF OF ARGENTINE GOVERNEMENT AND OTHER	86,391,240
RIGHTS DERIVING FROM OTHER DERIVATIVE FINANCIAL INSTRUMENTS	0
RIGHTS DERIVING FROM REPO TRANSACTIONS	218,031,364
OTHER ASSETS	7,393,195
- Other Assets	7,393,195
TOTAL ASSETS	3,447,687,089
Rate of Exchange USD/$:	20.2665
LIABILITIES	
MONETARY BASE	1,022,485,529
- Money in Circulation	758,048,979
Banknotes and Coins in Circulation	758,048,727
Pay-off Checks in Pesos	252
- Current Accounts in Pesos	264,436,550
MEANS OF PAYMENT IN OTHER CURRENCIES	1,684,956
- Pay-off checks in other currencies	2,432
- Certificates of Deposit for Investment	1,682,524
CURRENT ACCOUNTS IN OTHER CURRENCIES	253,971,612
DEPOSITS FROM NATIONAL ARGENTINE AND OTHER	21,519,036
- Other Deposits	21,519,036
OTHER DEPOSITS	236,688
IMF SPECIAL DRAWING RIGHTS	9,376,984
- IMF Special Drawing Rights	59,496,443

- SDR contra account	-50,119,459
OBLIGATIONS WITH INTERNATIONAL AGENCIES	**3,973,093**
- Obligations	19,562,363
- Contra Account of the Use of the Reserve Tranch	-15,589,270
SECURITIES ISSUED BY THE BCRA	**1,359,364,865**
- Bills and Notes issued in Foreign Currency	0
- Bills and Notes issued in Argentine pesos	1,359,364,865
LEBAC y NOBAC	1,248,605,506
LELIQ	110,759,358
CONTRA ACCOUNT TO ARGENTINE GOVERNMENT CONTRIBUTIONS	**59,130,381**
TO INTERNATIONAL AGENCIES	
DUE TO OTHER DERIVATIVE FINANCIAL INSTRUMENTS	**0**
DUE TO REPO TRANSACTIONS	**265,738,774**
DUE TO MULTILATERAL CREDIT AGREEMENTS	**1,323,682**
OTHER LIABILITIES	**215,259,466**
PROVISIONS	**4,051,552**
TOTAL LIABILITIES	**3,218,116,618**
NET EQUITY	**229,570,471**
TOTAL LIABILITIES + NET EQUITY	**3,447,687,089**
Rate of Exchange USD/$:	**20.26650**
control:	0

North America

Mexico

Summarized Balance Sheet of Banco de México

Assets

International Reserves 1/	3,210,235.7	3,268,211.1
International Reserves (In millions of U.S. dollars)	172,910.3	173,004.5
Gross international reserves	3,291,276.5	3,343,976.0
Liabilities of less than 6 months	-81,040.7	-75,765.0
Credit to the Federal Government	0.0	0.0
Securities	0.0	0.0
Government Securities 2/	0.0	0.0
Other Securities	0.0	0.0
Credit to Financial Intermediaries & Debtor Repurchase Agreements	273,251.3	193,995.6
Debtor repurchase agreements	271,447.3	192,189.0
Commercial banks	1,804.0	1,806.7
Development banks	0.0	0.0
Fobaproa	N/E	N/E
Fameval	N/E	N/E
Development trust funds	0.0	0.0
Credit to public sector agencies	0.0	0.0
IPAB	0.0	0.0

Net Liabilities and capital

International Monetary Fund	0.0	0.0
Financial Authorities Abroad	0.0	0.0
Monetary Base	1,475,768.8	1,489,481.8
Currency in circulation	1,473,082.3	1,486,518.1
Current account bank deposits 3/	2,686.5	2,963.8
Banco de México's Bonds (BREMS) 4/	0.0	0.0
Federal Government Deposits 5/	656,303.0	585,287.8
Monetary Regulation Liabilities	1,265,725.2	1,247,363.4
Federal Government Deposits 6/	917,238.7	897,152.7
Banks Deposits 7/	215,172.2	215,486.4
Commercial banks	182,452.6	182,719.0
Development banks	32,719.6	32,767.4
Banco de Mexico's Bonds (BREMS L) 8/	105,087.5	105,240.9
Other Financial Intermediaries Deposits & Creditor Repurchase Agreements	28,226.7	29,483.3
Creditor repurchase agreements	0.0	0.0
Commercial banks 9/	25,925.3	29,483.3
Development banks 10/	2,301.4	0.0
Fobaproa	N/E	N/E
Fameval	N/E	N/E
Trust funds	0.0	0.0
Mexican Oil Fund	19,008.9	18,497.1
Other Liabilities and Capital, Net from Other Assets	66,681.1	121,576.5

Canada

Bank of Canada
Statement of Financial Position
As at December 31, 2017
(Millions of dollars)

UNAUDITED

ASSETS			LIABILITIES AND EQUITY			
Cash and foreign deposits		14.6	Bank notes in circulation			85,855.9
Loans and receivables			**Deposits**			
Securities purchased under resale agreements	9,478.5		Government of Canada	21,454.2		
Advances	-		Members of Payments Canada	500.3		
Other receivables	4.5		Other deposits	2,274.3		
		9,483.0				24,228.8
Investments						
Treasury bills of Canada	18,370.4		**Securities sold under repurchase agreements**			-
Government of Canada bonds	82,087.0		**Other liabilities**			520.0
Other investments	403.6					
		100,861.0				110,604.7
Property and equipment		569.0	**Equity**			
Intangible assets		40.1	Share capital	5.0		
Other assets		132.6	Statutory and special reserves	125.0		
			Available-for-sale reserve	365.6		
						495.6
		111,100.3				**111,100.3**

United States

H.4.1

5. Consolidated Statement of Condition of All Federal Reserve Banks
Millions of dollars

Assets, liabilities, and capital	Eliminations from consolidation	Wednesday Mar 21, 2018	Change since			
			Wednesday Mar 14, 2018		Wednesday Mar 22, 2017	
Assets						
Gold certificate account		11,037		0		0
Special drawing rights certificate account		5,200		0		0
Coin		1,859	-	18	-	62
Securities, unamortized premiums and discounts, repurchase agreements, and loans		4,333,349	-	5,801	-	76,650
Securities held outright[1]		4,192,285	-	5,256	-	62,662
U.S. Treasury securities		2,424,723	+	161	-	39,251
Bills[2]		0		0		0
Notes and bonds, nominal[2]		2,293,885		0	-	46,526
Notes and bonds, inflation-indexed[2]		111,220		0	+	5,319
Inflation compensation[3]		19,618	+	161	+	1,957
Federal agency debt securities[2]		4,391		0	-	8,938
Mortgage-backed securities[4]		1,763,171	-	5,417	-	14,474
Unamortized premiums on securities held outright[5]		155,105	-	569	-	14,914
Unamortized discounts on securities held outright[5]		-14,054	+	26	+	922
Repurchase agreements[6]		0		0		0
Loans		14	-	1	+	5
Net portfolio holdings of Maiden Lane LLC[7]		1,708		0	+	1
Items in process of collection	(0)	88	+	14	+	39
Bank premises		2,197	+	1	-	2
Central bank liquidity swaps[8]		77	+	13	-	942
Foreign currency denominated assets[9]		22,163	-	113	+	1,958
Other assets[10]		23,544	-	131	-	1,354
Total assets	(0)	4,401,222	-	6,036	-	77,014

Note: Components may not sum to totals because of rounding. Footnotes appear at the end of the table.

5. Consolidated Statement of Condition of All Federal Reserve Banks (continued)
Millions of dollars

Assets, liabilities, and capital	Eliminations from consolidation	Wednesday Mar 21, 2018	Change since			
			Wednesday Mar 14, 2018		Wednesday Mar 22, 2017	
Liabilities						
Federal Reserve notes, net of F.R. Bank holdings		1,587,391	-	269	+	100,086
Reverse repurchase agreements[11]		249,149	+	11,870	-	246,569
Deposits	(0)	2,520,162	-	16,103	+	73,212
Term deposits held by depository institutions		0		0		0
Other deposits held by depository institutions		2,135,068	-	55,075	-	178,894
U.S. Treasury, General Account		298,973	+	62,813	+	244,728
Foreign official		5,254		0	+	83
Other[12]	(0)	80,867	-	23,840	+	7,295
Deferred availability cash items	(0)	239	-	115	-	247
Other liabilities and accrued dividends[13]		5,110	-	1,431	-	2,101
Total liabilities	(0)	4,362,051	-	6,047	-	75,619
Capital accounts						
Capital paid in		31,670	+	10	+	1,105
Surplus		7,500		0	-	2,500
Other capital accounts		0		0		0
Total capital		39,170	+	10	-	1,395

Note: Components may not sum to totals because of rounding.

1. Includes securities lent to dealers under the overnight securities lending facility; refer to table 1A.
2. Face value of the securities.
3. Compensation that adjusts for the effect of inflation on the original face value of inflation-indexed securities.
4. Guaranteed by Fannie Mae, Freddie Mac, and Ginnie Mae. The current face value shown is the remaining principal balance of the securities.
5. Reflects the premium or discount, which is the difference between the purchase price and the face value of the securities that has not been amortized. For U.S. Treasury securities, Federal agency debt securities, and mortgage-backed securities, amortization is on an effective-interest basis.
6. Cash value of agreements, which are collateralized by U.S. Treasury and federal agency securities.
7. Refer to table 4 and the note on consolidation accompanying table 6.
8. Dollar value of foreign currency held under these agreements valued at the exchange rate to be used when the foreign currency is returned to the foreign central bank. This exchange rate equals the market exchange rate used when the foreign currency was acquired from the foreign central bank.
9. Revalued daily at current foreign currency exchange rates.
10. Includes accrued interest, which represents the daily accumulation of interest earned, and other accounts receivable.
11. Cash value of agreements, which are collateralized by U.S. Treasury securities, federal agency debt securities, and mortgage-backed securities.
12. Includes deposits held at the Reserve Banks by international and multilateral organizations, government-sponsored enterprises, designated financial market utilities, and deposits held by depository institutions in joint accounts in connection with their participation in certain private-sector payment arrangements. Also includes certain deposit accounts other than the U.S. Treasury, General Account, for services provided by the Reserve Banks as fiscal agents of the United States.
13. Includes the liability for earnings remittances due to the U.S. Treasury.

Appendix II
Abbreviations

APF	Asset purchase facility
ARMA	Autoregressive moving average
ATM	Automatic teller machine
BIS	Bank for International System
CBN	Central Bank of Nigeria
DGD	Domestic Government Debt
ECB	European Central Bank
EME	Emerging market economies
FA	Foreign assets
Fed	Federal Reserve, U.S.
FX	Foreign exchange
GDP	Gross domestic product
HP	Hodrick-Prescott
IASB	International Accounting Standards Board
IFS	International Financial Statistics
IMF	International Monetary Fund
LB	Liabilities to Banks
LG	Liabilities to Government
LRAD	Long-run aggregate demand
LRAS	Long-run aggregate supply
MBS	Mortgage backed securities
NCB	National central bank
OECD	Organization for Economic Cooperation and Development
QE:	Quantitative easing
RBA	Reserve Bank of Australia
RBC	Real business cycle
SARB	South Africa Reserve Bank
SNB	Swiss National Bank
SVAR	Structural vector autoregression
WBDI	World Bank Development Indicator

DOI 10.1515/9781547400577-013

References

Abbassi, P and T Linzert (2011): "The effectiveness of monetary policy in steering money market rates during the recent financial crisis," *ECB Working Paper Series*, No 1328, April.

Aït-Sahalia, Y, J Andritzky, A Jobst, S Nowak and N Tamirisa (2012): "Market response to policy initiatives during the global financial crisis," *Journal of International Economics*, Vol 87, No 1, pp 162–177.

Allen, W A (2012): "Quantitative monetary policy and government debt management in Britain since 1919," *Oxford Review of Economic Policy*, Vol 28, No 4, pp 804–836.

Allen, W A and R Moessner (2010): "Central bank co-operations and international liquidity in the financial crisis of 2008–9," *BIS Working Papers*, No 310, May.

Araújo, A, S Schommer and M Woodford (2015): "Conventional and Unconventional Monetary Policy with Endogenous Collateral Constraints." *American Economic Journal: Macroeconomics,* Vol. 7, No.1, pp. 1–43.

Archer, D and P Moser-Boehm (2013): "Central bank finances," *BIS Papers*, No 71, April.

Auerbach, A and W Gale (2009): "The economic crisis and the fiscal crisis: 2009 and beyond," mimeo, University of California, Berkeley.

Bank of England (2005): "Reform of the Bank of England's operations in the sterling money markets: A paper on the new framework by the Bank of England," April.

Bauer, M D and G D Rudebusch (2012): "The signalling channel for Federal Reserve Bond Purchases," *International Journal of Central Banking*, Vol 10, No 3, pp 233–289.

Benford, J, S Berry, K Nikolov and C Young (2009): "Quantitative easing," *Bank of England Quarterly Bulletin*, Q2, pp 90–100.

Bernanke, B, S. (2015): "Monetary Policy in the Future," Speech at the IMF's Rethinking Macro Policy Conference III, April 2015. Blanchard, Olivier, 2016, "Currency Wars, Coordination and Capital Controls," NBER Working Paper No. 22388.

BIS (2009): *Issues in the governance of central banks*, May.

_____. (2013): *Central bank collateral frameworks and practices: A report by a Study Group established by the Markets Committee*, March.

Blinder, A S (2010): "Quantitative easing: Entrance and exit strategies," *Federal Reserve Bank of St. Louis Review*, Vol 92, No 6, pp 465–47, November/Decemeber.

Blommestein, H J and P Turner (2012): "Interactions between sovereign debt management and monetary policy under fiscal dominance and financial instability," in: BIS (ed.), "Threat of fiscal dominance," *BIS Papers*, No 65, May.

Borio, C (2001): "A hundred ways to skin a cat: Comparing monetary policy operating procedures in the United States, Japan and the euro area," in: BIS (ed.), "Comparing monetary policy operating procedures across the United States, Japan and the euro area," *BIS Papers*, No 9, December.

Borio, C, G Galati and A Heath (2008): "FX reserve management: trends and challenges," *BIS Working Papers*, No 40, May.

Borio, C and P Disyatat (2010): "Unconventional monetary policies: An appraisal," *The Manchester School*, Vol 78, No s1, pp 53–89.

Brainard, Lael, (2017) : "Cross-Border Spillovers of Balance Sheet Normalization," Speech at NBER's Monetary Economics Summer Institute, New York, NY, July 13, 2017

Buiter, W H (2008): "Can central banks go broke?" *CEPR Discussion Paper*, No DP6827, May.

DOI 10.1515/9781547400577-014

Caruana, J (2012): "Why central bank balance sheets matter," in: BIS (ed.), "Are central bank balance sheet in Asia too large?" *BIS Papers*, No 66, pp 2–9.

Cassola, N and A Durré (2011): "Implementing monetary policy in crisis times – the case of the ECB," in: ECB (ed): *"Approaches to monetary policy revisited – lessons from the crisis,"* ECB.

Cecchetti, S G (2013): "Central bank independence – a path less clear," remarks prepared for the International Conference held to commemorate the 20th anniversary of the autonomy of the Bank of Mexico, Mexico City, 14 October.

Cecchetti, S G, R N McCauley and P M McGuire (2012): "Interpreting TARGET2 balances," *BIS Working Papers*, No 393, December.

Chadha, J S, P Turner and F Zampolli (2013): "The interest rate effects of government debt maturity," *BIS Working Papers*, No 415, June.

Chen, H, V Cúrdia and A Ferrero (2012): "The macroeconomic effects of large-scale asset purchase programmes," *The Economic Journal*, Vol 122 (November), pp F289-F315.

Chen, Q, A Filardo, D He and F Zhu (2012): "International spillovers of central bank balance sheet policies," in: BIS (ed.), "Are central bank balance sheet in Asia too large?" *BIS Papers*, No 66, pp 220–264.

_____. (2015): "Financial Crisis, U.S. Unconventional Monetary Policy and International Spillovers," IMF Working Papers 15/85 (Washington: International Monetary Fund).

Cheun, S, I von Köppen-Mertens and B Weller (2009): "The collateral frameworks of the Eurosystem, the Federal Reserve System and the Bank of England and the financial market turmoil," *ECB Occasional Paper Series*, No 107, December.

Cho, Dongchul, and Changyong Rhee, (2013): "Effects of Quantitative Easing on Asia: Capital Flows and Financial Markets," Asian Development Bank Working Paper Series No. 350.

Christensen, J H E and S Krogstrup (2014): "Swiss unconventional monetary policy: Lessons for the transmission of quantitative easing, *Federal Reserve Bank of San Francisco Working Paper Series*, No 2014–18, July.

Christensen, J H E, J A Lopez amd G D Rudebusch (2013): "A probability-based stress test of Federal Reserve assets and income," *Federal Reserve Bank of San Francisco Working Paper Series*, No 2013–38, December.

Cincibuch, M, T Holub and J Hurník (2008): "Central bank losses and economic convergence," *Czech National Bank Working Paper*, No 3, March.

Clark, John, Nathan Converse, Brahima Coulibaly, and Steven Kamin (2016) :"Emerging Market Capital Flows and U.S. Monetary Policy", Federal Reserve Board, IFPD Notes. Federal Open Market Committee, 2017, Minutes of the February Meeting, March 15.

Coeuré, B (2013): "Non-standard monetary policy measures: Where do we stand?" speech delivered at the International Monetary Seminar "Sovereign Risk, Bank Risk and Central Banking" organized by the Banque de France, 10 July 2013.

Cook, D and J Yetman (2012): "Expanding central bank balance sheets in emerging Asia: A compendium of risks and some evidence," in: BIS (ed.), "Are central bank balance sheet in Asia too large?" *BIS Papers*, No 66, pp 30–75.

CPSS (2003): "The role of central bank money in payment systems," *CPSS Reports*, No 55, August.

Cúrdia, V and A Ferrero (2013): "How stimulatory are large-scale asset purchases," *Federal Reserve Bank of San Francisco Economic Letter*, No 2013–22, August.

Cúrdia, V and M Woodford (2011): "The central bank balance sheet as an instrument of monetary policy," *Journal of Monetary Economics*, Vol 58, No 1, pp 54–79.

D'Amico S and T B King (2013): "Flow and stock effects of large-scale treasury purchases: Evidence on the importance of local supply," *Journal of Financial Economics*, Vol 108, No 2, pp 425–448.

ECB (2006): "The accumulation of foreign reserves," *Occasional Paper Series*, No 43, February.

_____. (2011): *The monetary policy of the ECB*, May.

_____. (2013): *Collateral eligibility requirements: A comparative study across specific frameworks*, July.

Eisner, E A Martin and Y Søvik (2018): What is the composition of central bank balance sheets in normal times?

Engert, W, T Gravelle and D Howard (2008): "The implementation of monetary policy in Canada," *Bank of Canada Discussion Paper*, No 2008–9, July.

Fawley, B W and C J Neely (2013): "Four stories of quantitative easing," *Federal Reserve Bank of St. Louis Review*, Vol 95, No 1, pp 51–88, January/February.

Filardo, A and J Yetman (2012): "Key facts on central bank balance sheets in Asia and the Pacific," in: BIS (ed.), "Are central bank balance sheet in Asia too large?," *BIS Papers*, No 66, pp 10–29.

Forbes K, M Fratzscher, and R Straub, (2015) : "Capital-flow Management Measures: What Are They Good For?" *Journal of International Economics,* Elsevier, Vol. 96, S1, pp. S76-S97.

Fostel A, J Geanakoplos, and G Phelan (2017) : "Global Collateral: How Financial Innovation Drivers Capital Flows and Increases Financial Instability," Cowles Foundation Discussion Papers 2076, Cowles Foundation for Research in Economics, Yale University

Frait, J and T Holub (2008): "Exchange rate appreciation and negative central bank capital: Is there a problem?" in: S Milton and P Sinclair (eds.), *The Capital Needs of Central Banks*, Routledge.

Fratscher, M, M, Lo Duca and R Straub (2012): "A global monetary tsunami? On the spillovers of US quantitative easing," *CEPR Discussion Paper Series*, No 9195, October.

Fratzscher M, M Lo Duca, and R Straub (2013) : "On the International Spillovers of US Quantitative Easing," Discussion Papers of DIW Berlin 1304, DIW Berlin, German Institute for Economic Research.

Gagnon, J E, M Raskin, J Remache and B Sack (2011): "The financial market effects of the Federal Reserve's large-scale asset purchases," *International Journal of Central Banking*, Vol 7, No 1, pp 3–43.

Gagnon, J, and B Sack (2014): "Monetary policy with abundant liquidity: A new operating framework for the Federal Reserve," *Peterson Institute for International Economics Policy Brief*, No PB14–4, January.

Gambacorta, L, B Hofmann and G Peersman (2012): "The effectiveness of unconventional monetary policy at the zero lower bound: a cross-country analysis," *Journal of Money, Credit and Banking*, Vol 4, No 4, pp 615–642.

Geanakoplos, J (1997) : "Promises, Promises," in W.B. Arthur, S. Durlauf, and D. Lane, eds., *The Economy as a Complex, Evolving System, II,* Reading, MA: Addison-Wesley, 1997. 27

Geanakoplos, J and H Wang (2017) : "Quantitative Easing, Collateral Constraints, and Financial Spillovers," Work in Progress.

Geanakoplos, J and W. R. Zame, (2013) : "Collateral Equilibrium: A Basic Framework," Cowles Foundation Discussion Paper No. 1906 .

Goodfriend, M (2011): "Central banking in the credit turmoil: An assessment of Federal Reserve practice," *Journal of Monetary Economics*, Vol 58, pp 1–12.

Goodhart, C A E (2010): "The changing role of central banks," *BIS Working Papers*, No 326, November.

Greenwood, R and D Vayanos (2008): "Bond supply and excess bond returns," *NBER Working Paper*, No w13806.

Greenwood, R, Samuel G. Hanson, and Jeremy C. Stein, (2016): "The Federal Reserve's Balance Sheet as a Financial Stability Tool," 2016 Economic Policy Symposium. Jackson Hole: Federal Reserve of Kansas City. International Monetary Fund, World Economic Outlook, Chapter 2, April 2016.

_____. (2014) "Emerging Market Volatility: Lessons from the Taper Tantrum", IMF Staff Discussion Note No. 14/09 (Washington: International Monetary Fund)

_____. (2015): "Measures which are Both Macroprudential and Capital Flow Management Measures: IMF Approach". (Washington: International Monetary Fund)

HM Treasury (2009): *The nationalisation of Northern Rock*, report by the comptroller and auditor general, March.

Ho, C and F-L Michaud (2008): "Central bank measures to alleviate foreign currency finding shortages," in: Fender, I and J Gyntelberg (2008): "Global financial crisis spurs unprecedented policy actions," *BIS Quarterly Review*, September, pp 14–15.

IMF (2010): "Reserve accumulation and international monetary stability," *Policy Paper Series*, April.

Jean-Philippe C, J Elmeskov, and A Mourougane (2018) : "Estimates of Potential Output: Benefits and Pitfalls from A Policy Perspective" OECD Economics Department.

Jobst, C and S Ugolini (2014): "The coevolution of money markets and monetary policy, 1815–2008," paper prepared for Norges Bank's bicentenary project conference Of the Uses of Central Banks, Oslo, 5–6 June 2014 (http://www.norgesbank.no/pages/100044/01_Jobst_and_UgoliniCoevolutionMoneyMarketCentralBanks2014.pdf)

Joyce, M, A Lasaosa, I Stevens and M Tong (2011): "The financial market impact of quantitative easing in the United Kingdom," *International Journal of Central Banking*, Vol 3, No 3, pp 113–161.

Joyce, M and M Tong (2012): "QE and the gilt market: A disaggregated analysis," *The Economic Journal*, Vol 122, No 564, pp. F348–384.

Kok Sørensen, C and J M Puigert Gutiérrez (2006), "Euro area banking sector integration: Using hierarchical cluster analysis techniques," *ECB Working Paper Series*, No 627.

Krishnamurthy, A and A Vissing-Jorgensen, (2011): "The Effects of Quantitative Easing on Interest Rates: Channels and Implications for Policy," Brookings Papers on Economic Activity, Economic Studies Program, The Brookings Institution, Vol. 43, No. 2, Fall, pp. 215–287.

Krugman, P (2009): "Competition, Coordination, and the crisis," speech at the Conference on Industrial Competitiveness, EU Commission, Brussels, 17 March, (http://ec.europa.eu/enterprise/enterprise_policy/industry/doc/conference_17_march_2009/krugman_speech_slides.pdf)

Kyle D. Allen, Scott E. Hein, and Mathew D. Whitledge (2015) : "The Evolution of Federal Reserve's Term Auction Facility and Community Bank Utilization" Texas Tech University.

Lautenschläger, S (2014): "How innovative should central banks be?" speech at Wirtschafsgipfel 2014 "Wirtshaft neu denken – die Kraft der Innovations, 29 November (http://www.ecb.europa.eu/press/key/date/2014/html/sp141129.en.html)

Lombardi, M and F Zhu (2014): "A shadow policy rate to calibrate US monetary policy at the zero lower bound," *BIS Working Papers*, No 452, June.

Lenza, M L Reichlin and H Pill (2010): "Monetary policy in exceptional times," *Economic Policy*, Vol 25, No 4, pp 295–339.

Mark Grant (2017):"The Risk in Central-Sheets are Clear : the Fed is virtually unique in regards to the safety of its holdings. Other banks, not so much" https://www.bloomberg.com/view/articles/2017-12-07/the-risks-in-central-bank-balance-sheets-is-clear-mark-grant

Meaning, M and F Zhu (2012): "The impact of Federal Reserve asset purchase programmes: another twist," *BIS Quarterly Review*, March 2012, pp 23–30.

Miles, D and J Schanz (2014): "The relevance or otherwise of the central bank balance sheet," *Journal of International Economics*, Vol 92, pp S103-s116.

Nagel, J (2012): "Understanding central bank balance sheets," *International Economy Magazine*, No 26, August.

Naudon, A and A Yany (2016): "The Impact of the U.S. Term Premium on Emerging Markets" in Challenges for Central Banking—Perspectives for Latin America, ed. Yan Carriere-Swallow, Luis Jacome, Hamid Faruqee, and Krishna Srinivasan (Washington: International Monetary Fund).

Obstfeld, M, J C Shambaugh and A M Taylor (2010): "Financial stability, the trilemma and international reserves," *American Economic Journal: Macroeconomics*, Vol 2, pp 57–54.

Obstfeld, M and A M Taylor (1998): "The Great Depression as a watershed: international capital mobility over the long run," in: "*The defining moment: The Great Depression and the American economy in the twentieth century,*" edited by M D Bordo, C Goldin and E N White, University of Chicago Press.

Otaviano Canuto and M Cavallari (2017): "The Mist of Central Bank Balance Sheets" EconoMonitor

Pattipeilohy, C (2013): "A descriptive analysis of the balance sheet and monetary policy of De Nederlandsche Bank: 1900–1998 and beyond," *DNB Occasional Studies*, Vol 11, No 3.

Pattipeilohy, C, J W van den End, M Tabbae, J Frost and J de Haan (2013): "Unconventional monetary policy of the ECB during the financial crisis: An assessment and new evidence," *DNB Working Paper*, No 381, May.

Peersman, G (2011): "Macroeconomic effects of unconventional monetary policy measures in the euro area," *ECB Working Papers*, No 1397, November.

Potter, Simon, (2016), "Money Market After Liftoff: Assessment to Date and the Road Ahead", February 22, Columbia University, New York. https://www.newyorkfed.org/newsevents/speeches/2016/pot160222

Restrepo, J, L Salomé and R Valdés (2009): "Macroeconomìa, polìtica monetaria ypartimonia del Banco Central," *Documentos de Trabajo/Working Papers*, No 497.

Singh, Manmohan, (2011) : "Velocity of Pledged Collateral- Analysis and Implications", IMF Working Paper No. 11/256 (Washington: International Monetary Fund)

_____. (2015): "Managing the Fed's Liftoff and Monetary Policy Transmission," IMF Working Paper No. 15/202 (Washington: International Monetary Fund).

_____. (2017a): "Collateral Reuse and Balance Sheet Space," IMF Working Paper 17/113, (Washington International Monetary Fund).

_____. (2017b): "Why shrinking the Fed balance sheet may have an easing effect," *Financial Times*, Alphaville, April 24. https://ftalphaville.ft.com/2017/04/24/2187716/guest-post-why-shrinking-the-fed-balancesheet-may-have-an-easing-effect/

Spiegel, M (2001): "Quantitative easing by the Bank of Japan," *Federal Reserve Bank of San Francisco Economic Letter*, No 2001–31, November.

Stella, P (1997): "Do central banks need capital?" *IMF Working Paper*, No WP/97/83, July.

_____. (2008): "Central bank financial strength, policy constraints and inflation," *IMF Working Paper*, No 49, February.

Summers, Larry, (2016) : "Macroeconomic Policy and Secular Stagnation". Mundell-Fleming Lecture, International Monetary Fund,

Taylor, J B and J C Williams (2009): "A black swan in the money market," *American Economic Journal: Macroeconomics*, Vol 1, No 1, pp 58–83.

The Investment Management Practice Group (2008): "Federal Reserve Announces Money Market Investor Funding Facility."

Tobias Adrian, Karin Kimbrough, and Dina Marchioni (2011) : "The Federal Reserve's Commercial Paper Funding Facility" *FRBNY Economic Policy Review*.

Turner, P (2011): "Fiscal dominance and the long-term interest rate," *Financial Market Group Special Paper Series*, No 199, April.

_____. (2014): "The exit from non-conventional monetary policy: What challenges?" *BIS working Papers*, No 448, May.

Vayanos, D and J L Vila (2009), "A preferred-habitat model of the term structure of interest rates," *NBER Working Papers*, No w15487, November 2009.

Ugai, H (2006): "Effects of the quantitative easing policy: A survey of empirical analysis," *Bank of Japan Working Paper Series*, No 06E10, July.

Zampolli, F (2012); "Sovereign debt management as an instrument of monetary policy: An overview," in: BIS (ed.), "Threat of fiscal dominance," *BIS Papers*, No 65, May.

Index

DOI 10.1515/9781547400577-015